THE PICADOR BOOK OF

African Stories

THE PICADOR BOOK OF

African Stories

Edited by Stephen Gray

PICADOR

First published 2000 by Picador
an imprint of Macmillan Publishers Ltd
25 Eccleston Place, London SW1W 9NF
Basingstoke and Oxford
Associated companies throughout the world
www.macmillan.com

ISBN 0 330 48540 7 (HB)
ISBN 0 330 39630 7 (TPB)

1 3 5 7 9 8 6 4 2

A CIP catalogue record for this book is available from
the British Library.

Typeset by SetSystems Ltd, Saffron Walden, Essex
Printed and bound in Great Britain by
Mackays of Chatham plc, Chatham, Kent

Contents

Introduction

WHEN WITH THE FIRST FREE democratic elections in South Africa in 1994 my country joined the rest of its continent at last, I felt freed as well – to discover that whole mainland from which for most of my life I had been excluded. I happened to meet Caryl Phillips then; he encouraged me to outline a project for Macmillan, the firm which we knew had a longstanding network of interests in Africa, albeit in largely educational publishing, and would not look askance at the notion of a literary survey.

So I proposed *The Picador Book of African Stories*, together with a beginner's scheme of things, and hunkered down actually to take stock of the African short stories that I had, I realized, been collecting for such a purpose. Six years later the present anthology is the upshot; and I end where I began, asking Caryl Phillips to endorse the results of the research he had suggested would be richly worth undertaking.

From the first I was determined that this *Picador Book* should not – as some recent anthologies of African writing have done – give the impression that all the literature of the continent worth reading is really written in English, with perhaps the odd translation attached. Only nineteen out of forty pieces here were originally written in English, a fair proportion. French being my reading language, I have always been able to keep abreast of French-language developments, and here have convinced a team of translators to make rare, choice texts in French which I feel should not be overlooked available in English (in all thirteen pieces derive from the Francophone African world).

New Portuguese material I was aware of through colleagues like Luís Rafael and Richard Bartlett, two out of many translators dedicated to making Lusophone African literature – which, although largely unfelt, flanks and enwraps my country – more widely known to non-Portuguese-speakers (five items here). Afrikaans, my other home language, I felt should not be completely written off (one item).

And then there is also literature in Arabic (two items), yet another language exotic to Africa, for a knowledge of which, like so many other English-speakers, I am reliant on a prolific translator like Denys Johnson-Davies. Readers may take it that a sample of his work being placed first

on the contents page is by way of a tribute to *his* usefulness in the world
of African short fiction. I recall Sylvia Pankhurst, who learned that method
of understanding Africa – doing translations.

The problem of representation also proved complicated. How to
encompass the products of no less than fifty-two countries (fifty-three
with the recent founding of Eritrea), only one of them still colonized
(Western Sahara by Morocco), across which the experience of achieving
independence and modern nationhood has been protracted (Egypt in
1954, Sudan, Morocco and Tunisia in 1956, Ghana and Guinea in 1957 . . .
through to Zimbabwe, 1980, and Namibia, 1990)? The big producers of
African fiction, known in the West thanks to a long process of successful and compatible exporting, would remain predominant. Here Egypt,
Nigeria and Mozambique have three entries, while South Africa has five. I
was determined that some smaller countries, such as Equatorial Guinea,
never a big scorer in the anthology stakes, should not be edged out (in
the event I failed to raise any item from the Spanish). Niger caused a
flurry of excitement with its first ever collection of nine new French-
language stories, published by Editions du Ténéré as late as 1995, but that
came to naught. By chance in 1997 I was sent by the French Institute of
South Africa on one of those agreeable writers' exchanges – to the Red
Sea republic of Djibouti. I am delighted that, as a result, Djibouti now, for
the first time ever, scores two brilliant places in an English-language
anthology designed for an international readership.

The Southern region (the concluding Part Five here) has, thanks to
circumstances of citizenship and scholarly interest, long been my area of
research. Despite the grim apartheid years, for fellow writers of the region
the flow of information never seemed that prohibited: exchanges took
place, our developments were mutually monitored. Nor were its nine
other countries entirely out of bounds to a white South African writer. So
I feel safest in making the choice in this final part.

But during those pre-1994 years I also had unlimited entry to the
region of Part Four, which comes in with a small share, but at least is an
entity of its own, almost never previously collected. I had become convinced that there was a distinct literature of what is here called the 'Indian
Ocean African Islands', hardly known to the rest of the world, let alone to
the mainland to which they do after all belong, yet of course perfectly
well known to themselves (in the Seychelles, Comores, Mauritius,
Réunion, Madagascar and so on). Part Four at least provokes future
anthologizers into not neglecting that whole new region. And in Abouba-

car Ben Saïd Salim's delicious fantasy, it is tiny Moroni that pacifies the entire world, no less.

With those two familiar parts planned out, the North of Part One (of Egyptian and Maghrebine literatures, with Naguib Mahfouz's wonderful opening piece), the Sub-Saharan West of Part Two (best known on syllabuses and on major bookshelves in the Heinemann African Writers Series) and its East and Central counterpart in Part Three, readily fell into shape.

Then an advertisement I placed, calling for submissions of unpublished work, brought in a huge number of unexpected items, leading to the first appearance of some pieces, as the notes on contributors make clear (see Tanure Ojaide, Kanchana Ugbabe and Édouard Maunick, for example).

But from some earlier anthologies I had learned how out of convenience, possibly as an editor's nervous tic, some writers are all too often tagged and typified (Ama Ata Aidoo the 'Ghanaian', Nawal El Saadawi the 'Egyptian woman Arabic-language' writer), as if quotas are of more than symbolic importance and have to be filled. I have tried to allow room for those irregulars who, because they are hard to classify, have often been excluded from grand representative schemes. So, here is Albert Taïeb the *Tunisian*, writing about *neo-colonials* – in the *Ivory Coast*; Sylvie Kandé of Senegal in *Paris*; the inimitable Nuruddin Farah uniquely of Mogadiscio – in *London*. And here is M. G. Vassanji's young Indian lady on the East Coast falling for ... a *Ghanaian*. I have attempted to undo the kind of classificatory separations Peter Clarke outlines in his perfect record of how ethnicities became identified and thrust apart in the old South Africa. For my purposes Ahdaf Soueif's 'Sandpiper' exemplifies the new approach as it refuses to be restricted to the one locale, connects up others. My conviction was to be suspicious of nationalistic literatures anyway, because they tend to be self-regarding and even archaic, rejecting the foreign, and so negating what is really germane to the avant-garde – its transgressive way of assessing and confronting the singular and different.

To outsiders the nature of African literature is often summed up in one word: oral. But from the beginning my intention was not to compete here with a treasure-trove such as Chinweizu's *Voices from Twentieth-Century Africa: Griots and Towncriers* (Faber, 1988), which honours that huge spoken tradition, particularly in the autochthonous languages of the continent. All too often tourists wish African to be no more than exotic, folkloric, other. They demand tale-spinning with digressions, animals spouting those age-old, now incomprehensible proverbs, wise parables become reduced to cartoons.

But the parallel written African short fiction is also a longstanding continuum of distinction; it is *that* tradition, very recognizable to Western readers, that I have attempted to summarize here. So the closest this collection comes to acknowledging any oral mode is in Tahar Ben Jelloun's and Taban Lo Liyong's contributions, both of which wreak havoc with its lazy conventions.

Rather be it noted that the African *written* story has developed some interesting characteristics of its own: the use of the mode of testimony and of denunciation (as in the two major pieces of Rachid Mimouni and Emmanuel Dongala); the treachery of writing back to an adversary in the adversary's very own language; the group enterprise of mastering that small, intricate, imported form (the classic short story) and turning it to an appropriately African usage.

After the Second World War anthologies such as this began modestly enough with Cullen Young's still extraordinary *African New Writing* in 1947 (fourteen stories by seven writers, no less than five being by the dazzling Cyprian Ekwensi – six were West African and one was from down South). In 1957 Mbari Publications in Ibadan founded *Black Orpheus*, there was *Transition* from Kampala fostering Africa-based story writers (while novelists could always publish abroad); there was the clearing-house of *Okike, Contrast* ... through to *La Serpent à Plumes*. There was always *The London Magazine* where writers from Luís Bernardo Honwana to Bessie Head and Ben Okri could make their debuts, where Doris Lessing and Nadine Gordimer were regulars ...

In 1962 the fine anthologist Ezekiel (now Es'kia) Mphahlele pointed out in his *The African Image* that, while vernacular literature in the English-language realm was often reduced down to serving schools only, through the magazines and the press (as in his own *Drum* experience) the supple short story form in the old colonial languages had become preferred as the most common medium for adult debate. Mphahlele even went as far as classifying it in two ways, into the escapist (popular) and the protest (socially aware) types. However, another practitioner, Henri Lopes (in the *Research in African Literatures* of Spring 1993), talking of African writers of the 1950s and 1960s in general, warned that should they continue to repeat themselves they were in danger of becoming their own undistinguished successors, leading to a dead-end. But it was the short story that he advocated as the way forward to generate that critical humour 'that begets democracy'. Lo Liyong had said it tongue-in-cheek: *fixions* – short pieces about people in big fixes.

The characteristics of the modern African short story were defined by

Emmanuel Dongala (in an interview in *Notre Librairie*, October–December 1992) in a manner with which no one may take exception. It is indebted to the tradition of Chekhov and Maupassant, Mansfield and Hemingway; it is concentrated ('une perle' – a pearl); its relationship to the expansive novel is that of poetry to prose; it is solely the creation of its individual author, written for experienced short story readers, rather than any written reduction from orature. This is the distinction between *nouvelles* and *contes*, the same one made in the translator's preface to José Luandino Vieira's *Luuanda* stories of 1980, between *histórias* (stories) and *estórias* (tales).

Dongala continues saying that no one should think writing stories is easier because they are shorter. Short stories have always put a premium on writerly skill, on cleverness in the condensation. Therefore, the short story should stand as a major genre of its own.

Accordingly I thought to trace this developing use of the short story form in Africa, beginning with the historical perspective: with Kobina Sekyi's irresistible portrait of cultural mixtures in 'The Anglo-Fanti' of 1918; with Tawfiq Al Hakim's 'The Artistes' of 1927, recounting the train journey of those dancing girls who leave Cairo in mourning only to arrive in Alexandria in full song; with a piece of R. R. R. Dhlomo captured from the mouldering pages of Stephen Black's *The Sjambok* in Johannesburg in the late 1920s; with Adelaide Casely-Hayford's 'Mista Courifer', about the respectable coffin-maker whose detribalized son reverts to indigenous costume for his outrageous wedding; with Jean-Joseph Rabearivelo's 'Un Conte de la Nuit', not a 'tale' but a 'story' really; with Birago Diop's 'Sarzan' of 1947 about the thwarted sergeant, uprooter of heathen gods in Senegal, and with other works that the late Dorothy S. Blair enabled us to read thanks to her elegant translations; with Albert Camus's crucial 'The Adulterous Woman' of 1957, about the European who commits her so-called infidelity by falling for the African interior; with Sylvain Bemba's archetypal 'The Dark Room' of 1964, about the alienated African author in dank Europe, a theme which recurs in a story such as Sylvie Kandé's here. There were the early Chinua Achebes (*Girls at War* of 1972), Gordimers and Richard Rives ... I wanted to make a sample of Williams Sassine's work available, assert the memory of innovative Dambudzo Marechera, introduce some fresh Angolans such as Uanhenga Xitu and Manuel Rui ...

There was also the allied form of the novella to be honoured, for reasons of its bulk nearly always ruled out of bounds in a short story collection. There were those several masterpieces of Sembène Ousmane, there was Leila Abouzeid's *Year of the Elephant*, about a Moroccan woman's journey to independence (translated from the Arabic by Barbara Parmenter). But how may the presence of an author occupying seventy pages be justified, while so many others would be left out altogether? Only three items here run over the five thousand word mark (by Ojaide, Ngugi and Dongala), which technically makes them 'long short stories'. At the other extreme there are several 'short shorts' (Ananissoh, Cheney-Coker, Aucamp), and some brief sketches which none the less use the full short story techniques (Akalay, Bebey).

Related was the question of selecting from story collections planned as book-length works. Bessie Head's *The Collector of Treasures* of 1977, and Assia Djebar's stories based on interviews of the late 1970s, translated as *Women of Algiers in their Apartment* (1992), are difficult to excerpt from without damaging their connective tissue. Only Vassanji's reasonably autonomous 'Breaking Loose' here is taken from a linked sequence.

Nor is there much of a scholarly apparatus to assist the researcher in following the development of the African short story. The American *Research in African Literatures*, founded in 1970 as the most comprehensive of English-language scholarly journals covering all the literatures of Africa, did not manage to deal with the short story until its sixteenth year, and then only with an article paying attention to Ayi Kwei Armah's early stories, treated as trial runs for the novels, and another on Ekwensi's exceptional career, yet with the stress on his novels as well. The Canadian journal *Ariel: A Review of International English Literature* did not get around to any coverage of the African short story until the second number of its fifteenth volume (in April 1984), where Jean de Grandsaigne made the obvious comment that clearly, in most scholarly circles, the African short story was widely seen as a mere apprentice form, soon abandoned for the prestigious and award-winning novel as commodity.

Another practitioner, Adewale Maja-Pearce (in a review in the *RAL* of Winter 1986, responding to the publication of Achebe and C. L. Innes's very influential *African Short Stories* in 1984 and its aftermath), rehearsed the argument that, as the circumstances of black writers often made it difficult to engage in a sustained creation like the novel, the hit-and-run skirmish of the short story form was for them perhaps a more appropriate and appealing manoeuvre (though he pointed out many exceptions). He maintained that, whereas the novel had fallen into coping with the African past, the story tended to deal with immediate contemporary, especially city experience in a 'slice-of-life' manner, and inevitably that, following the European and American publishing fashion, the short story in Africa had likewise fallen into a steep decline. He might well have added that in

making selections of stories suitable for educational purposes, anthologizers were also in danger of puerilizing the entire field.

The annual *African Literature Today*, founded in 1968, took until issue
number seventeen of 1991 to carry an article entirely devoted to the short
story. This was by F. Odun Balogun, another practitioner and a champion
of the form, whose *Tradition and Modernity in the African Short Story: An
Introduction to a Literature in Search of Critics* (Greenwood Press, 1991) has
been both a tease and an inspiration here. In this first ever general survey
Balogun points out that the short story *inside* Africa often enjoys a wider
audience than any other form; that it should not be considered as a by-
product or some experimental first draft of any other genre; and that both
singly and in collections the body of short stories obviously represents
a hugely complex and original achievement in its own right. And, as
Jacqueline Bardolph commented in a review of Balogun's pioneering effort
(in the *RAL* of Spring 1992), that all may undoubtedly be true within the
English-language realm, but in the French-speaking, Portuguese-speaking,
Arabic, etc., these matters just happen to be arranged differently.

*

Pursuing all these directions would have resulted in a somewhat massive
historical reader, not really what is expected of a *Picador Book* – a survey
of continuing, present activity.

Then, although only one essay in Derek Wright's groundbreaking
collection, *Contemporary African Fiction* (published by Bayreuth African
Studies in 1997) is devoted to the history and the art of the short story, it
nevertheless provided the stimulus needed for me to change my old,
locked-in position on African writing. Wright and his contributors argue
along these lines: that with Achebe's *Things Fall Apart* (1958) and for the
independence generation of the 1960s African literature became interesting essentially as a counter-discourse, writing back from Africa to foreigners. The next generation's work (for example, Armah's) was characterized
by anger and disillusionment, to be sure, but with the shifting of blame
to indigenous rulers. But then – Wright reckons – 1980 became the
watershed year that shaped today, with a diverse school of writers now in
pursuit of authentic African models, making attempts on cultural management (Ngugi wa Thiong'o, Ken Saro-Wiwa), with the hybridization of new
subject matters and with hugely increased formal innovation (Ben Okri).
Also there is the arrival of women on the publishing scene (El Saadawi,
Aidoo, Lília Momplé and Sheila Roberts) and even the occasional other-
than-black (Mia Couto, for example, is a white male).

Since 1980, with three Nobel Prizes at last won by Africans (Wole Soyinka, 1986; Mahfouz, 1988; Gordimer, 1991), the continent has achieved some status, too, as far as world literary affairs are concerned. And Wright's team names the pioneering writers who now typify present movements, many of whom are indeed represented here: Ben Jelloun, Okri, Ngugi and Farah, through to Yvonne Vera and Chris van Wyk. Wright delimited the new African literary shop-window in which I may now exhibit a choice of wares.

The threshold of 1980 has not been ruthlessly applied here, however. Often for a general reader with a not very professional access to the entire production of such a varied and vast region, the psychological 'date' of a text is the one when he or she first discovers it. Cape Verdean literature, to give one puny example, arrived for many English-speakers only in 1988 with the appearance of *Across the Atlantic* – so the inclusion of Teixeira de Sousa's story, albeit from as early as 1972, is in a sense justified, if only as a prelude to the later works of the region to which it is attached. Honwana's 'lost' story of 1971 is also out of the time-frame, but here its uncovering by its first translator (in 1998) is what perhaps counts today. (The same may be said of no less than another fifteen translations, which also appear here for the first time.)

There were other limits about which it is best to be frank. Some stories are too terrible to be told. Ever since Joseph Conrad's perennial *Heart of Darkness* (1902) that began the century now closed, British and American readers have seemingly developed a bottomless appetite for the very untold horrors that Conrad's work was meant to deplore and which the 'Dark Continent' appears – at least in the media version – only too willing to keep feeding. For obvious reasons, more than half of the contributors here do not live in their home countries. One story by Augustin Ruhabura of Rwanda, about the police raiding, robbing and raping the very citizens they are meant to protect, proved just too strong for my staunch readers' panel. Another one on the shortlist was Festus Iyayi's title story to his collection, *Awaiting Court Martial*, published in Lagos in 1996 by Malthouse. This is the monologue of an executioner involved in secret firing-squad activities, torturing and finally wiping out enemies of the military regime, who is called upon to arrange the quick, secret dispatch of his own kid brother. During the action the cruelties are so grotesque (children with kneecaps removed, led stumbling to the target-range; truckloads of dismembered bodies heading through the night for mass pit-burials) that my panel was unable to stomach such atrocities; indeed the English language is not accustomed to carry such depictions. One may only marvel at Iyayi's courage in writing so explicitly, and at the daring of his publishers, which no Western publisher may match. But in the end I felt 'Awaiting Court Martial' should not take its deserved place here for fear that it became misread. The furthest this book may stretch literary decorum is demonstrated in Mimouni's piece (against fundamentalism), in Okri's (against famine) and in Dongala's (facing dictatorial rule).

*

Several friends – from Texas to Singapore, and Venice to Gaborone – have generously assisted me with material from their collections, as recommenders, advisers and as preliminary readers. Others have accepted commissions as translators with grace and speed. Those to whom I have become indebted over the years for many other services are too numerous to mention. But to them my gratitude.

STEPHEN GRAY
Johannesburg, 2000

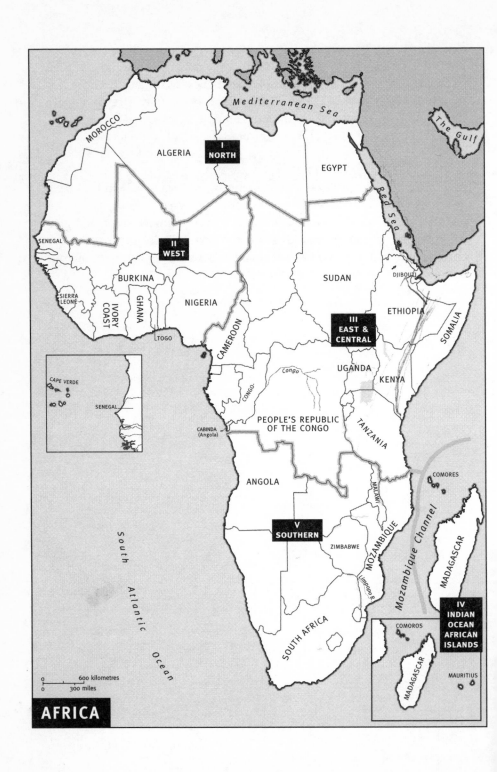

PART ONE

NORTH

Naguib Mahfouz

Half a Day

Translated from the Arabic by Denys Johnson-Davies

Naguib Mahfouz, born in Cairo, Egypt, in 1911, is the pioneer of modern fiction in Arabic with some forty books to his name in a career of over sixty years. These include novels such as the classics of Middle Eastern literature, *Miramar* (1967) and *Wedding Song* (1981), and some fourteen volumes of Cairene short stories. He was awarded the Nobel Prize for Literature in 1988 and more than half of his œuvre is now available in English. An English volume of his short stories, ranging from 1962 to 1984, was made available by the American University in Cairo Press in 1991 under the title, *The Time and the Place and Other Stories* (now Doubleday). 'Half a Day' is taken from this selection, and the original first appeared in a collection in Cairo in 1989.

Denys Johnson-Davies is a Vancouver-born scholar, trained in Arabic at London University, who has since become the distinguished translator of numerous Arabic-language authors, including Mohamed El Bisatie, Tawfiq Al Hakim and Alifa Rifaat.

I PROCEEDED ALONGSIDE MY FATHER, clutching his right hand, running to keep up with the long strides he was taking. All my clothes were new: the black shoes, the green school uniform and the red tarboosh. My delight in my new clothes, however, was not altogether unmarred, for this was no feast day but the day on which I was to be cast into school for the first time.

My mother stood at the window watching our progress, and I would turn towards her from time to time, as though appealing for help. We walked along a street lined with gardens; on both sides were extensive fields planted with crops, prickly pears, henna trees and a few date palms.

'Why school?' I challenged my father openly. 'I shall never do anything to annoy you.'

'I'm not punishing you,' he said, laughing. 'School's not a punishment. It's the factory that makes useful men out of boys. Don't you want to be like your father and brothers?'

I was not convinced. I did not believe there was really any good to be had in tearing me away from the intimacy of my home and throwing me into this building that stood at the end of the road like some huge, high-walled fortress, exceedingly stern and grim.

When we arrived at the gate we could see the courtyard, vast and crammed full of boys and girls. 'Go in by yourself,' said my father, 'and join them. Put a smile on your face and be a good example to others.'

I hesitated and clung to his hand, but he gently pushed me from him. 'Be a man,' he said. 'Today you truly begin life. You will find me waiting for you when it's time to leave.'

I took a few steps, then stopped and looked but saw nothing. Then the faces of boys and girls came into view. I did not know a single one of them, and none of them knew me. I felt I was a stranger who had lost his way. But glances of curiosity were directed towards me, and one boy approached and asked, 'Who brought you?'

'My father,' I whispered.

'My father's dead,' he said quite simply.

I did not know what to say. The gate was closed, letting out a pitiable screech. Some of the children burst into tears. The bell rang. A lady came along, followed by a group of men. The men began sorting us into ranks. We were formed into an intricate pattern in the great courtyard surrounded on three sides by high buildings of several floors; from each floor we were overlooked by a long balcony roofed in wood.

'This is your new home,' said the woman. 'Here too there are mothers and fathers. Here there is everything that is enjoyable and beneficial to knowledge and religion. Dry your tears and face life joyfully.'

We submitted to the facts, and this submission brought a sort of contentment. Living beings were drawn to other living beings, and from the first moments my heart made friends with such boys as were to be my friends and fell in love with such girls as I was to be in love with, so that it seemed my misgivings had had no basis. I had never imagined school would have this rich variety. We played all sorts of different games: swings, the vaulting horse, ball games. In the music room we chanted our first songs. We also had our first introduction to language. We saw a globe of the Earth, which revolved and showed the various continents and countries. We started learning the numbers. The story of the Creator of the universe was read to us, we were told of His present world and of His

Hereafter, and we heard examples of what He said. We ate delicious food, took a little nap and woke up to go on with friendship and love, play and learning.

As our path revealed itself to us, however, we did not find it as totally sweet and unclouded as we had presumed. Dust-laden winds and unexpected accidents came about suddenly, so we had to be watchful, at the ready and very patient. It was not all a matter of playing and fooling around. Rivalries could bring about pain and hatred or give rise to fighting. And while the lady would sometimes smile, she would often scowl and scold. Even more frequently she would resort to physical punishment.

In addition, the time for changing one's mind was over and gone and there was no question of ever returning to the paradise of home. Nothing lay ahead of us but exertion, struggle and perseverance. Those who were able took advantage of the opportunities for success and happiness that presented themselves amid the worries.

The bell rang announcing the passing of the day and the end of work. The throngs of children rushed towards the gate, which was opened again. I bade farewell to friends and sweethearts and passed through the gate. I peered around but found no trace of my father, who had promised to be there. I stepped aside to wait. When I had waited for a long time without avail, I decided to return home on my own. After I had taken a few steps, a middle-aged man passed by and I realized at once that I knew him. He came towards me, smiling, and shook me by the hand, saying, 'It's a long time since we last met – how are you?'

With a nod of my head, I agreed with him and in turn asked, 'And you, how are you?'

'As you can see, not all that good, the Almighty be praised!'

Again he shook me by the hand and went off. I proceeded a few steps, then came to a startled halt. Good Lord! Where was the street lined with gardens? Where had it disappeared to? When did all these vehicles invade it? And when did all these hordes of humanity come to rest upon its surface? How did these hills of refuse come to cover its sides? And where were the fields that bordered it? High buildings had taken over, the street surged with children and disturbing noises shook the air. At various points stood conjurors showing off their tricks and making snakes appear from baskets. Then there was a band announcing the opening of a circus, with clowns and weight lifters walking in front. A line of trucks carrying central security troops crawled majestically by. The siren of a fire engine shrieked, and it was not clear how the vehicle would cleave its way to reach the blazing fire. A battle raged between a taxi driver and his passenger, while the passenger's wife called out for help and no one answered. Good God! I was in a daze. My head spun. I almost went crazy. How could all this have happened in half a day, between early morning and sunset? I would find the answer at home with my father. But where was my home? I could see only tall buildings and hordes of people. I hastened on to the crossroads between the gardens and Abu Khoda. I had to cross Abu Khoda to reach my house, but the stream of cars would not let up. The fire engine's siren was shrieking at full pitch as it moved at a snail's pace, and I said to myself, 'Let the fire take its pleasure in what it consumes.' Extremely irritated, I wondered when I would be able to cross. I stood there a long time, until the young lad employed at the ironing shop on the corner came up to me. He stretched out his arm and said gallantly, 'Grandpa, let me take you across.'

Nawal El Saadawi

The Veil

Translated from the Arabic by Shirley Eber

Nawal El Saadawi is one of the few Arabic women writers widely published in the West, where her novels *Woman at Point Zero* (1984) and *God Dies by the Nile* (1985), both translated into English by her husband, Sherif Hetata, are favourites. She was born in the village of Kafr Tahla, trained as a medical doctor and rose to become Egypt's Director of Public Health. She lives in Cairo. 'The Veil' was written in Addis Abeba in 1978, was first published in an English translation in Cairo in an anthology in 1987, and featured in the 1993 *Passport to Arabia*. In 1987 it was also included in the selection of her stories, *Death of an Ex-Minister* (Methuen), translated by Shirley Eber. The same translator has also produced another selection of stories of hers, *She has No Place in Paradise* (1989). She has recently published her autobiography, *A Daughter of Isis*.

Shirley Eber has written articles on African authors for the *Guardian* and *Index on Censorship*; she translates into English both from Arabic, as here, and from the French (see Rachid Mimouni's story on page 20).

ALL OF A SUDDEN I AWAKE to find myself sitting, a bottle of wine in front of me of which only a little remains, and an ashtray full of cigarette ends of a strange kind I think I have not seen before, until I remember that they are the new brand I began smoking three or four years ago.

I look up from the ashtray to see a man I've never seen before. He is naked, apart from a silken robe which is open to reveal hairy chest and thighs. Between the chest and thighs are a pair of close-fitting striped underpants. I raise my surprised eyes to his face. Only now do I realize that I've seen him before. My eyes rest on his for a moment and I smile a strange, automatic smile, as fleeting as a flash of light or an electric current, leaving behind no trace other than a curious kind of perplexity like the eternal confusion of a person in search of God or happiness. Why is there such confusion in the world and in my body at this particular moment, even though each day my eyes meet hundreds or thousands of eyes and the world and my body remain as they are? But it is soon over. The world and my body return to normal and life continues as usual. It is three or four years since I saw him for the first time and I'd almost forgotten him in the tumult of work and home and people.

My eyes fall on to his naked body and hairy thighs once more. The expression on my face, as I look at his body, is not the same as when I look into his eyes, for my problem is that what I feel inside shows instantly on my face. His eyes are the only part of his body with which I have real contact. They dispel strangeness and ugliness and make my relationship with him real in the midst of numerous unreal ones. Three years, maybe four, and every time I run into him in a street or office or corridor, I stop for a moment in surprise and confusion. Then I continue on my way, knowing that while this relationship is very strange, it is at the same time familiar and accepted, among numerous unfamiliar and unaccepted relationships.

When we began meeting regularly or semi-regularly, my relationship with him did not extend to parts of his body other than his eyes. For long hours we would sit and talk, my eyes never leaving his. It was a sort of meeting of minds, and gratifying, but the gratification was somehow lacking. What did it lack?

I asked myself whether it was the body's desire for contact with another body? And why not? In the final analysis, isn't he a man and I a woman? The idea strikes me as new, even strange, and a frightening curiosity takes hold of me. I wonder what the meeting of my body with his could be like. A violent desire to find out can sometimes be more violent than the desire for love and can, at times, draw me into loveless contacts simply in order to satisfy that curiosity. And every time that happens, I experience a repulsion, certain in my mind that my body repulses the body of a man except in one situation – that of love.

I understand the cause of this repulsion. It's an explicable repulsion linked not to the body but to history. To the extent that man worships his masculinity, so woman repulses him. A woman's repulsion is the other face of the worship of the male deity. No power on earth can rid woman of her repulsion other than the victory of love over the male deity. Then history will go back six thousand years to when the deity was female. Will love be victorious? Is the relationship between us love? I do not know. I have no proof. Can love be proved? Is it the desire which rises to the surface of my crowded life, to look into his eyes? Like a person who, from time to time, goes to a holy water spring to kneel down and pray and then goes home? I do not kneel down and neither do I pray. I recognize no deity other than my mind inside my head. What is it that draws me to his eyes?

Is love simply a fairy tale, like the stories of Adam and Eve or Cinderella or Hassan the Wise? All the fairy tales came to an end and the veil fell from each of them. Many veils fell from my mind as I grew up. Each time a veil fell, I would cry at night in sadness for the beautiful illusion which was lost. But in the morning, I'd see my eyes shining, washed by tears as the dew washes the blossom, the jasmine and the rose. I would leave the mirror, trample the fallen veil underfoot and stamp on it with a new-found strength, with more strength than I'd had the previous day.

He has filled the tenth or twentieth glass. My hand trembles a little as I hold it, but the deity inside my head is as steady and immobile as the Sphinx. My eyes are still on his and do not leave them, even though I realize, somehow, that he is no longer wearing the silken robe nor even the tight striped underpants.

I notice that his body is white, blushed with red, revealing strength, youthfulness, cleanliness and good eating. My eyes must still have been staring into his, for in another moment, I realize that he has taken my head in his hand and moved it so that my eyes fall on to his body.

I look at him steadily and once again see the strength and youthfulness and cleanliness and good eating. I almost tell him what it is I see.

But I look up and my eyes meet his. I do not know whether it is he who looks surprised or whether the surprise is in my own eyes. I tell myself that the situation calls for surprise, for it is nearly three in the morning. The glass is empty. There is no one in the house and the world outside is silent, dark, dead, fallen into oblivion. What is happening between my body and his?

When I next turn towards him, he is sitting, dressed in the robe with the belt carefully tied around his waist, hiding his chest and thighs. I no longer see anything of him other than his head and eyes and feet inside a pair of light house shoes. From the side, his face looks tired, as though he's suddenly grown old and weary. His features hang loose, like a child needing to sleep after staying up late. I put out a hand, like a mother does to stroke the face of a child, and place a tender motherly kiss on his forehead.

In the street I lift my burning face to the cold and humid dawn breeze. Mysterious feelings of joy mingle with strange feelings of sadness. I put my head on my pillow, my eyes open, filled with tears. My mind had got the better of the wine until I put my head on the pillow; but then the wine took over and sadness replaced joy.

When I open my eyes the following day, the effect of the wine has gone and the veil has lifted from my eyes. I look in the mirror at my shining eyes washed with tears. I am about to walk away from the mirror, like every other time, to trample on the fallen veil at my feet and stamp on it with new-found strength. But this time I do not leave my place. I bend down, pick up the veil from the ground and replace it once again on my face.

Ahdaf Soueif

Sandpiper

Ahdaf Soueif was born in Cairo and educated in Egypt and in England, where she now lives. She has contributed stories (written in English) to the *London Review of Books*. Her first collection, *Aisha* (1983), was much praised for its presentation of sexual politics in modern Africa. 'Sandpiper' first appeared in *Granta*, number 40 (Autumn 1994), and was collected in the volume of short stories to which it gave its title, *Sandpiper* (Bloomsbury, 1996). Her second novel, *The Map of Love*, was shortlisted for the Booker Prize in 1999.

OUTSIDE, THERE IS A PATH. A path of beaten white stone bordered by a white wall – low, but not low enough for me to see over it from here. White sands drift across the path. From my window, I used to see patterns in their drift. On my way to the beach, I would try to place my foot, just the ball of my foot, for there never was much room, on those white spaces that glinted flat and free of sand. I had an idea that the patterns on the stone should be made by nature alone; I did not want one grain of sand, blown by a breeze I could not feel, to change its course because of me. What point would there be in trying to decipher a pattern that I had caused? It was not easy. Balancing, the toes of one bare foot on the hot stone, looking for the next clear space to set the other foot down. It took a long time to reach the end of the path. And then the stretch of beach. And then the sea.

I used to sit where the water rolled in, rolled in, its frilled white edge nibbling at the sand, withdrawing to leave great damp half moons of a darker, more brownish-beige. I would sit inside one of these curves, at the very midpoint, fitting my body to its contour, and wait. The sea unceasingly shifts and stirs and sends out fingers, paws, tongues to probe the shore. Each wave coming in is different. It separates itself from the vast, moving blue, rises and surges forward with a low growl, lightening as it approaches to a pale green, then turns over to display the white frill that slides like a thousand snakes down upon itself, breaks and skitters up the sandbank. I used to sit very still. Sometimes the wave would barely touch my feet, sometimes it would swirl around me then pull back, sifting yet another layer of sand from under me, leaving me wet to the waist. My heels rested in twin hollows that filled, emptied and refilled without a break. And subtle as the shadow of a passing cloud, my half moon would slip down the bank – only to be overtaken and swamped by the next leap of foaming white.

I used to sit in the curve and dig my fingers into the grainy, compact sand and feel it grow wetter as my fingers went deeper and deeper till the next rippling, frothing rush of white came and smudged the edges of the little burrow I had made. Its walls collapsed and I removed my hand, covered in wet clay, soon to revert to dry grains that I would easily brush away.

I lean against the wall of my room and count: twelve years ago, I met him. Eight years ago, I married him. Six years ago, I gave birth to his child.

For eight summers we have been coming here, to the beach-house west of Alexandria. The first summer had not been a time of reflection; my occupation then had been to love my husband in this – to me – new and different place. To love him as he walked towards my parasol, shaking the water from his black hair, his feet sinking into the warm, hospitable sand. To love him as he carried his nephew on his shoulders into the sea, threw him in, caught him and hoisted him up again; a colossus bestriding the waves. To love him as he played backgammon with his father in the evening, the slam of counters and the clatter of dice resounding on the patio while, at the dining-room table, his sister showed me how to draw their ornate, circular script. To love this new him, who had been hinted at but never revealed when we lived in my northern land and who, after a long absence, had found his way back into the heart of his country, taking me along with him. We walked in the sunset along the water's edge, kicking at the spray, my sun-hat fallen on my back, my hand, pale bronze in his burnt brown, my face no doubt mirroring his: aglow with health and love; a young couple in a glitzy commercial for life insurance or a two-week break in the sun.

My second summer here was the sixth summer of our love – and the last of our happiness. Carrying my child and loving her father, I sat on the beach, dug holes in the sand and let my thoughts wander. I thought about our life in my country, before we were married: four years in the cosy flat, precarious on top of a roof in a Georgian square, him meeting me at the bus stop when I came back from work, Sundays when it did not rain and we sat in the park with our newspapers, late nights at the movies. I thought of those things and missed them – but with no great sense of loss. It was as though they were all there, to be called upon, to be lived again whenever we wanted.

I looked out to sea and, now I realize, I was trying to work out my coordinates. I thought a lot about the water and the sand as I sat there watching them meet and flirt and touch. I tried to understand that I was on the edge, the very edge of Africa; that the vastness ahead was nothing compared to what lay behind me. But – even though I'd been there and seen for myself its never-ending dusty green interior, its mountains, the big sky, my mind could not grasp a world that was not present to my senses – I could see the beach, the waves, the blue beyond, and cradling them all, my baby.

I sat with my hand on my belly and waited for the tiny eruptions, the small flutterings, that told me how she lay and what she was feeling. Gradually, we came to talk to each other. She would curl into a tight ball in one corner of my body until, lopsided and uncomfortable, I coaxed and prodded her back into a more centred, relaxed position. I slowly rubbed one corner of my belly until *there*, aimed straight at my hand, I felt a gentle punch. I tapped and she punched again. I was twenty-nine. For seventeen years my body had waited to conceive, and now my heart and mind had caught up with it. Nature had worked admirably; I had wanted the child through my love for her father and how I loved her father that summer. My body could not get enough of him. His baby was snug inside me and I wanted him there, too.

From where I stand now, all I can see is dry, solid white. The white glare, the white wall and the white path, narrowing in the distance.

I should have gone. No longer a serrating thought but familiar and dull. I should have gone. On that swirl of amazed and wounded anger when, knowing him as I did, I first sensed that he was pulling away from me, I should have gone. I should have turned, picked up my child and gone.

I turn. The slatted blinds are closed against a glaring sun. They call the wooden blinds *sheesh* and tell me it's the Persian word for glass. So that which sits next to a thing is called by its name. I have had this thought many times and feel as though it should lead me somewhere; as though I should draw some conclusion from it, but so far I haven't.

I draw my finger along a wooden slat. Um Sabir, my husband's old nanny, does everything around the house, both here and in the city. I tried, at first, at least to help, but she would rush up and ease the duster or the vacuum cleaner from my hands. 'Shame, shame. What am I here for? Keep your hands nice and soft. Go and rest. Or why don't you go to the club? What have you to do with these things?' My husband translated all this for me and said things to her which I came to understand meant that tomorrow I would get used to their ways. The meals I planned never worked out. Um Sabir cooked what was best in the market on that day. If I tried to do the shopping the prices trebled. I arranged the flowers, smoothed out the pleats in the curtains and presided over our dinner parties.

My bed is made. My big bed which a half-asleep Lucy, creeping under the mosquito net, tumbles into in the middle of every night. She fits herself into my body and I put my arm over her until she shakes it off. In her sleep she makes use of me; my breast is sometimes her pillow, my hip her footstool. I lie content, glad to be of use. I hold her foot in my hand and dread the time – so soon to come – when it will no longer be seemly to kiss the dimpled ankle.

On a black leather sofa in a transit lounge in an airport once, many years ago, I watched a Pakistani woman sleep. Her dress and trousers were a deep yellow silk and on her dress bloomed luscious flowers in purple and green. Her arms were covered in gold bangles. She had gold in her ears, her left nostril and around her neck. Against her body her small son lay curled. One of his feet was between her knees, her nose was in his hair. All her worldly treasure was on that sofa with her, and so she slept soundly on. That image, too, I saved up for him.

I made my bed this morning. I spread my arms out wide and gathered in the soft, billowing mosquito net. I twisted it round in a thick coil and tied it into a loose loop that dangles gracefully in mid-air.

Nine years ago, sitting under my first mosquito net, I had written, 'Now I know how it feels to be a memsahib.' That was in Kano; deep, deep in the heart of the continent I now sit on the edge of. I had been in love with him for three years and being apart then was a variant, merely, of being together. When we were separated there was for each a gnawing lack of the other. We would say that this confirmed our true, essential union. We had parted at Heathrow, and we were to be rejoined in a fortnight, in Cairo, where I would meet his family for the first time.

I had thought to write a story about those two weeks; about my first trip into Africa: about Muhammad Al Senusi explaining courteously to me the inferior status of women, courteously because, being foreign, European, on a business trip, I was an honorary man. A story about travelling the long, straight road to Maiduguri and stopping at roadside shacks to chew on meat that I then swallowed in lumps while Senusi told me how the meat in Europe had no body and melted like rice pudding in his mouth. About the time when I saw the lion in the tall grass. I asked the driver to stop, jumped out of the car, aimed my camera and shot as the lion crouched. Back in the car, unfreezing himself from horror, the driver assured me that the lion had crouched in order to spring at me. I still have the photo: a lion crouching in tall grass – close up. I look at it and cannot make myself believe what could have happened.

I never wrote the story, although I still have the notes. Right here, in this leather portfolio which I take out of a drawer in my cupboard. My Africa story. I told it to him instead – and across the candlelit table of a Cairo restaurant he kissed my hands and said, 'I'm crazy about you.' Under the high windows the Nile flowed by. Eternity was in our lips, our eyes, our brows – I married him, and I was happy.

I leaf through my notes. Each one carries a comment, a description meant for him. All my thoughts were addressed to him. For his part he wrote that after I left him at the airport he turned round to hold me and tell me how desolate he felt. He could not believe I was not there to comfort him. He wrote about the sound of my voice on the telephone and the crease at the top of my arm that he said he loved to kiss.

What story can I write? I sit with my notes at my writing table and wait for Lucy. I should have been sleeping. That is what they think I am doing. That is what we pretend I do: sleep away the hottest of the midday hours. Out there on the beach, by the pool, Lucy has no need of me. She has her father, her uncle, her two aunts, her five cousins; a wealth of playmates and protectors. And Um Sabir, sitting patient and watchful in her black *jalabiyyah* and *tarha,* the deckchairs beside her loaded with towels, sun-cream, sun-hats, sandwiches and iced drinks in thermos-flasks.

I look, and watch, and wait for Lucy.

In the market in Kaduna the mottled, red carcases lay on wooden stalls shaded by grey plastic canopies. At first I saw the meat and the flies swarming and settling. Then, on top of the grey plastic sheets, I saw the vultures. They perched as sparrows would in an English market square, but they were heavy and still and silent. They sat cool and unblinking as the fierce sun beat down on their bald, wrinkled heads. And hand in hand with the fear that swept over me was a realization that fear was misplaced, that everybody else knew they were there and still went about their business; that in the meat market in Kaduna, vultures were commonplace.

The heat of the sun saturates the house; it seeps out from every pore. I open the door of my room and walk out into the silent hall. In the bathroom I stand in the shower tray and turn the tap to let the cool water splash over my feet. I tuck my skirt between my thighs and bend to put my hands and wrists under the water. I press wet palms to my face and picture grey slate roofs wet with rain. I picture trees; trees that rustle in the wind and, when the rain has stopped, release fresh showers of droplets from their leaves.

I pad out on wet feet that dry by the time I arrive at the kitchen at the end of the long corridor. I open the fridge and see the chunks of lamb marinating in a large metal tray for tonight's barbecue. The mountain of yellow grapes draining in a colander. I pick out a cluster and put it on a white saucer. Um Sabir washes all the fruit and vegetables in red permanganate. This is for my benefit since Lucy crunches cucumbers and carrots straight out of the greengrocer's baskets. But then she was born here. And now she belongs. If I had taken her away then, when she was eight months old, she would have belonged with me. I pour out a tall glass of cold, bottled water and close the fridge.

I walk back through the corridor. Past Um Sabir's room, his room, Lucy's room. Back in my room I stand again at the window, looking out through the chink in the shutters at the white that seems now to be losing the intensity of its glare. If I were to move to the window in the opposite wall I would see the green lawn encircled by the three wings of the house, the sprinkler at its centre ceaselessly twisting, twisting. I stand and press my forehead against the warm glass. I breathe on the window-pane but it does not mist over.

I turn on the fan. It blows my hair across my face and my notes across the bed. I kneel on the bed and gather them. The top one says, 'Ningi, his big teeth stained with kola, sits grandly at his desk. By his right hand there is a bicycle bell which he rings to summon a gofer – ', and then again: 'The three things we stop for on the road should be my title: "Peeing, Praying and Petrol."' Those were light-hearted times, when the jokes I made were not bitter.

I lie down on the bed. These four pillows are my innovation. Here they use one long pillow with two smaller ones on top of it. The bedlinen comes in sets. Consequently my bed always has two pillows in plain cases and two with embroidery to match the sheets. Also, I have one side of a chiffonier which is full of long, embroidered pillowcases. When I take them out and look at them I find their flowers, sheltered for so long in the dark, are unfaded, bright and new.

Lying on the bed, I hold the cluster of grapes above my face and bite one off as Romans do in films. Oh, to play, to play again, but my only playmate now is Lucy and she is out by the pool with her cousins.

A few weeks ago, back in Cairo, Lucy looked up at the sky and said, 'I can see the place where we're going to be.'

'Where?' I asked, as we drove through Gabalaya Street.

'In heaven.'

'Oh!' I said. 'And what's it like?'

'It's a circle, Mama, and it has a chimney, and it will always be winter there.'

I reached over and patted her knee. 'Thank you, darling,' I said.

Yes, I am sick – but not just for home. I am sick for a time, a time that was and that I can never have again. A lover I had and can never have again.

I watched him vanish – well, not vanish, slip away, recede. He did not want to go. He did not go quietly. He asked me to hold him, but he couldn't tell me how. A fairy godmother, robbed for an instant of our belief in her magic, turns into a sad old woman, her wand into a useless stick. I suppose I should have seen it coming. My foreignness, which had been so charming, began to irritate him. My inability to remember names, to follow the minutiae of politics, my struggles with his language, my need to be protected from the sun, the mosquitoes, the salads, the drinking water. He was back home, and he needed someone he could be at home with, at home. It took perhaps a year. His heart was broken in two, mine was simply broken.

I never see my lover now. Sometimes, as he romps with Lucy on the beach, or bends over her grazed elbow, or sits across our long table from me at a dinner party, I see a man I could yet fall in love with, and I turn away.

I told him too about my first mirage, the one I saw on that long road to Maiduguri. And on the desert road to Alexandria the first summer, I saw it again. 'It's hard to believe it isn't there when I can see it so clearly,' I complained.

'You only think you see it,' he said.

'Isn't that the same thing?' I asked. 'My brain tells me there's water there. Isn't that enough?'

'Yes,' he said, and shrugged. 'If all you want to do is sit in the car and see it. But if you want to go and put your hands in it and drink, then it isn't enough, surely?' He gave me a sidelong glance and smiled.

Soon I should hear Lucy's high, clear voice, chattering to her father as they walk hand in hand up the gravel drive to the back door. Behind them will come the heavy tread of Um Sabir. I will go out smiling to meet them and he will deliver a wet, sandy Lucy into my care, and ask if I'm okay with a slightly anxious look. I will take Lucy into my bathroom while he goes into his. Later, when the rest of the family have all drifted back and showered and changed, everyone will sit around the barbecue and eat and drink and talk politics and crack jokes of hopeless, helpless irony and laugh. I should take up embroidery and start on those Aubusson tapestries we all, at the moment, imagine will be necessary for Lucy's trousseau.

Yesterday when I had dressed her after the shower she examined herself intently in my mirror and asked for a French plait. I sat behind her at the dressing-table blow-drying her black hair, brushing it and plaiting it. When Lucy was born Um Sabir covered all the mirrors. His sister said, 'They say if a baby looks in the mirror she will see her own grave.' We laughed but we did not remove the covers; they stayed in place till she was one.

I looked at Lucy's serious face in the mirror. I had seen my grave once, or thought I had. That was part of my Africa story. The plane out of Nigeria circled Cairo airport. Three times I heard the landing-gear come down, and three times it was raised again. Sitting next to me were two Finnish businessmen. When the announcement came that we were re-routeing to Luxor they shook their heads and ordered another drink. At dawn, above Luxor airport, we were told there was trouble with the undercarriage and that the pilot was going to attempt a crash-landing. I thought, so this is why they've sent us to Luxor, to burn up discreetly and not clog Cairo airport. We were asked to fasten our seat belts, take off our shoes and watches, put the cushions from the backs of our seats on our laps and bend double over them with our arms around our heads. I slung my handbag with my passport, tickets and money around my neck and shoulder before I did these things. My Finnish neighbours formally shook each other's hands. On the plane there was perfect silence as we dropped out of the sky. And then a terrible, agonized, protracted screeching of machinery as we hit the tarmac. And in that moment, not only my head, but all of me, my whole being, seemed to tilt into a blank, an empty radiance, but lucid. Then three giant thoughts. One was of him – his name, over and over again. The other was of the children I would never have. The third was that the pattern was now complete: this is what my life amounted to.

When we did not die, that first thought: his name, his name, his name became a talisman, for in extremity hadn't all that was not him been wiped out of my life? My life, which once again stretched out before me, shimmering with possibilities, was meant to merge with his.

I finished the French plait and Lucy chose a blue clasp to secure its end. Before I let her run out I smoothed some aftersun on her face. Her skin is nut-brown, except just next to her ears where it fades to a pale cream gleaming with golden down. I put my lips to her neck. 'My Lucy, Lucia, *Lambah*,' I murmured as I kissed her and let her go. Lucy. My treasure, my trap.

Now, when I walk to the sea, to the edge of this continent where I live, where I almost died, where I wait for my daughter to grow away from me, I see different things from those I saw that summer six years ago. The last of the foam is swallowed bubbling into the sand, to sink down and rejoin the sea at an invisible subterranean level. With each ebb of green water the sand loses part of itself to the sea, with each flow another part is flung back to be reclaimed once again by the beach. That narrow stretch of sand knows nothing in the world better than it does the white waves that whip it, caress it, collapse on to it, vanish into it. The white foam knows nothing better than those sands which wait for it, rise to it and suck it in. But what do the waves know of the massed, hot, still sands of the desert just twenty, no, ten feet beyond the scalloped edge? And what does the beach know of the depths, the cold, the currents just there, there – do you see it? – where the water turns a deeper blue.

Rachid Mimouni

The Escapee

Translated from the French by Shirley Eber

Rachid Mimouni was born in 1945 in a village to the east of Algiers, where he was a teacher of economics at the National Institute of Production and Industrial Development. Of his several distinguished novels in French, *The Honour of the Tribe*, which shows the destruction of community life affected by heedless modernization, appeared in English translation in 1992. His stories, *La Ceinture de l'Ogresse*, published in Algiers and Paris in 1990, received the Prix de la Nouvelle de l'Academie Française in 1991, and appeared as *The Ogre's Embrace* in 1993 in a translation by Shirley Eber. 'The Escapee' is the concluding piece there. In the same year he went into exile in Morocco, and died in Paris in 1995.

IN HIS INFINITE SOLICITUDE, for his birthday, the Supreme Leader, beloved of the people and awesome forger of History, has decreed this Wednesday a legal holiday, public and generously paid, for the personnel of all administrations and enterprises, including those remunerated by the hour or by the day; a school holiday for pupils, students and scholars, to whom will be distributed free of charge a meal accompanied by little flags with his effigy which should, when the time comes, be waved frenetically and ceaselessly before the cyclopean eye of cameras released on to the streets of the capital, more exuberant than crazed young calves longtime quarantined. To the lower steps of his sheltered residence, the peasants will come to deposit their most beautiful fruits, the poets to declaim their most beautiful verses and the most beautiful girls to howl their adulation. The shops in the town have received an imperious order from the administration not to lower their shutters until past midnight despite their impoverished windows which will have to remain illuminated through the night; just like the cafés which throughout the day have, on orders from on high, taken delivery of cargoes of multicoloured lemonades and a variety of juices; like the restaurants with starved menus which, for the occasion, will be able to offer their fortunate guests not only meat, red and white, and ten varieties of fish but even, for dessert, exotic fruit so long missing from our traders' stalls that our children are unaware of their existence; and the bars, always watched over like dens of intellectuals, will be licensed by a permit from the Prefecture to serve male bacchantes until dawn with beer that froths and all sorts of liqueurs imported with hard currency, whose bottles of a thousand shapes have ended up adorning shelves more naked than the languid pose of a mistress with eyes for the lover whose desire is appeased, and the sight of which brings tears of nostalgia to the eyes of the old drunkards who recall times more distant than joy. This evening they will shamelessly overindulge in those drinks of yesteryear miraculously reappeared.

For the great day, they have repainted all the buildings in uniform blue and white, dusted down the sickly and scrofulous trees, given lights to the blinded lamps, flushed down the arteries of the town to the detriment of the inhabitants who know they must pay for this liquid prodigality with several days of sterile taps. They have stopped the drains from emptying into the streets, the beggars and tramps from showing themselves, restricted to their homes the few intellectuals still at liberty, erased the cases of suicide and hysteria from the statistics, remembered to wind up the public clocks which forgetfulness has made arthritic, decorated with multicoloured bulbs and sky-blue slogans the façades of buildings, cloaked with integrity all the officials of the Great Party of the People, proceeded to rewrite all the Books of History, expelled the foreign journalists, called on the sky to obliterate its clouds, stifled in his hotel room the last political opponent whom they had earlier decided provisionally to reprieve in order that he might serve as a scapegoat for future popular disturbances, embellished the curricula vitae of the high dignitaries of the regime with great exploits and subtly trimmed down those of their wives, ordered all the bigots to shave their beards and peopled the streets with a profusion of banners required simply to flutter in spite of the ardent breeze.

Motorists will be able to hoot their horns to their hearts' content and park where they want. Foreign embassies have been authorized to accept every visa request, but for the one glorious day only and on condition that they immediately hand over to the police names of the applicants for travel. Common convicts will be able to watch on television the scenes of public rejoicing.

Adolescent boys know that the girls will come out, priggish or provocative, but they will only dare approach them under cover of the shadows or, more easily still, the throngs of pseudopodia who will enliven the great public places around orchestras equipped with infernal sound systems imported by the planeload from countries that worship music.

The newspapers have announced that a generous amnesty, decided by the Supreme Leader, beloved of the people and awesome forger of History, has liberated a thousand prisoners. Released: the bakers, starvers of the masses, who speculated on the weight and price of a loaf; the unscrupulous grocers who trafficked in the powdered milk of sucklings by mixing it with plaster; the pharmacists, peddlers of out-of-date medicines; the distracted printer who gave blue eyes to the portrait of the Supreme Leader, beloved of the people and awesome forger of History; the young hooligans who plundered the flowers of the few public gardens by way of protest against the slow death planned for them; and, finally, the solitary demonstrator whose death from a heart attack the press had announced one month previously.

Towards the middle of the afternoon, the people invade the streets en masse. The populous areas spew out the contents of their entrails into the great boulevards. The cinemas can no longer lure in customers to dream, the patisseries are besieged by ravenous young girls who jostle each other, each buttock tenderized by precious silk chafing against the coarse cotton of jeans. The illicit street vendors of coloured stones see their prices and products take off.

The crowd flows with more and more difficulty and thickens in the squares where stands for the orchestras have been erected.

*

It was at dusk of the great day, as the festivities were beginning, that the Chief of State Security received the news. This night-bird who handled such dark secrets that he'd had all the windows of his office walled up, more inaccessible than the path to paradise, had bit by bit transformed himself into a chthonic monster, deformed and vicious, of which only the eyes glowed with a day-blind beauty. He lived for his dossiers more cherished than his four children, to fabricate or dismantle the wiliest of plots with the joyful ferocity of a moray eel attacking its prey. He had undertaken to assassinate all the Comrades whose past might cast a shadow over the Supreme Leader, beloved of the people and awesome forger of History; to kidnap and torture to death all political opponents, even those who'd taken refuge abroad; to compromise in scandalous affairs all potential rivals who found themselves condemned to perpetual solitary confinement, and in their prison died one by one of an epidemic of heart failure; to exile to the most forgotten of embassies any would-be dauphins who dared to believe in their future; to recommend the immediate resignation of competent ministers; to infiltrate all the workers' unions however strictly obedient, just as he had planted his own agents in the universities and the ministerial cabinets, the businesses and the mosques, the dark corners of the town and the queues in front of the supermarkets. His disquieting tentacles spread throughout the country and the mention of his name sowed terror.

There was only one man whom he had managed neither to corrupt nor intimidate nor diminish. Thus he'd had him locked up in the most terrible of prisons.

'He has escaped!'

The Chief of State Security immediately convened the gaoler of the prison, the chiefs of staff of the three armies and a mysterious stranger with a beard.

As though gripped by nausea, the barracks surrounding the capital began vomiting up their soldiers, their police, their parachutists, their elite units, their rapid intervention groups, their social guards, their shock commandos, their anti-riot brigades, their anti-terrorist sections, their man-hunting experts all armed with pistols, shotguns, grenades, machine-guns and all sorts of apparatus of detection, of location, of listening, of jamming, of tracking, of clearing. Motorbikes, police cars marked and unmarked, trucks, half-tracks, jeeps, armoured cars on wheels, on tracks, amphibian, overland, poured out at full speed into the streets, while the sky was enlivened by a saraband of helicopters, of hunting planes and of bombers.

*

He had been shut away for so long that he had forgotten the face of his mother, lost his childhood memories, no longer knew the colour of the sky. He did not know what the babbling of an infant was like and no longer felt nostalgia for an old refrain casually hummed. For centuries, he had lived only the nocturnal hours whose darkness reinforced the anguish, amid the thud of boots, the clank of loaded firearms, the passwords murmured behind his back. He dreaded above all the intrusion of those occult and icy emissaries who never lost either their temper or their heart. They obstinately returned to the charge, asking the same question for the thousandth time, receiving with candour the same response that was noted with the same application. They never wavered from their cold restraint except, from time to time, to venture some false confidence by way of a menace. These polite and respectable men seemed to know nothing about the torturers who followed on their departure and who did not leave until the pale dawn light. And the prisoner came to realize that he feared the first more than the second.

His past had been more closely examined than the life of the Prophet, and the least of his acts and gestures gave rise to long exegeses.

Against a single word, they had promised him everything: radiant mornings for the last of men; for the most nostalgic, return to the past; public admission by the leaders of all errors committed, of their denials of justice and abuses of power; the end of potato shortages and a kilo of meat less dear than the smile of my last-born; for every citizen the right to denounce the meanness of their bosses, and once every decade the assurance of making them eat their words; for him a salary higher than the highest mountain in the country, not counting the various perks and the possibility of converting every year the equivalent of his monthly pay into hard currency, the granting of an armoured car directly imported from Japan which would bid him welcome the moment the door opened, a tri-coloured card which would allow him access without having to queue at the most prestigious of shops reserved for the buying of all the cheeses of the world, not to mention butter which melts in the sun like my heart under the caresses of my wife, the assurance of having his children educated in Switzerland, transported by private aeroplane, morning and night, together with those of high dignitaries; the abolition of surtax on whisky; the possibility for the citizen to go abroad without fuss or hard currency and for the most desperate, the right to say 'shit'.

Against a single word, they promised him everything.

He told them 'shit'.

*

He set off at a run across town, instinctively taking the most obscure paths, the narrowest streets, the least used, the least usable, in the hope of emerging in the quarter of his birth, the only possible refuge. But they were not to be found – the street of his childhood, the street of the butchers with bloody stalls, of the tanners with their sickening pits of steeping skins, the dyers with skeins of multicoloured wool dripping in the sun, the braziers barely visible in their dark hovels, the street of illicit vendors of merchandise pilfered from smart shops, itinerant second-hand dealers offering their own clothes for sale, the street of pickpockets whose strict professional code of ethics prohibits them from robbing an inhabitant of the quarter, the street of brothels of the poorest quality, alone in

surreptitiously accepting minors on condition that the latter relieve themselves in less than one minute, which hardly presents them with a
problem, the street of all contraband, of vagrants and beggars of all sorts,
of layabouts, drunkards, unemployed, orphans, the hungry, the infirm ...

But everything had changed in the town, once comely and inviting,
smiling in her sunlit mornings, coquettishly allowing herself to be photographed by tourists, today turned in on herself like a porcupine under
attack, fearful and menacing, hostile to strangers, with her new boulevards
at angles too acute, her avenues leading nowhere, her quarters cut off,
her imperious hoardings, her neurasthenic colours, her nights forsaken.
More serious still, the town had repudiated the sea which lapped at her
feet and had mislaid the populous quarters which the fugitive sought.
From alley to alley, the escapee collided against the impassability of
carriage gateways, always rejected and out of breath, resumed his disor-
derly course of a blind bumble-bee towards other doorways just as
indifferent, and the same inhospitable pavements.

Suddenly he emerges into a semicircular square, illuminated to profusion by one thousand pitiless searchlights. He falls to his knees, panting.
He blinks his eyes. Blinded, the bird of night. Too late to turn back.
Already some passers-by are surrounding him. The man gets up painfully.
He is immense, as though mounted on stilts. Equilibrium ill-assured, he
sways on his long legs, torso bending, ventures some hasty steps to regain
his stability, and the strollers recoil, frightened, making a space which
isolates him. His bulging eyes, staring, are crazed, a false smile making
ape-like his face which sweats with fear. The large red cloak in which he
is covered turns him into an entertainer of revellers who gather round in
a semicircle.

He is cornered, can no longer flee.

He recoils, backwards, to trust his back to the wall. He tries to catch
his breath, swallows, mouth open. Grotesque efforts.

He advances once more, awkwardly.

'Brothers, help me,' he croaks with an effort from the depths of his
being.

His glance sweeps over the spectators, more rapid than a kaleidoscope.
The deep lines which furrow his cheeks accentuate the singularity of his
tormented face. The oldest, attentive to the constrained smile, believe
they detect in it an air of familiarity. It was long ago, so long ago,
generations before, when the nights of the town were still animated, the
bars properly stocked with liquor, political opponents alive and at liberty
to express themselves, magazines and newspapers open to writers, prisons

transformed into museums not yet reconverted into prisons, when books packed the shelves in bookshops, when the universities were forbidden to the police, when the Great Party of the People tolerated opposition, when girls dressed as they wanted without dread of being assaulted, when dignitaries dared to go shopping without fear of being lynched, when one could still sing in the street, even in the rain, without the risk of being hauled up before the Court of State Security, when they knew how to make the country work without the help of the crutch of petroleum, when the maritime pines stood tall and proud, heads held high towards the sky, and my violinist friend took pride in the tribulations of his art, when a baguette was four times cheaper, when all my friends were unemployed but not yet drunkards, when the American embassy, ransacked on a day of popular rage, was still in ruins, the cinemas usable, the books of History uncensored and the sea still there playing with the petticoats of the town. In those times immemorial, the face of this man brightened the front page of newspapers, illuminated the screen of televisions. He was seen everywhere, a familiar profile immediately recognized and celebrated, in meetings and popular demonstrations, processions and days of voluntary service, come to support dockers on strike, with peasants from the hinterland, at the pillage of the American embassy today rebuilt, or simply in the street strolling about at nightfall.

And then abruptly the man had disappeared, seized by the snare of nothingness. The old newspapers in which his name and photograph appeared had to be pulped, certain images had to be expurgated from the documentary films of the period, the chair which he had occupied in workers' assemblies and congresses had to be emptied, all his confidants and friends locked up, the place of his birth put under strict surveillance, before deciding to relocate it, the citation of his name forbidden and all namesakes obliged to change theirs, the house in which he had lived razed in order to lay out a public garden, all the books in his library burned after having been leafed through in search of secret or compromising documents, several pages ripped from the books of History, his face erased from the memories of the common people.

'Since the leaders of this country cannot be moved to pity, help me corrupt them. Pour out before me mountains of money, your wives' gold and jewellery, what you've received in inheritance, what you've been able to steal from the coffers of banks or the purses of housewives, by cheating the State with the complicity of foreign companies or, on the contrary, what you've been able to save patiently, each day weighed down by labour, each night of bad wakefulness. For the lowest in the hierarchy, it will take a fortune of which the wildest imagination cannot conceive, so much have they grown used to luxury and muddle, to bathrooms with taps of solid gold electronically controlled from their innumerable bedrooms which oblige them to get up throughout the night to enjoy all their beds, their wives bedecked in jewellery more heavy than the branches of the pomegranate tree at the end of autumn, the whims of their children more demanding than the film star of my dreams, their offices as tellingly decorated as an up-market brothel with their obsession with the wives of others, to their hunger for foreign gadgets to the accumulation of products complacently offered by companies of State.'

He pulled himself up, more protracted than a day of absence of a loved one.

'You and I know that power has made them more overbearing than the monarchs of Divine Right, more arrogant than victorious generals on the eve of battle, more ferocious than the lions of our legends, more contemptuous towards us than towards their wives whom they humiliate, unfailingly morning and night, the more so towards all other fallen women, more hypocritical than a famished crocodile, more nauseating than the garbage cans of the residential quarters which the hurried collectors forget to empty, more crafty than the chameleon lying in wait for its prey, ready to take on all colours and qualities, prepared to hold all discourses, cheerfully cursing that which they adored yesterday to adore today that which they have damned, more corrupt than assistants in the state-run shops, but also more anxious than peasants hoping for the first rains, than mothers keeping an eye on the fever of their child, than an unemployed person in his apprehension of tomorrow, than a fiancée awaiting the return from exile of the beloved in order to melt against him in a passionate embrace but whose conscience, initial desire assuaged, will be titillated by suspicions of infidelity, the more unfair since she knows nothing of the bitterness of exile and its atrocious nights of solitude, the torments of the lonely darkness that hugs the sides of the streets searching for an untraceable kindred spirit. Yes, they are even more anxious, and if you want, this evening, shoulder to shoulder, we can march towards the area where, in the shade of the large trees, their residences shamefully hide. We will go via the streets of people who at first invitation will agree to follow us. On the way, we will slash the huge hoardings which display their deceitful smiles, we will set fire to the special cooperatives where they supply themselves shamelessly with pure imported produce. Our rage will make the walls of their air-conditioned offices quake. And, if you feel like it, we will go and ransack the beauty

salons where their wives go to patch up their appearance. In passing, we
will not forget to pillage the premises of the radio which bores us to death
with syrupy talks and to pull to pieces all the gleaming state cars along
the way. It will be easy for us to overrun the barricades and the lines of
spikes which they are bound to erect to contain us, to turn against them
the rifles of the guards whom they pay at the price of gold but who have
always hated them. And when fear has jammed their automatic machine-
guns treacherously ensconced at the corners of the streets, rendered
mute their alarm sirens relayed direct to all the barracks of the country,
demobilized the delicate mechanisms of the locks of their armoured
doors, entombed the secret tunnels at the exit of which helicopters ready
for take-off await, then we will discover them stripped bare, faces decom-
posed by terror.'

A child's smile has just illuminated his face.

'We will make them admit everything. They must tell us why their
mothers refused to sing over their cradles, why their wives found
their way to suicide or to asylum, why their children are repulsed
by their smile, why the air shudders when they appear, the animals flee,
the young girl in love stops singing, the sky rumbles in anger, the flowers
wither, the springs dry up, the babies cry, God trembles in fear. They must
tell us at the cost of how many assassinations they took power, at the cost
of how many others they have held on to it, by what miracle they were
able in so short a time to squander the riches of the country, for what
reason they entrusted everything from our subsoil to the air we breathe
to foreigners: factories to be constructed, hotels to be run, roads and
railways to be laid, their illnesses to be treated, mosques to be built,
sanctuaries to be erected, hospitals to be equipped, their children to be
educated, subways to be excavated, their wives to be clothed, statues of
national heroes to be sculpted, the secrets of our finances to be scruti-
nized. They must tell us how to distinguish the true from the false plots
which they have announced, how this spy condemned for delivering to
wicked foreigners that which no longer remains our State secret and
executed for high treason, how he was able to become a high dignitary
once more. They must explain to us why they traffic in information, in
History, in ballot boxes, in GMT, in meteorology, in the figures of national
book-keeping.'

The semicircle continues to thicken.

'After having stripped their archives and their recording tapes, we will
put them on public trial. We will expose all their depravity, their infamy,
their shady dealings, their ignoble hagglings, their black manoeuvrings

and all their villainy. We will publish all useful documents and hold them accountable for their crimes before a serene assembly. We do not seek vengeance but fair punishment. We will scrupulously see to it that they enjoy all the rights granted them by the texts which thousands upon thousands of times they have flouted but which they themselves had conceived strictly for their own convenience.'

He falls silent, and the murmurs of the crowd approve his speech.

'Then we will have to choose the wisest among us and ask them to prescribe for us regulations and laws which mistrust all powers. In spite of that, we will remain vigilant.'

The crowd is ready to follow him.

Slowly, the mysterious stranger with the beard breaks through the semicircle and advances on the square gleaming with light, pistol in hand. The orator, who has just recognized him, recoils, back to the wall. The man points his weapon at the temple of the escapee and presses the trigger once. Then he turns and calmly walks away.

Nobody has moved.

Tahar Ben Jelloun

The Blue Viper

Translated from the French by Anne Fuchs

Tahar Ben Jelloun was born in 1944 in Fès, Morocco, which was to become independent from France in 1956. He studied philosophy in Rabat before emigrating to France in 1961. He has been publishing novels since 1973, notably on the dilemmas of France's North African immigrant and Beur communities. In 1987 his *La Nuit Sacrée* (translated into English as *The Sacred Night*) won him the esteemed Prix Goncourt. His short stories of twenty years were collected together in 1995 under the title *Le Premier Amour est Toujours le Dernier*, from which the entertainment 'The Blue Viper' – newly translated for this anthology – is taken.

Anne Fuchs is British-born, resident in France and recently retired from the University of Nice-Sophia Antipolis, where she has researched African Francophone and Anglophone drama and edited several collections of essays on those topics.

I LIKE TRAVELLING BY BOAT. In these times of speed and air-traffic congestion, boats are a luxury. You can take your time over a journey. It's an opportunity for emptying your mind and for preparing to enter into a new rhythm. This summer I was on the *Marrakech*, a liner making the crossing between Sète and Tangiers. I had just embarked when a short man of about fifty welcomed me with open arms, and embraced me. I had never seen this man before. Rather perturbed, I did not say anything. To all appearances, it was a misunderstanding, a mistake or he had got me mixed up with someone else. No, it wasn't any of that.

The man reassured me: 'My name is Hadj Abdelkrim and I was born in Marrakech on an exceptionally hot day; I am married to a Sicilian and father to three children who know and love you. As for myself, more's the pity, I don't read. My wife reads for me. I don't read but I have a great experience of life, of the visible and the invisible. My trade, if you are interested, is trying to make foreigners love my country by showing it to them in all its beauty and its complexity. But why I wanted to meet you – and I have been waiting a long time for this – is because I wanted to tell you a story, a true story. You are a writer, aren't you? Well, listen to this. It's about Brahim, a quiet, good sort of man trying to make a living for his family. It's the story of someone whose fate is lying in wait for him along the path of Evil. Listen . . .'

Hadj Abdelkrim was in the centre of the saloon and the other passengers had rushed up to listen to him.

*

For ages now, tourists no longer stopped in front of Brahim and his snakes. Too old and tired, lacking in conviction, the snakes no longer responded to their master the snake-charmer's music. Even when he changed his flute or his tune, they scarcely showed their haggard or sleepy heads. In order to make the performance attractive once again there was only one solution: change the animals rather than the instruments. Brahim decided to make a sacrifice and buy a young, lively and brilliant viper. This was brought to him from a village renowned for its snakes. He fondled and got it excited and then played it a piece of music of his own composition. The viper who was very gifted had a manner of dancing which was quite exceptional, at will twisting and turning to the rhythm with precision and darting out its tongue to punctuate the sequence. Brahim regained his confidence. The other snakes were enchanted by the beautiful blue viper.

The following night Brahim had a strange dream: the big square was deserted and lit by the full moon. He was seated in the centre, cross-legged. He couldn't move. It was as if he were stuck to the ground with a special glue. Facing him appeared the viper, but in the guise of a blue young woman. He couldn't tell whether she was wearing a blue veil or it was her skin that was coloured. She had the body of a woman and the head of a viper. She spoke as she circled round him: 'This afternoon I played the game and showed you what I was capable of. I am not who you think I am. You are not going to condemn me to a life of twisting and turning to please your tourists. I am worth better things, I am young, I want to live, to stroll in the meadows, to experience emotions and pleasures and have memories for my old age. If your tourists want thrills, they have only to go to Amazonia or to a country where the stones are gifted with memory. I am warning you, if you put me on show, you will regret it ... or rather, I am not sure you will have time to regret anything.'

While she spoke, she was circling round him, brushing his hand or his hip. He tried to reply, but his voice got stuck in his throat. He was hypnotized.

Self-confident, she went on with her speech: 'Don't try and explain your problems to me so that I will take pity on you. Give me up and you will have peace. I've too many things to do. It's the harvest season and I have to crawl back under the stones. I love the cool hands of the girls who stoop to pick up the corn. Your tourists make me sick. They are not very beautiful. And you, you are pleased with their ridiculous tips. Be a bit more dignified. And now you can leave. The square is going to fill up. The sun will rise. And as for you, go and think about this. But if you want peace, give me back my freedom.'

Brahim woke with a start, trembling and feverish. He inspected the box where the snakes slept. The viper was there, peacefully plunged in a deep sleep.

Reassured, he washed himself and then recited his morning prayer. On that particular day he joined his hands and asked God for help and protection: 'Allah, Thou art the greatest and most merciful. Keep Evil and the unscrupulous away from me. I am a poor man. I earn my living thanks to animals. I have no way of fighting Evil or of changing my trade. Times are difficult. In our family, snake-charming has been passed down from father to son. I was born and brought up among reptiles. I have never trusted them completely. They are treacherous. As a good Muslim, I don't believe in reincarnation, but sometimes I do meet people with the heart and soul of former vipers, transformed into hypocrisy and false smiles.'

It wasn't his habit to indulge in prayers and self-justification. For years now he had been plying his trade without question. But last night's dream had shaken him. There had been something real about it. Brahim was frightened. Frightened of an accident or the evil eye.

That day he was due to charm his snakes in a big hotel in front of a group of tourists who had paid extra to watch this spectacle, the exoticism of which was guaranteed: the sight of a viper dancing to the music of a hill-dweller. Brahim recited a prayer before leaving home, avoided taking his bicycle and fastened a silver hand round his neck. In theory his fears had been exorcized. He turned up at the hotel at the appointed time. The tourists had just finished eating a couscous. They had drunk their rosé wine or beer. They were full up and a bit drowsy. The organizer introduced Brahim: 'Ladies and gentlemen, here we now present what you have often heard of but never seen, here we have what makes the difference between the North and the South, here we do not have magic but poetry, here we have the most famous snake-charmer in the region, here is the man who risks his life to give you thrills, here is Brahim and his snakes . . .'

The cameras were all ready. Some of the tourists didn't look impressed; they were drinking their mint tea and eating pastries in the shape of gazelle horns. Brahim made his appearance, looking frail and hesitant. He bowed to the audience. But while bending down he thought he caught sight of the blue lady of his dream. She had a bird's head, was wearing a tightly fitting blue djellaba and had practically no breasts. She was sitting on the branch of a tree and swinging her legs like a child. Brahim just played his flute, putting off the moment for opening the snake box. The tourists were no longer drowsy. They all had their eyes glued to the box. Brahim pushed open the lid and plunged his hand into the box. He caught the viper. Actually, it was rather the viper which caught on to his wrist. Just when he was going to stroke its head, it bit him. It still had all its venom. And yet it had had its venom removed right in front of Brahim when he bought it. He fell down stone-dead, his mouth full of blood and white froth. This froth was the venom. The tourists believed it was all a bad joke. Some felt cheated and complained; others were so upset by this death they vomited all their lunch up. Photos were taken. A souvenir of instant death. A souvenir of the artist who dies on stage.

Brahim's body was removed to the main mortuary and placed in drawer number 031.

*

Ali and Fatima, the two children portrayed holding hands on their way to school on the cover of the Primary School reader, have grown up. Promised to one another since childhood, they could have become a staid middle-class couple with no problems, as in the picture which became the dream of thousands of schoolchildren. They had got married because they were in love and no one could have stopped the marriage. But in spite of appearances, they were separated by too many things: Ali had been able to continue his studies and worked in a private sector company; Fatima came from a poor background and scarcely knew how to read or write. Ali was what is called a man 'whose glance could strike down a bird in full flight'; to signify his passion for women, it was also said that he had 'green eyes', although these were in fact black. He liked to drink, drive fast cars and steal the wives of others. Fatima was a good housewife and spent her time looking after her home. She devoted herself completely to the husband she was perpetually waiting for and to their two children. A woman resigned to her lot, she was not very bright but always available, never gave her husband any kind of surprise and held no more mystery for him; a woman of great sincerity and goodwill, she was defenceless and her excessive kindness even resembled stupidity. Like her mother and grandmother before her, Fatima settled into a kind of peaceful feebleness, right up until the day she decided to react, to do something to keep Ali at home.

But his life was elsewhere. Apparently, nothing could any longer keep him in this home of dismal and oppressive routine. When Fatima dared to protest, Ali slapped her twice and left slamming the door. He didn't hide his numerous conquests. He ran after the girls, didn't deny it and considered he was not accountable to anyone. This only exacerbated Fatima's jealousy. Jealousy made her ill and the doctors could not bring her husband back. They prescribed tranquillizers. Fatima didn't dare confide in her family, but those around her guessed at her unhappiness.

One day she decided to consult a fortune-teller. 'Your husband is handsome. He deceives you and will always do so. It is more powerful than he is. I can see a crowd of pretty women around him who want to embrace him. He has the gift of great potency. He gives women what other men cannot. It could be said that he was born to satisfy all those whom fate has allotted only the impotent. His role is to repair the damage. You won't be able to do anything about it. This kind of man isn't made for marriage and family life. Even if you hide him in a prison, women will find him and take him away from you. Be brave! It is all I can say, my daughter!'

Fatima was desperate. She confided in Khadouj, a neighbour who was a nurse at the local hospital. Khadouj was bound to feel a certain complicity with Fatima. She herself had tried to attract Ali, but unsuccessfully. Not only did she understand her friend's jealousy and distress, she also shared them. She suggested going to see a sorcerer, a woman who was well-known for solving marriage problems. She had an office in a small flat and saw people only by appointment. She was a modern young woman who had studied applied psychology. She did not seem like the old sorcerers who were one-eyed and frightening. She asked Fatima to state her problem. She took notes and asked precise questions.

'You want to get your husband back, you want him to be yours and only yours? I could prescribe pills to dissolve in his morning coffee, but it's not certain this would work. There is also this herb which must be mixed in the bread, but there could be a risk of its being toxic. You want to get him back, I suppose, in good health . . .'

Fatima whispered something to Khadouj, then addressed the technician: 'I don't want him to become impotent or a weakling. I want him the same as he used to be, just as I love him, strong, loving and tender.'

'In that case, I am going to prescribe for you the good old recipe of our ancestors: a ball of unleavened dough which has spent a whole night in a corpse's mouth, preferably that of a fresh corpse, not one which has been forgotten about at the mortuary. Your husband only has to bite this dough and eat it; he will then change and come back to you just as you dreamed. In fact, the dough must pass from the corpse's mouth straight into his. It's possible to do it during his sleep if you can't make him eat it.'

Fatima brought up the problem of finding a corpse. Khadouj gave her a sign. She paid the secretary whose office was at the entrance just next to a waiting room.

That same afternoon the dough was ready. Khadouj wrapped it in a handkerchief and went off to the hospital. That night she was on duty. Her luck was in, as sometimes happens. She went down to the mortuary and opened a few drawers, looking for the freshest corpse to place the dough in its mouth. Number 031 was still lukewarm. Its mouth was half open. There was still some white froth and blood around it. The nurse had no difficulty in sticking the dough between the corpse's teeth. Early in the morning she took the dough back in the same handkerchief. Ali was in a deep sleep. Fatima gently opened his mouth, where she placed the dough. He bit into it without even realizing. Ali did not wake up. He was dead. The poison was still active.

Fatima fainted. And it was then that the blue woman with the viper's head appeared before her and spoke as follows: 'Sorcery does not exist. But stupidity does. One person wanted to hold on to me against my will and he died. The other tried to swim against the current of the river and she lost everything. The one lacked dignity and the other pride. In whichever case, I am the one who points the moral of the story: one should beware of vipers, especially when they have been cursed by the moon on an evening when it's full of bitterness and disdain. Farewell, my daughter. You will at last sleep in peace and for eternity. As you see, I am not completely wicked . . .'

Lotfi Akalay

Colour Blues

Translated from the French by Pius Adesanmi

Lotfi Akalay is a Moroccan author whose *Les Nuits d'Azed* depicts the comedy of the sexes in everyday Maghrebian life. 'Dis, Papa!', which appeared on New Year's Day 1997, in *Jeune Afrique*, is an early comedy piece which led to his regular fortnightly 'Tout Va Bien' columns there.

Pius Adesanmi is Nigerian-born, a critic and scholar of Francophone African literature, graduated from the Universities of Ilorin and Ibadan, at present studying at the University of British Columbia. His translation of 'Dis, Papa!' as 'Colour Blues' first appeared in the *Post Express Literary Supplement*, Lagos, in April 1997.

'HEY, DAD, where is this Morocco?'

'In Africa.'

'Over there where there're giraffes and hippos?'

'No, higher up – in North Africa.'

'So what's there in Morocco?'

'Arabs.'

'I thought all the Arabs live in Arabia . . .'

'Well, the Arabs are everywhere, even in the Metro. In Morocco the Arabs are Berbers.'

'But Berbers are barbarians, aren't they?'

'No, the barbarians were completely another thing – they were hordes of invaders.'

'Yes, but yesterday when you were watching the television, you complained that our dear France has been invaded by Arabs.'

'Ah yes ... but it's not exactly the same thing. There are quite nice Arabs, like Brahim the neighbourhood grocer.'

'But only the day before yesterday you called him a thief because he capitalizes on peak hours to hike his prices.'

'I said that because I was a bit angry, that's all.'

'Do you know any Moroccans?'

'Not really, but I do meet some in the street sometimes.'

'Which language do you speak to them?'

'I don't say a word to them because I don't know them.'

'But if you don't know them, how do you know that they are Moroccans and not Americans?'

'Well, Americans are white.'

'Like Miles Davis and Carl Lewis?'

'No, those ones are from Africa.'

'Now I'm getting all mixed up. Brahim is white like you and I, he is not black and yet you say he is an Arab.'

'That's because there are white Arabs, but Moroccans come in various colours. Some have a very dark skin, while some have skin as white as any Dutchman, you see?'

'But ... well, on Sunday on the television I watched the Dutch football team. And half the team was black!'

'But that's not at all the same. In the world of sport there are lots and lots of blacks.'

'There is only one in tennis. In golf, in swimming and in horse-riding I've never seen even one.'

'That's not my doing, is it? Go and ask your mother to explain and let me finish my forecast on the horse race.'

'It's Mum who told me to ask you these questions. She is busy in the kitchen and she's complaining that you never help her. I have one more question to ask you. My friend Anabelle is completely black and she swears she is French. She's a liar, isn't she, Dad?'

'But your little friend is from Martinique and that does make her French.'

'So there are Frenchmen who are black and Moroccans who are white, is that it?'

'Yes. Yes. Now let's change the topic.'

'Yes ... but Anabelle has very curly hair, you know, like a sheep.'

'Moroccans also have the same curly hair.'

'Well, my pal Momo is Moroccan, but his hair is really very sleek.'

'Some come like that.'

'Once he told me that we, the French, were colonizers. Is there any truth in what he said?'

'What utter rubbish!'

'He said that long ago we actually invaded his country and that we treated them quite badly.'

'We did go to his country and we settled there for a bit, that's all.'

'But the same with them, they come to us and settle a bit. Tomorrow I'm going to tell Momo that he, too, is a colonizer!'

'No, it's different again. To come to our country Moroccans have to have an entry visa!'

'Didn't we need one as well, when we went to them?'

'No, in those days there weren't any visas, and things were much more straightforward. All we had to have was a gunboat!'

PART TWO

WEST

Teixeira de Sousa

In the Court of King Dom Pedro

Translated from the Portuguese by Don Burness

Teixeira de Sousa was born in 1919 in the island of Fogo of the volcanic Cape Verde archipelago, on the old sea route between Portugal and Brazil, three hundred miles from the African coast; he is a medical doctor by profession. Besides novels about the fall of the wealthy Cape Verdean estate owners, on the eve of independence from Portugal (in 1975) he published a collection of stories (*Contra Mar e Vento*, 1972) from which 'In the Court of King Dom Pedro' is taken. It was translated more recently for inclusion in the collection *Across the Alantic: An Anthology of Cape Verdean Literature* (1988).

Don Burness is the noted scholar of Portuguese-language writing in Africa, editor of *Critical Perspectives on Lusophone African Literature* (1981) and of several translations; he is a poet as well, and teaches at Franklin Pierce College, Rindge, New Hampshire.

ON THE TOP OF THE HILL Raimundo leaned against the balustrade of the Church of São Pedro – at the side of Vicente Cardoso – and looked down majestically at the rest of the small town that extended at his feet to the bottom of the gorge. In the moonlight the roofs of the houses looked like cascades. The paths descended and wound their way through the line of houses, like rivers of silver. Streets, alleys and paths formed the texture of this noble and proud town of São Filipe. Silence was interrupted only by the sound of the waves down below, breaking against the shore.

He wore a royal coat made of sacking, which covered his body and trailed along the ground. With his arms uplifted and his head also raised to the heavens, Raimundo began his fantasy of the all powerful monarch.

'I am King Dom Pedro, Lord and Master of all the houses in this town. The house of Senhor Jerónimo belongs to me. The shop of Senhor Caetano Mendonça belongs to me. The felucca *Adelina* also belongs to me. I am the richest man in the world. I have sixty thousand measures of corn kept in the government warehouse. The coffee of Mount Queimado is all mine. When there is hunger on the island, all come to me, for I am great, I am wealthy and I provide food for all the people of my kingdom.

'I am King Dom Pedro who can have the Chief Administrator arrested and the Governor fired if they provoke me. I have no fear of the police or the soldier with his bayonet.

'I am King Dom Pedro. I am King Dom Pedro. Shit, I am King Dom Pedro.'

Marking time with his index fingers, he began to warble with a throbbing voice:

> The youth of King Dom Pedro
> The mill with its singing dove
> The wife that God gave to me
> Ai, the life of he who loved!
>
> O la la la
> La la la la
> Dom Pedro Cru is my name
> And Dona Inêz is my wife.

Vicente Cardoso – also leaning against the balustrade of the church of São Pedro, on this silent Christmas Eve – was searching for images of times gone by. It was not quite midnight and no one was strolling on the square. Not a single light was shining in the windows of the church. What had happened to the groups of another time which used to fill the town with Christmas carols? Hadn't Jesus Christ been born in former times in a manger in Bethlehem? A tombstone had descended over everyone and everything. Doors were closed to the celebration of the Holy night. People had become insensitive to the poetry of Christmas. Only he, Vicente Cardoso, persisted in the search for what no longer existed, like a stranger in quest of feeling.

Over there was the very place. Exactly as it was. Even including the blue ochre of the façade and the white strips of the cornice and the door jambs – they were the same. To the north the roof came down on the large veranda where the family used to attend. São João's tournament of horses. In that house the festival of Christmas used to be celebrated with turkey and cakes, champagne and port wine. The family would gather around the large table that was covered with food. Uncles and cousins appeared. Cups were raised and toasts were offered to those present and absent. On a silver tray were coins to give to groups of carollers.

The ground floor was occupied by the shop with its desk. In the warehouse of the interior courtyard was deposited various merchandise. Pineseeds, castor-oil, maize, beans, tiles, lime, skins, salt, petroleum. There were galvanized grain containers. The beasts of burden which carried heavy loads had their own separate enclosure in the estate of Senhor Jerónimo Cardoso. At times he and his brothers witnessed restless quarrels among the horses and mules. If there were a mare present, it was a more serious case.

His father was a wealthy businessman and landowner in the town. His uncle's firm went bankrupt. Objects were sold way below their value to satisfy impatient creditors. Old Jerónimo underwrote letters of credit to help during this time of trouble. Until, one fine day, the Bank resolved to collect payment from the brothers Cardoso and all relatives who held promissory notes. Jerónimo Cardoso lost everything, including his living quarters where he continued to live but had to pay rent.

There were eleven children. Five girls and six boys. The oldest had gone off to study in Lisbon. Three sisters went to the College of Bom Sucesso. Four boys attended the College of São Fiel in Campolide. Vicente, the youngest, had left for Lisbon during that year of financial ruin. He couldn't continue. The brothers who were studying had to return immediately. His father felt an enormous sense of disgust and cut off relations with his bankrupt brothers. The old man was so distraught that his body became covered with sores from head to foot. Dr Barreto had said that these problems might cause skin irritation. This was during the rainy season. Flies were everywhere. Finally, his father built a sort of cage of mosquito netting large enough to hold a man. He spent all his time there reading novels to pass the time. People who passed by stopped to see Senhor Jerónimo in his cage. Schoolchildren wasted endless minutes staring at that bizarre old man. The same thing was true on the large veranda facing the road, where the old man would sit down protected from flies and microbes.

A woman with a foul-smelling tin plate on her head passed by. Dona Sara's dog barked, but without conviction, at the spectre that descended the slope in the direction of the old apothecary shop. As soon as the creature vanished further on, beyond the tamarind tree, silence again fell over the town. Only the moon was shining gloriously in the vastness of the sky. It was Christmas Eve.

My father's skin rash was never cured up to the day he closed his eyes. He tried all of Dr Barreto's remedies and even some herbal baths. These at least reduced the oozing from the sores. The doctor said that it was a kind of eczema caused by nerves and only personal wellbeing and happiness could make him better, but he never again experienced even the slightest contentment. This continued even after his death, for Princepe de Ximento refused to dress the cadaver of Senhor Jerónimo Cardoso. All those who dressed corpses admitted their repugnance towards that body covered with scabs and pus. Finally, it was his own children who shrouded the cadaver of their dead father before it was placed in its tomb. God grant him eternal rest.

*

For a long time Raimundo was silent, his head hung down over the parapet. The sacking cloak that wrapped him in that position brought to mind the coverings of mules that drew carriages in the season of the flies. He was either sleeping or praying, beseeching the Lord for better fortune for his kingdom. When the rains don't come, thousands of his subjects fall down in black misery. And were it not for his providing succour to the hungry through public works, the repairing of local roads and building of walls everywhere, these thousands of poor sinners would die of starvation, swollen and sore, infested like Senhor Jerónimo Cardoso.

He was King Dom Pedro who had everything and who could do everything. He commanded the Chief Administrator as well as the Governor seated in the capital of Praia singing dispatches.

He had come to his island to buy cattle. This was in reality the activity of Vicente Cardoso. Living for many years on São Vicente, on Mount Sossego, he never succeeded in establishing himself in any occupation. Like the blowing of the wind.

By chance, on one particular occasion, he was successful. He bought fifty-five head of cattle at a good price. Then, arriving at São Vicente, he planned a business deal with the butchers. He wasn't going to let himself be taken advantage of. He bought fodder for the animals so that he would not have to sell them precipitously. No, he would wait for a better opportunity. Once there was a shortage of meat in the butcher's shop, he would then bring his cattle. Taking everything into account, he hoped to earn about twenty contos from the fifty-five head of cattle. With the twenty contos, he would then explore some business deals in lumber in Guinea. Happily he still had a good reputation among the wood merchants of Guinea.

Raimundo the Madman abruptly lifted himself up and stared at the moon which was floating lazily in the sky.

'I am King Dom Pedro and Dona Inêz is my wife. I am the Master of

Fogo and of all the estates of white folks. I am the owner of the felucca *Aleluia*! Hallelujah! Hallelujah! Hallelujah! Hallelujah! I have money coming out of my ears. I can assuage the hunger of all the people on the islands!'

Vicente Cardoso felt his stomach grind with hunger. He had had dinner quite early and eaten only two slices of fried fish with three spoonfuls of rice. If he could find some coffee house still open, he would order something to eat. It would be, when all is said and done, his Christmas dinner. He remembered the good times when he had a sumptuous and happy repast in the dilapidated old blue two-storey house with its interior courtyard and veranda, in the home of his parents who are already up there in the peace of the Lord.

It seems that only at that moment did Raimundo become aware of the presence of someone next to him. With a presumptuous air, he went over to Vicente de Nhô Jerónimo to ask for a cigarette. He held out his hand to his childhood friend, pleading with him for just one cigarette, for the love of God. Vicente took his tortoise-shell cigarette case from his pocket, putting it in the outstretched hand of the madman. The latter, with his hands shaking, reached for the row of cigarettes. By the time he finally succeeded in taking out a cigarette, the son of Nhô Jerónimo had pulled out his lighter.

The flame appeared and only then did he notice how old and frail Vicente had become, he who had been the most valiant and determined lad in school. What a sad fate had besieged Raimundo de Veiga! Nevertheless, he continued to spend his evenings shouting that he was the most wealthy and generous man on the island and that he was King Dom Pedro who was Lord and Master of everyone and everything.

'Are you hungry, Raimundo?'

In between cigarette puffs, Dom Pedro answered Vicente's question with a prolonged guffaw.

'Tell me if you feel like eating anything.'

Raimundo continued to laugh and cough at the same time, choking on the smoke from his cigarette. When he finished laughing, he made the following observation to this friend of former times: 'Do you honestly believe in São Vicente one can find something to eat or drink at any time of the day?'

He was still, up to a certain point, the same wise and clever Raimundo he had been in the class of Senhor Pereira. That rapid and lucid outburst of King Dom Pedro impelled Vicente to act. He resolved right then to invite the monarch to dine with him, somewhere, on this Christmas Eve.

'Let's go to Nhô Quirino's coffee house. Just a short while ago his place was open.'

Raimundo followed his friend down towards the lower part of the town, his cloak of sacking trailing along the streets beneath the light of the moon. The same dog of Dona Sara barked at His Majesty and his friend Vicente Cardoso as they were passing on their way to Nhô Quirino's coffee shop, filled with dignity and hunger.

Along the way Raimundo did not remain quiet, laughing his ironic and sceptical laugh. And he was reiterating that on Fogo one could not eat or drink at that hour. On São Vicente, yes, there was always a tavern open, even after midnight.

'Do you know São Vicente?'

'You must be kidding. Don't you remember that's where I did my military service? Company, present arms! Fall out! Company, eyes left!'

'It's true. It was a long time ago!'

Finally, King Dom Pedro became more approachable, more human. He descended his throne to accompany his friend Vicente to Nhô Quirino's coffee house, and off they went again in friendly conversation as they passed near the old elementary school where they had once been students.

'Do you remember Senhor Pereira?' asked Vicente.

'Of course. He was a brute. He could only teach by beating students with a palmatoria. He sure was a wild boar.'

'Oh, but he knew a lot.'

'Knew what? He didn't know anything.'

'Poor fellow, he died a few months ago.'

'Serves him right. No one misses him.'

They arrived at Nhô Quirino's. It was closed. Vicente pounded on the door as hard as he could. No one answered. He leaned his ear against the keyhole but was unable to hear any sound indicating that anyone was inside. Once again Raimundo laughed triumphantly.

The son of Senhor Jerónimo Cardoso hammered on the door with clenched fists. Someone from the recesses of the second floor answered in a hoarse and hollow voice: 'Who's there?'

'Vicente Cardoso.'

Nhô Quirino looked out of the window with his bald head shining, illuminated by the moon. He was a man who never laughed. He was always ill-humoured. In spite of this, he was successful in business. He sold a lot in his coffee house.

'What do you want at this time of night?' asked the old man.

'Could you fix us up something to eat?'

'What for?'

'To eat.'

'To eat? You're not right in the head. Who did you come with?'

'With . . .'

'With whom?'

'King Dom Pedro is with me.'

'Look, go play with your grandmother.'

And he rudely shut the window in their face, disappearing from the sight of bold Vicente and his mad companion.

Smiling ironically, Raimundo got ready to set off towards the old fort with his cape open like the wings of a bat, while Vicente Cardoso, propped against the wall of the coffee house, ruminated on Nhô Quirino's insult. Life has its ups and downs. Who would have thought that the son of Senhor Jerónimo Cardoso would one day be offended by the son of a former slave of his grandmother! The same grandmother the old man had referred to as he shut the window in his face.

King Dom Pedro began to climb the staircase leading to the old fort. A gentle breeze penetrated his royal robe and his guffaws echoed like the spasmodic rat-a-tat of a machine-gun. He was disappearing among the acacias of the large square.

A little while later, once again, he began his tirade of a deposed monarch, still powerful, still opulent, still humanitarian.

'I am King Dom Pedro, Lord and Master of Fogo and Brava and Lord also of the felucca *Aleluia.* Hallelujah! Hallelujah! Folks, come meet the richest man in the world.'

Théo Ananissoh

Coming Home

Translated from the French by Elsa Glenn

Théo Ananissoh is a French-language Togolese writer, born in the Central African Republic in 1962, and a noted scholar of comparative African literature, who currently lives in Germany. He has contributed articles to *Palabres* and to *Études Littéraires Africaines*. His collection of four pieces, including the novella 'Matthieu', was published as *Yeux Ouverts* by the Centre Togolais de Communication in Lomé recently, with 'Retour au Pays' ('Coming Home') as its tailpiece.

Elsa Glenn, daughter of the well-known translator Catherine Lauga du Plessis, a sample of whose work is also included here, is a student of French at the University of Cape Town and undertook this task as a study project.

'THE POST BOX NUMBER, it is not much.'

I had returned to this defective usage of a French I had all but forgotten. I understood what he meant; in truth, I was expecting it. I had been confronted with the same demand all those years earlier when I was leaving. But I pretended to be embarrassed and surprised.

The immigration official continued: 'Must put the name of the street and the number of the house where you going to stay.'

Then, after a calculated, nonchalant motion of the head, he rested on me his bloodshot eyes, almost lost in the mass of his bloated face. I thought to myself, 'This is Africa.' Six years earlier, in another terminal of the airport – the departure terminal – another official dressed like him had made the same demand without any concern for reality. I was leaving a town where the streets had no name. The official facing me knew it; he himself lived in a street without a name. But the departure form required this information.

Exaggerating my false surprise, I tried to argue my case: 'But ... it's all I have for an address ...'

'What area is it?'

'Bè-Gbényédzi ...'

'What?'

He was busy scribbling something and he had not paid any attention to my reply. I couldn't see what so engrossed him, nor what he was doing with my arrival form. Immigration control took the shape of a long counter manned by two officials. A few metres behind that was a conveyor belt bringing in the passengers' luggage. I spotted my suitcase and this only increased my impatience. I leaned towards him and repeated: 'It's in Bè-Gbényédzi Kopé, on the way to Akodesséwa.'

The other passengers who had disembarked at the same time – about ten people – were slowly disappearing beyond the control zone. The one official at the counter finally lifted his head and looked me in the eye.

'Get out of way.'

There was nobody behind me. The last person to get off the plane, a man who seemed to be Lebanese, was putting his passport back into his pocket in front of the other official. I was the only one left.

'Done.'

I didn't know if this was a question or a statement. I kept quiet.

'You ... what year you leave the country?'

He was making a great effort not to use the familiar 'tu' form of address and to stick to the formal, respectful 'vous'.

'In '86.'

He looked down again at whatever had been occupying him behind the counter.

'Where you coming from?'

'I beg your pardon?'

He raised his voice to an unpleasant pitch. 'Where you coming from?'

This was actually written on my arrival card.

'From Amsterdam via Lagos.'

'You wait.'

He had finally lapsed into the familiar 'tu' form. He got up. The situation was beginning to worry me. He waved to the colleague standing next to the luggage to come across. A large bellied man, stuffed into a uniform with damp marks under the arms. He walked over, taking his time. My official pointed his forefinger to the arrival form, probably to the block meant for the address.

'He has no street.'

Still this bad French. The large bellied official rested his damp eyes on me.

'Which street is it, Mr Lawson?'

'I don't know, sir. I have been trying to explain to your colleague. It's been six years since I left and at that time the street did not have a name.'

He glanced over the arrival form.

'What?' he mumbled after a few seconds.

I calmly repeated myself. 'When I left in 1986 the street did not have any name.'

'Yes, but without the name of the street and the number of the house you cannot go through. Post box number isn't enough.'

I looked at him disconcertedly.

'Who are you going to stay with?' he asked suddenly.

'With my parents ...'

'Your father?'

'Yes.'

'Where does he work?'

'He is retired, he used to work for the UAC.'

'Can't you give us anyone's address?'

I thought for a moment, suppressing the urge to reply in the negative.

'I know the phone number of our neighbour, Mr Améganvi. He's the boss of a building firm.'

That neighbour had rebuilt a section of the airport some time before I left. Such a piece of information would probably be useless. The official handed me the white form.

'Fill that in.'

Above the post box number I scribbled the name of the neighbour, the acronym of his firm – inventing half of it – and then added his phone number. The official retrieved the piece of paper and read it.

'Mr who?'

'Améganvi.'

I dreaded another refusal and, this getting the better of me, I added: 'It's his firm that does the building work for this very airport!'

He looked at me, then once again lowered his eyes to the form.

'National Enterprise ...'

'Of Construction and Renovation Works!'

'He's the boss?'

'He is.'

'Where's his office?'

'In Tokoin, but the telephone number I have written in is his home number.'

The rest happened in a flash. He lifted the rubber stamp and snapped it down on my passport. The other official who had dealt with me earlier moved away.

'Thank you, sir.'

'Pleasure.'

Albert Taïeb

When a Dog is Worth Nine Children

Translated from the French by Catherine Lauga du Plessis

Albert Taïeb was born in 1936 in the coastal town of Sousse in Tunisia, and is qualified as a social psychologist. For thirteen years he headed the Institut de Formation et de Recherches Appliquées in Abidjan, Côte d'Ivoire. In his preamble to his very popular *Chroniques Abidjanes*, published in Paris in 1995, he states that each of his two dozen sketches is derived, not from his imagination, but from common knowledge or from newspaper reports about life in the capital. (At the time of the publication of 'Quand un Chien Vaut Neuf Enfants' one hundred CFA francs were the equivalent of one French franc.)

Catherine Lauga du Plessis is the French-born translator of English-language African authors such as J. M. Coetzee and Zakes Mda into French. She has also with her students of translation at the University of Cape Town published versions in English of Sembène Ousmane's novellas, *Niiwam* and *Taaw*.

SCOTTIE WAS A MAGNIFICENT bulldog bitch. In good health, affectionate, lively.

Robert and Adeline were leaving Ivory Coast, headed for Tahiti, stopping in France en route. It really would have been pretty complicated for them to take Scottie with them. They did not have to search too hard before they found a new master for Scottie: Romain, my four-year-old son, just adored that dog and we were quite fond of her as well. What is more, as we lived in a villa and our nice watchman, Bourema, was a little inclined to snooze rather than be on the lookout – how can we blame him? – we thought Scottie would be a suitable addition to our security system.

In short, to everybody's satisfaction Scottie came to live with us.

I put Bernardin, our houseboy, in charge of the dog: he was to look after her, wash her and especially feed her. Our Scottie was to have the fanciest treatment. She had all the required inoculations. We often took her for a run on the beach. Generally speaking we were extra careful to keep her in good condition, especially as Robert and Adeline insisted on regular health reports.

Then we had the first alarming episode. One day, as I came home at lunch-time, I found our Scottie stretched out on the marble floor, panting heavily; my son was crying next to her.

The boy came up and said: 'You must take her to the doctor, I don't understand why she is sick. It started after she ate, half an hour ago.'

I didn't stop to think. I took Scottie to the young vet who had just opened a surgery nearby. He examined her very thoroughly.

'I don't know what's wrong with her. It may be a passing attack that will go away. Be careful what you feed her. I think it's nothing to worry about. Make sure she has these tablets and bring her back if it starts up again. By the way, is it the first time she is like this?'

'Yes, the very first. Otherwise she is in great shape.'

'She's a really beautiful dog. I think it is nothing serious.'

Our Scottie was soon her own cheerful self again and I forgot the incident. But, a fortnight later, once again I found her spreadeagled on the floor, panting and limp. The young vet was really puzzled.

'I just don't understand. All the tests are negative. I really think it is a passing thing, like the first time. You'll just have to watch what she eats. I'm giving her a much longer treatment against infections.'

Scottie was soon her cheerful self again, but as for myself, I had lost my peace of mind. All this puzzled me, worried me, and I did not know why. All the servants were questioned, but to no avail. I decided to report the matter to a more seasoned vet who had been recommended to me by some friends.

'Look,' he said, 'everything you tell me is rather odd. It is difficult for me to say what is wrong with her if I don't see her, and preferably when she has an attack. Next time bring her as quickly as you can. I hope she is just upset and nothing more.'

I questioned him on what he really thought. He replied that he had a hint of an idea about what was ailing Scottie, but he hoped he was wrong. Then he bombarded me with very specific questions on how Scottie was fed and cared for and, just generally, how we treated her.

A few days later, as had already happened twice, Scottie collapsed. But this time things looked more serious. She was drooling profusely, she was spitting blood and moaned very loudly. Immediately I took her to the older vet who had a good look at her, examined her.

'Just what I thought,' he said. 'I'll need a few tests to be absolutely sure. But there is no hope for your bitch and, in my opinion, you should put her down rather than leave her in such agony. There is nothing more we can do for her.'

I was sad. I was staggered . . .

'But really, doctor, I do not understand what you are saying. Here is a magnificent animal, in perfect health, clean, well fed, well cared for. And all of a sudden, just like that, nothing can be done for her.'

'You're going to have to understand. Last time you came, you remember, I asked you a whole series of questions: what did your dog eat and drink? Who looked after her? What shampoo was used to keep her clean and so on? Your dog was treated like a queen, wasn't she?'

'Of course . . .'

The vet interrupted me. 'That's just it. Forgive me for being so blunt, but you've made a big psychological mistake. If we add up what you spend every month to keep your bitch beautiful, well fed and healthy it comes out as forty thousand CFA francs. How much do you pay your houseboy, the one who was supposed to look after the dog?'

'Fifty thousand a month.'

'And how many children has he got?'

'Nine, or ten, I think.'

'Could anyone bear it for long feeding a dog at a cost which could practically support a whole family with ten children?'

'So you think the houseboy did it?'

'He may have, or the watchman, or the garden boy or all of them. I am quite sure your dog was poisoned. Everyone in your household knows how much you like to spend on her. Your little white lad, they don't mind you spoiling him, but the bitch they can't understand. Oh, I am not saying that the dog always gets poisoned in cases like this. But it does happen. Don't worry, you are not in the least likely to be poisoned yourself. Social inequality, that they can understand, they can accept. But if you want to keep a dog, then look after it yourself, unless someone else volunteers to do the job.'

The tests did show traces of poison with delayed effect in Scottie's stomach and gut. The vet explained that the dog had taken several weeks to die because very small doses had been used to poison her.

I had learnt my lesson in psychology, and I vowed to be more careful in future. I did not tell anybody about Scottie, I did not tell the houseboy, the garden boy, the watchman, and no one asked any questions, except for Romain. I told him that Scottie could not really live in a house, so we had sent her out to the bush. Did he believe my explanation?

Scottie gave me the measure of poverty. In time I came to understand and to accept how insufferable and contemptuous it was to compare the fate of servants with the fate of animals.

Sylvie Kandé

In This Goddamned Messed-up Land

Translated from the French by Christopher Winks

Sylvie Kandé, the daughter of a Senegalese father and a French mother, now teaches Francophone literature in the French department at New York University. With the publisher L'Harmattan in Paris she has edited two books on the theme of mixed racial identity (metissage), in Sierra Leone during the eighteenth and nineteenth centuries, and in the Francophone context generally. One of her short stories ('Journey') was published in *Europe* in 1997, and she has contributed to *Callaloo*. In a review in *Research in African Literatures* (Summer 1996) she described the state of mutism African women experienced under colonialism, how they are still obliged to remain reserved and are discouraged from making disclosures. This is the first appearance of her 'Dans Ce Sacré Foutu Pays...', translated especially for this anthology; it is dedicated to Léon Gontran Damas and Daniel Biyaoula.

Christopher Winks is the managing editor of *Black Renaissance/Renaissance Noire*, the Pan-African journal of culture and politics. He has taught at New York University, specializing in Caribbean, African-American and African literatures.

GO AWAY!
  She's waiting.
  Have pity!
  She ain't got none.

*

Even on Sundays, she manages to be up before everybody else. To whirl and spin around the room that does triple duty as bedroom, kitchen and study. Scratching the bottom of empty stewpots with the tips of her nails – claws she paints with red polish – deliberately opening and closing the refrigerator door, which takes a while to come unstuck and which every time starts up the irregular hissing of the motor, even trying to force open the upper window-frame sealed shut by the frost. She's moved back in with them for a week now, and ever since it's been the same old routine. They're lucky that this morning she hasn't tried to slip her cold, bony body into either of the beds. She'd be quite capable of doing so! Well anyhow, she's satisfied with moving about like crazy and then standing stock-still in the very centre of the room, her arms crossed, relishing the disruption she has hurled into their fragile slumber.

Biram is the first to toss and turn on his camp-bed, his usual throat noises accompanied by sighs and rapid swallows. On the other hand, nothing stirs in the corner occupied by Marie-Jo and Abdou. Under an acrylic blanket in a large flower pattern (Li'l Brother's Christmas present, here you are lovebirds I've brought you something useful), their bodies, wedged together, form a hump – the navel of the one stuck like a limpet to the small of the other's back, unless it's the other way around. These two share a rather soft bed, made of two mattresses stacked atop each other, and a profound love made of two separate anguishes locked in an embrace. Silence surrounds their repose like a mosquito net: however, it's a good bet that they're just lightly dozing, but are still avoiding the outside world. The thing is, they haven't the slightest desire to confront, so early in the day, their companion's ungrateful face.

Impelled by a deliberate resolution, Biram casts aside a flap of the sleeping-bag in which he has been cocooned and folds up his bed with the movements of an automaton. He can be heard walking over to the sink in the tiny bathroom, scrubbing his face under a thin trickle of water (a shudder to think that it could well be freezing), meticulously brushing his teeth. Under his breath he starts singing a pachanga from the night before, not yet daring to turn on the radio and plug the world into their garret. Just hang on; she'll take care of that. Besides, there she is already, pushing the buttons, moving from one station to the next until she finds a holiday broadcast where a master chef is explaining the complicated recipes for a successful New Year's Eve dinner.

'Cause pity, she ain't got none of that.

Stoically Biram gives her the cold shoulder and starts (it might be guessed) rummaging through the cupboard, for cups, spoons and jars clatter on the formica table. A tap spills into the bottom of a saucepan, which is then set down abruptly on the stove. A match crackles: the water will be boiling two or three minutes from now. Just enough time to cobble together a few crazy images for a future dream, when one really feels like dreaming. Finally, a drop of boiling water falls into each cup, giving the small spoon enough wherewithal to stir the thick, powdery substance adhering to the bottom of the porcelain (lent by the compassionate landlady, but take good care of them, they mean a lot to me, you know, and that phoney shy look she drops) and to make the sugar granules dissolve by means of the applied force. Faster and faster, with greater and greater ease as the water is added, turns the spoon, turning as it scrapes the porcelain cup, the porcelain of a dream for two that is cracking, as it scrapes the inside of our bellies polished by a time of waiting where a pain twists and turns, acquires a voice, thunders forth and then reproaches itself.

Have pity, have pity, I tell you.

She ain't got none.

*

'The Nescafé's on, Tata!' announces Biram in his tender voice.

People like Biram, thanks to that way he has of mothering the woes of the group, with an affectionate gesture, a kind word, a crude joke that puts the blues off until tomorrow. All three of them, now seated wherever they can, inhale almost simultaneously a sip of hot, creamy, sugary liquid that has nothing, absolutely nothing in common with plain old instant coffee. The odours of the night scatter, the rest of the morning is spent on trifles: Marie-Jo has to finish reading a difficult article that she had dipped into last night; and while Biram sets about washing down and scrubbing the Turkish toilets on the landing, Abdou takes a long shower. In the meantime, the witch strikes poses before the mirror.

Sidi comes by around eleven, the usual thing of shooting the breeze and now and then to see if.

'Monday for sure,' says Biram, who loves only hope.

But he ought to know that the cheques never arrive on the first of the month and that most of the offices are closed on holidays. And besides (Abdou's getting mad), it could well be that the grant stipends had been suspended, that's been an issue for quite some time, there's been a lot of debate over that on campus, have you forgotten, Plan B, Plan C, go back home to poverty, stay here in poverty, fear of fighting, fed up with not daring to, still in our country these people were a bunch of spoiled brats, and neither Marx nor Lenin's written anything serious to help us think about our situation, which just goes to show.

That's blasphemy, Sidi shouts. They close in on each other. They break it up. Biram takes half a kola-nut from a jar, divides it. Sidi, upset, takes his share with trembling fingers and claims a prior engagement. They hold him back.

'You too, Sidi, stay a little longer . . .'

They all make fun of Marie-Jo who prefers to chew a stick of gum. Stubbornly Abdou contrives as usual to have the last word or to read the chosen excerpt and sentence that prove his point.

I too have been hungry in this goddamned messed-up land . . .

Biram pushes aside Abdou and his same old song to take his large sailor's peacoat out of the cupboard. It's one of the two coats he owns. Truth be told, the real coat is the other one, in beige tweed, not too worn out, the long and lined coat he wears for the first two weeks of the month, from November to March. The peacoat is the garment for lean times, which is what they call (not without a certain tenderness) the end of the month. And it's true that Biram, despite his broad shoulders, looks skinny under the ample dark blue fabric, equipped with deep buckled pockets that look like baskets sewn with large stitches, as if for conscience's sake. Watching good old Biram button his bad-times garment in the middle of a bad Sunday, they know the plan he has in mind, but pretend to be unaware of it – eyes cunningly lowered over the porcelain cups filled with hot water where a Lipton's teabag is steeping (let's save the rest of the Nescafé). Nobody will even look up to answer his farewell when, already on the landing, he turns around and, at an angle, frames his placid face with its fogged-over glasses in the embrasure of the door: 'See you real soon, Tata! Need anything? Sidi, Abdou, see you, guys!'

When she hears his voice receding, the slut opens wide the door to the room and a ferocious wind rushes in. With disordered gestures, she pursues Biram to the stairway and, out of breath, dogs his footsteps. So why is it that, once the door has been shut, her presence is still felt inside?

*

For hours on end they'll pretend not to be waiting for Biram. Sidi's left for his rendezvous. Shortly after, Abdou goes out to look for cigarettes: on Sundays you have to walk a good distance to find an open tobacconist's. Marie-Jo resolves to ask him to clarify some points about the Asiatic mode of production when he gets back, but takes advantage of his absence to listen to the same Barry White record ten times in a row:

Baby, sweet baby, my babe / What am I gonna do with you? / Tin-din-din.

That much she understands, even if she doesn't know English: too bad, it'd be nice to know the rest of the song. Abdou comes back, throws his keys and his Gitanes on the bed.

'Turn that off! A name like that, give me a break. The Asiatic mode of production? We talked about that last week at Savannah's, were you asleep or what?'

And there they are, tearing at each other, embracing each other, in order not to lose a single part of this rare moment when it's just the two of them, in order to adorn the advancing afternoon, in order not to confess their shame, their fear and everything else.

*

It's really something, the fuss they make over Biram when he sets down on the table a large plastic bag labelled 'Supermarché Felix' containing a square box of Maggi bouillon cubes with a small cash-register receipt stuck to it. They start pulling on the linty sleeves of his peacoat.

'That can't be all, c'mon, that can't be all!'

Amid joyous yells Biram extracts, with an epic scowl, a package of red, *really* red meat from an inside pocket, from another a bag of biscuits; thick turkey drumsticks emerge from an outside pocket, and a big container of Dakatine from another hiding place. Oh yes, and also in his possession are some matches, plus a chocolate bar and tomato purée. As for rice, there's no shortage of that, there's always a bag in reserve. Two onions are languishing in the refrigerator and oil can be cadged from the neighbour in the back, the nice old lady who doesn't have running water. Meanwhile, our little shrew has started scratching at the door with her polished nails, but nobody pays her any mind. While Marie-Jo hangs the peacoat on a wall-nail for Biram, who is already getting busy over the stove, Abdou starts working on the pot of Dakatine with a blade and leaves it, still partly crowned with its metal lid, on the formica table where a spot of oil is spreading.

Dakatine's an amazing thing. It guarantees being able to prepare two and even three mafés, as long as the sauce isn't cooked too thickly. And furthermore, Dakatine alliteratively alludes to the name of a beloved, caressing city (hence the incongruity of those loud colours, blue, white and red, decorating the box). But when you get right down to it, what's most astonishing is the enigmatic gesture of the blue-eyed, red T-shirted child whose portrait takes up half the container: enraptured, he brings to his smiling, cherry-red mouth a slice of bread covered with a thick dollop of peanut butter. Dakatine, eaten straight and on a piece of bread? What good old Biram does is to cook it for a long time in a tomato purée seasoned with garlic and onions, until he obtains a smooth, orange sauce whose surface, splitting as it boils, forms tiny craters that quickly fill up with a reddish oil. Once, when Marie-Jo questioned him about it, Abdou answered, suddenly with feigned cruelty, 'You know, you just can't figure Americans out!'

But why should he be American, that child on the jar (she restrained herself from asking)? Because of his cheeks swollen from good eating? Because of that joyous assurance that lights him up just as he's about to carry out the most absurd gesture (swallowing a piece of bread covered in raw peanut butter)?

Why American and not Parisian and not Chinese and not Dakarois?

Why thirteen / and not fifteen / and not twenty / and not thirty?

Besides, Abdou said it well the other day: 'Really, you just can't figure our compatriots out!'

So he could well be Dakarois, that little Dakatine boy, except that he's devouring peanut butter on white bread with gusto.

*

Skinny and graceless, Abdou has stretched out on the bed and unfolded a newspaper which he comments on in a low voice.

'Registration fees are going up again! That just happened last year too. And what about us, what are we going to do with our limited work permits? (Marie-Jo, take the phone tokens out of my shirt pocket and go call Li'l Brother, Sidi and Jacqueline.)'

Tata (that's Biram's nickname for her) has already put her shoes on and, her mind a blank, knots a scarf over her coat collar.

'Ah, the election results. Goddamn it, Biram (and tell them to bring), are you listening to me, big guy? (a baguette and yeah, some beer!)'

Voiceless and weightless, with a single fluttering of her wings Marie-Jo descends the increasingly narrow spirals of the staircase, just as in that old dream that keeps coming back to her intermittently at night.

*

That evening they'll be there, crowded around the enamel bowl filled with good meat mafé: Sidi of course, and Jacqueline, unless she hasn't done her past week's course reading. Maybe Savannah will be there, too – what an artist that guy is, with his peroxide Afro and always carrying his latest daubings with him. Li'l Brother will bring dried fruit for dessert and lumps of sugar for mint tea. Most of the time he'll talk with Abdou, running his fingers through his ochre-coloured hair, with one knee on the cold tiled floor (mind you, less not to pay court to Abdou but to punish himself for that chronic feeling of superiority he drags around with him).

Once the meal is finished, while Biram washes the bowl, Abdou, with a sure hand, will trace arabesques of boiling liquid with the spout of the nickel-plated teapot, filling with foam the little glasses arranged in a circle on a tray placed on the very floor itself and all sticky with sugar, draining them repeatedly of their thick tea in the belly of the metallic utensil blackened by the flame of the primus stove and whose lid, held down by a sudden movement of his nervous wrist, clatters every time. All conversation is suspended for a moment to allow the aroma of mint to spread throughout the room.

*

That evening the bitch can knock, storm, raise a ruckus all she wants, she won't get in.

Go away!

She's waiting.

Anyway, laughter and music drown out her enraged cries: old pachangas, some beguines, Miles obviously (oh yeah, an absolute must), Ike and Tina Turner if ever, their stomachs filled with warmth, they fall asleep, despite all that tea-sipping.

'Cause pity, she ain't got none of that.

That whore Poverty.

Damn it! and hunger too.

Curled up on a cushion, Marie-Jo listens in her mind to her favourite Barry White song (the assembled company would get mad if she ever).

Baby, sweet baby, my babe / What am I gonna do with you?

Maybe one day, she'll know the rest of it.

Tin-din-din...

Syl Cheney-Coker

The Concert

Syl Cheney-Coker was born in Freetown, Sierra Leone, in 1945 and educated at universities in the United States. He has lived as a journalist and is currently in exile from his home country, teaching at James Madison University. His career in literature began as a poet, but in 1990 he published in the Heinemann African Writers Series his extraordinary fantasy-epic of West African history, *The Last Harmattan of Alusine Dunbar*. His 'The Concert' was a joint overall winner in the 1996 Commonwealth Short Story Prize and was first published in *Wasafiri* (autumn 1996).

OVER THE YEARS Ramatu Sow had become someone unwilling to leave anything to chance, especially when she was preparing for a concert. Eagerly, she would look forward to November, after the insufferable months of the rain, as she waited for the sun that the concerts brought into her life. So she approached this evening, when her future son-in-law arrived unexpectedly, with an almost messianic fervour. Earlier she had woken up and began to sing to herself, careful not to disturb her husband, her eyes misted over with thoughts of faraway places she would dream of every time an orchestra came to town.

Sitting on a low stool, she applied her make-up, lingered for a while in front of her mirror and, with only a small admission of vanity, examined the lines on her face.

'Life has been good to me,' she mused.

Early in the afternoon, the aroma of garlic fish cooked with sweet basil had filled the kitchen. Intent on showing off her culinary skills, she baked her husband his favoured cake, a chocolate delight. That done, she straightened the paintings and framed photographs on the living-room walls, noting that the latter were fading with genealogical oblivion. One photograph held her attention for a while; that of her mad father. Two small teardrops came to her eyes as she thought of him, but she quickly wiped them away, so as not to dampen her mood. Somewhat exhausted, she rested for a while, as age was catching up with her. Finally, at six p.m., one hour before the concert was to start, her face beamed with pleasure as she began to run her bath.

When she was lonely, Ramatu would wear one of her two chiffon dresses, adorn her beautiful neck with some of her equally well-preserved jewellery, then parade up and down her lawn like a dowager queen. On this occasion, however, she paid special attention to her looks, gorgeously resplendent in a simple black dress made expensive by a set of immaculate pearls. She wore her Salvatore Ferragamo shoes reserved for important occasions, and was just about to apply a touch of Estée Lauder when the maid announced the arrival of Lansana Kan.

'Show him in,' Ramatu replied, unable to conceal her anger from the maid.

'Evening, Mrs Sow,' Lansana greeted her, as he came into the living room.

'Aminatu has told me you have something important to say, but I am afraid it will have to wait.'

'It is all right, Mrs Sow,' said Lansana, 'I can always come back.'

'You won't have to,' Ramatu replied, trying to match his facetious air, 'but since you are here, you might as well attend the concert.'

*

She led him into the inner sanctum, offered him a seat, excused herself, then went to her bedroom. Waiting, Lansana's thoughts were filled with the beauty of the place, how to approach this haughty woman for her daughter, and of the idea of driving Ramatu to the concert, when he saw the most remarkable thing he had ever seen.

Holding her head in a regal manner, as if she had once inspired Cézanne, Ramatu emerged from her bedroom with her husband leaning on her shoulder. A stroke had crippled Abraham Sow's left side a bit, halting his career as a scientist, but he showed no sign of disability. Rather, he looked happy, as on the day he had married Ramatu. Three high-backed chairs had been positioned in front of the TV ten feet away, but Abraham needed only a little encouragement to go across that expanse, as he would have done anything for his wife.

Smiling to his future son-in-law, Abraham greeted Lansana. 'How are you, son?'

'Fine, sir; and you, sir?'

'Living according to God's plan,' Abraham replied.

*

Once she had made her husband comfortable in one of the chairs, Ramatu switched on the TV. Soon the rich sound of the Orchestra National Orpheus came into the room, with the *Symphonie Fantastique*, which to Lansana was the best choice of music for the evening. As the music filled the room Lansana watched Ramatu close her eyes, the lines of her beautiful face moving with the rise and fall of the crescendoes; that presto of the Rhine that was the composer's passion. It was the work of genius, so Ramatu took the hand of her husband, in an acknowledgement of his own thwarted genius.

There and then, Lansana knew he would have given anything to be so loved by their daughter, for whose hand he had come.

Ama Ata Aidoo

Lice

Ama Ata Aidoo, one of Africa's leading feminists and best-known writers, was born and educated in Ghana, where for a period until 1983 she was Minister of Education; she writes poetry, plays and novels. Her 1970 collection of stories, *No Sweetness Here*, included items first published in *Black Orpheus, The New African* and *New African Literature and the Arts* (1970), and later she made her debut in the United States, as did many other African writers, in Edris Makward and Leslie Lacy's *Contemporary African Literature* (Random House, 1972). She has lived in Zimbabwe and in the United States as a writer-in-residence at various institutions. Typical of her work is the story 'Lice', published in *West Africa* in London (23 March 1987). A new collection of hers is *The Girl Who Can* (1997).

LIFE HAS ITS PROBLEMS. Without further ruining one's already bad nerves listening to the World News first thing in the morning. And when you are

> just a woman
> an ordinary wife with a normal
> marriage
> ignored, double-timed
> a harassed mother
> a low-paid teacher in a rotten
> Third World educational system

what should you want with the World News anyway? It's like eavesdropping on gossip about humankind. In this last quarter of the twentieth century, you are bound to hear something nasty. If not about your own backyard, then about other people or some things you are stupid enough to care greatly about . . .

Sissie knew she should know better. Which she did. But then, doing better is another task altogether.

And she had been prepared quite well for the life everyone had suspected she was going to have to lead. Her mother advising her to remember counting her blessings. Actually, that was not her mother. That had been the kindly missionary nuns who ran her old secondary boarding school.

> They scurried among them
> like frightened white mice
> in a tropical forest,
> forever surprise in their eyes
> yet
> still managing to
> fuss,
> like all mothers.

And from her mother:

> 'My Child, don't complain
> so much. Always remember
> that it doesn't matter how
> bad your situation is, someone
> nearby is wishing they were
> you.'

Sissie's eyes flew open against her will. So she quickly shut them up again. Tightly.

Sissie knew she was awake. She also knew 'Baby' was lying by her ...

Really, she should stop herself and everybody else calling the poor child 'Baby'. After all, she was a grand old lady of five years. Plus she had got a name ... names.

The countryside of Euro-Africa and Afro-Europe is indeed cluttered with rubbish.

Ah no, she shouldn't start on that sort of track this morning. Instead, she should start counting her blessings.

One. She had got a husband: married to traditionally, legally, fully ...

She could remember the wedding. She could also remember the events leading to the ceremony ... Her Big Mother murmuring: 'Now our daughter has become a proper lady ... Ah-h-h, our daughter has become a proper lady!' while she tried, Big Mother would, to adjust the veil there, push a curl from the wig there ... All in an attempt to beautify things a little more, no doubt. But then Big Mother had ended up just upsetting the semi-professional wedding merchants hired for the occasion.

... the ceremony itself ... that night ...

Just as, without looking, Sissie knew her second child had crawled into the bed some time in the night, she also knew without looking that her husband was not occupying his side of the bed. In fact, he had not been home at all. And that made the third night he had not been. She knew he had been sneaking into the house when he was certain that she herself had gone to work, at least.

She wondered what stories he was telling at his workplace to explain his regular lateness ...

... The mind too is a countryside cluttered with rubbish. Why couldn't she mind her own business? Concentrate on her own troubles? Keep on counting her blessings?

Two. She had the children. Kofi was seven, and 'Baby' Efua Anamua was five. One boy, one girl.

'Wo mmpe yi.
Na.
Wope dien?'

'If you aren't grateful for this, then what the hell do you want?'
There were always two queues at the clinic. One was pregnant:

– women with just missed periods, seeking confirmation;
– women at mid-term, looking for general good health for the remaining half of the trip, and for insurance against post-partum disasters;
– women at full term. Only a few weeks or a few days due. All eyes shining, nostrils flared with certain exultation: the very toes in the sandals oozing with fulfilment.

The other queue, which was always twice as long or longer, was almost infertile, infertile or completely barren. Everyone in it was looking for a child. An addition to, or replacement for the one or two born some time ago, and which had lived or died. Or because they had never had any. Ever.

– young working girls whose tentative experiments with unplanned sex had not ended in the half-dreaded, half-desired pregnancies with which they had hoped to trap the relevant young men into marriage ...
– women who were actively looking for pregnancy. Their marriages depended on it. Their femininity. Their humanity. They were always very fashionable: well-dressed, delicately perfumed, their figures well-kept ... and since their men refused to go for check-ups with them, who knows, perhaps the doctor himself ... Or some other male accidentally

met, leading to a quick accidental you-know-what and leading to a baby...

– women who had lost all hope. But who still kept going back to the clinic. As much to keep appointments with the doctor as with one another. For wasn't it only here that they could still behave like human beings? Chat, exchange confidences and trade gossip?

Sissie's eyes were still tightly shut. Briefly, she asked herself where counting one's blessings ended and dwelling on other people's woes began?

Three ... three ... three ...

She could only remember her son, the inside of his school shorts soaked with blood. She wondered, very briefly, whether Blessing Number One would have bothered to come home if he knew their son had hurt himself falling off a tree in school ... The nursing sister on duty at the hospital had made jokes; in an attempt to keep her calm, perhaps.

'Madam, we have been lucky. Just think of it, if it was the precious weapon that had been ruined? Such a handsome young man, too. Think of it; what would our daughters have done? Hah, ha ha!'

Sissie had not felt at all like laughing.

'Madam,' the Sister had continued, 'please hold his hand.'

Sissie remembered taking hold of Kofi's hand. She remembered asking them what they were going to do.

'Ah, Madam,' Sister had crooned, 'we are so lucky. So-o-o lucky. We have got a li-i-ttle bit of antiseptic left, and we will clean the wound with it. But unfortunately, that's all. It is not serious enough to put him under general anaesthesia. And we don't have anything for a local either ... We'll give him *pethidine*. That will relax him. But please, hold his hand while we stitch the wound up?'

Sissie's eyes were still tightly shut. In the darkness she remembered clearly that the nurse's assurances had put her feelings under general anaesthesia. She had felt absolutely nothing for the next half hour. Her son screaming and screaming. And then after she had covered his mouth with her cupped hand, he just whimpered like a dying animal as the needle went in and out of his flesh. While the black silk thread looked unimpressively familiar. Nothing about it to say it wasn't the regular cotton used for plaiting hair and bought from the city market...

Blessing Number Three: she had a job.

This time, Sissie's body experienced a major spasm.

Yes, the ring and the 'Mrs' title had produced one definite result.

She did not have to be nervous entering the headmaster's office any longer. He had obviously taken the hint. Plus there were all those younger and juicier unprotected females that made a third of the student population...

Of course, she was beginning to live with the knowledge that as long as she taught in that school, the headmaster was never going to recommend her for promotion... Dear God, and her pay was still the same, and inflation daily shrinking its value. The whole lot would now not pay for one dress... But wasn't there something quite universal about that these days?

At her old school the advice had been even in the form of a song they used to sing. Something to the effect that

'Count your blessings
Name them one by one...'
Yes, at least, she had a job.
She could see the school where she taught.
With more than twice the number of students
it should have had in the dormitories;
empty science laboratories, other empty places that should have been
equipped; the pipes that were perennially dry from drought or leaked
the little water away with old age and rust...

Even chalk was often a problem. Sure, nothing much was coming from the ministry. But she also knew that what little came was equally shared between the headmaster and the bursar. From food for the boarders to exercise books and chalk. Well, they too had mouths to feed and relatives to impress.

Ugh. Sissie shuddered again.

Blessing Number Four. It was a Saturday. No school.

But she still had to take Kofi to the hospital to have his wound seen to. And how was she to do that? The hospital was on the other side of town. The car was definitely with Blessing Number One who had no doubt parked it outside the door of whoever's bed he had been sharing these past nights.

The car was half-broken down. Like everybody else's. But when it moved, it was a car. Half the money that had gone into buying it had been hers. You wouldn't guess it, would you? From the way she had to beg for rides in it? Her mother had called her a fool when she had told her about their plans two years earlier. Sissie had felt hurt at first, and then secretly consoled herself that her mother was only an uneducated villager who could not be expected to understand the intricacies of a modern marriage . . .

On a Saturday morning no taxi driver was going to drive to distant places from the centre of the city. No, not on his hard-won petrol, his threadbare tyres, his half-working gears . . .

So how was she going to get Kofi to hospital?

And when did she do the weekly shopping before the shops closed down for the weekend? And it wasn't even a question of dashing in and out of the shops picking this and that . . . the city market was still good. Thank God. But the shops! She would have to stand forever in the queues which no one paid any attention to, since she fell into no easily identifiable grouping.

She did not look obviously pregnant.
She did not carry the card of an ex-serviceman of the World Wars.
She was not a senior army or police officer.
She was not an important businessman or businesswoman.
She did not have any political connections.
She was not the manager's relative,
his wife, or
his girlfriend. And
She was not . . .

Oh Mother-Superior, why didn't you ever add that counting blessings can be quite a hard job too?

She should have gone to the bathroom a long time ago. Her bladder was full and hurting. But that would have meant some eye-opening. And she was not ready to face that this morning. So her eyes remained tightly shut as she moved to lie flat on her stomach. Her mind told her the dawn was breaking since totally shiny moving black things in her head were gradually turning to grey, spangled moving things. A happy bird was twittering somewhere nearby. A happy bird.

'Mammy . . . Mammy . . . Mammy!'

'Yes, Baby, what is it?'

'Wake up.'

'Why?'

'Mammy, just wake up.'

'Oh please, I am so tired.'

'Mammy, wake up.'

'Baby, I am very tired. And it is not morning yet.'

'Yes, it is. Look!'

'Please, Baby, leave me to sleep a little.'

'Mammy, wake up and sing me a song.'

Sissie's eyes remained tightly shut. Maybe the bird outside was singing because her child wanted her to? Except that she knew this morning she could not sing, no matter how much her daughter pleaded.

Baby crawled from her side and threw her body across Sissie's back.

'Mammy ... Mammy ... Mammy, my head is itching.'

Without opening her eyes, Sissie reached out her left hand and touched her daughter's head.

'Here, here, here,' cried the little girl. 'All over, Mammy.'

Sissie opened her eyes.

She reached out, moved Baby off her back, turned over and sat up. It was still not light enough to see the itching head.

She realized she had to run and go to the bathroom if she was not going to pour the contents of her bladder on the bed. She sighed. She put her feet on the floor.

'I am coming back,' she told the little girl and ran out of the room.

On her way back from the bathroom she went to peep in at Kofi. He was still sleeping. She touched his forehead. It was not hot. She left the room and shut the door softly behind her.

Back in the bedroom Sissie switched on the single overhead bulb. Baby was still scratching her head. So Sissie asked her to sit down on the floor while she had a look. She parted the child's hair at random. A huge louse was crouching on her scalp. Sissie groaned as she picked it and crushed it. She parted another part of the hair. She saw two lice. True enough, the little girl's hair was full of lice.

Sissie began to shiver. And then she felt funny in her stomach and on her chest. 'I am coming,' she told the little girl again and ran out to the bathroom. She held on to the wash basin. But she was not sick. It was just nausea. And apart from the fact that her skin felt damp, she was all right. She also felt her eyes beginning to smart with unshed tears. She quickly washed her face.

What was she to do? Yes, she wasn't sure what to do about what.

As she walked back to the bedroom the second time, she met Baby on her way to the toilet.

Sissie sat on the edge of the bed. 'No one should feel as I am feeling right now, so early in the morning,' she told herself aloud. That was when she realized her own head was itching. She began to scratch it. But the more she scratched, the worse it got. Then Baby returned from the bathroom, sat on the floor again as she remembered her mother had asked her to. One hand was in her hair, a finger of the other hand in her mouth, her eyes raised with some expectation at her mother.

Sissie let herself fall back on the bed, closed her eyes again, but this time with her scalp itching very badly. From the floor Baby began to wail again, 'Mammy, Mammy!' while Sissie's own mind whined: 'What am I going to do?'

'What am I going to do?'

She had not realized she had switched on the little transistor radio. But, sure enough, the news was on:

... President Reagan had won a landslide victory for a second term as President of the United States of America;

... there had been a monstrous explosion at a nation's petroleum depot in ... she had missed the name of the city and the country ... hundreds of people were feared dead ... hundreds of surrounding homes were destroyed ... thousands evacuated; ...

... world experts do not see the end of the drought in sight. In fact, Africa was in for a worse time next year. All that can be predicted was more of:

the appalling pictures of emaciated
children
the victims of war
the columns of refugees trailing across
a
dusty landscape into
urban squalor ...

Then she wasn't sure any more whether all of that was coming that minute out of the radio. Or was it her mind doing funny tricks with other bits of the news heard at other times? In any case, the room had begun to spin a little.

Sissie took hold of herself. Suddenly she knew what she had to do.

There was a little paraffin left in the gallon can.

Where had she heard that paraffin was the best remedy for getting rid of lice?

She went to the corner of the garage where they kept things like paraffin ... It wasn't much of a garage. Just a small open shed to protect the car from the rain and the sun. They normally backed out straight from it into the street. But it was better than nothing ...

She picked up the gallon can and returned to the bedroom. She looked for, and found, the wide-toothed wooden comb, and carefully combed Baby's hair. Then she combed her own hair.

When she removed the lid from the gallon can, the fumes of petrol jumped at her. She had picked the wrong petroleum product. She paused for just a fraction of a second . . .

After all, if paraffin can get rid of lice, petrol can do that and much more? . . .

Petrol should get rid of some of life's problems.
Petrol gets rid of some of life's problems. All of life's problems.

She soaked her little girl's head first. Thoroughly. Then she soaked up her own. She was by now in so much haste the stuff was spilling on herself, over the bed, on the floor . . .

Where were the matches?

She was feeling too tired to walk all the way back to the kitchen. But there was no need. On the dressing-table was one of Blessing Number One's discarded matchboxes. She jumped and picked it up.

Baby had sat through all that petrol dousing without a murmur. Now she said: 'Mammy, it smells.'

'Yes, Baby, only for now. Soon the smell will go away.'

How should she go about it? Ah, she knew. She should light Baby's head first. Then her own. She struck the match.

Loud coughing came from beyond the door. Of course it was Kofi who had coughed. There was also a sound of him turning restlessly in his sleep. He coughed again. Sissie heard it.

The matchbox and lighted stick fell from Sissie's head.

She sat on the edge of the bed. After a second during which she was perfectly still, she moved with the greatest effort she must have ever made in her whole life, and brought her left foot down on the glowing match.

Then she threw herself back on the bed and finally burst into tears.

To end the news, these were the main headlines: 'President Reagan . . .'

Tanure Ojaide

God and His Medicine-men

Tanure Ojaide, the Nigerian-born critic and poet, studied at the University of Ibadan and at Syracuse University. He has published several volumes of poetry, one of which won the Commonwealth Poetry Prize for the Africa region in 1987. He lectured at the University of Maiduguri in Nigeria and is now a professor of African-American and African Studies at the University of North Carolina at Charlotte. His recent memoir is *Great Boys: An African Childhood* (Africa World Press, 1998). 'God and his Medicine-men', published here for the first time, is the title story of a collection of his in preparation.

THEY LIVED IN IGBI STREET and we lived in Ginuwa Road. Igbi Street runs into Ginuwa Road where my father's house still stands. My friend's home was less than five minutes' walk from ours. From childhood, we played in the same churchyard, the Anglican mission. We children did not know any difference between the Catholic and Anglican churches as our parents did. Endurance's father was a pastor, an Anglican reverend. My father was a churchman of the Catholic faith and he went daily to Mass in the cathedral a half-mile away. After school the open Anglican schoolground was ours for play till we were tired. We girls played together, so we established a common bond.

Even though we went to different elementary schools, we ended up in the same Government Teachers' College at Bomadi for our Grade II Teacher's Certificate. Government was neither Anglican nor Catholic, so those of us who went to different denominational elementary schools converged in a government-run teachers' college. We girls in the college were not many and so knew ourselves very well. For me and Endurance who came from the same town and had known each other and played together for years, it appeared we were from the same family.

That's how we became even closer and I got to know not only Endurance's father but also Odele, two of God's medicine-men. That's how I also came to see Endurance's disappointing marriage as partly caused by me, even though in the end people should make their own choices. I thought I was helping my friend but I could have been playing the matchmaker without knowing.

Whenever Endurance was going to bed, she always double-checked to ensure that the doors were properly secured. Though it was unusual to padlock the door from the inside, her parents allowed her to do so. They believed their daughter was paranoid and hoped her fears would subside with more years. It was not that she was afraid that burglars would break in, but she could not identify the source of what was happening to her. She was determined to stop a burglary of another kind.

It was vacation time when her two other sisters and her brother were around. She shared one room with her sisters and so she did not sleep alone. She slept in one bed, but there were two other beds in the room. Even when she changed beds with her junior sisters, there was no reprieve from the strange intruder. And yet she was always on her guard.

Her mind travelled in all directions. Where could this stranger come from to be able to enter into her at will? She knew that for all the quarrels they had in daytime and which were tightly hidden from outsiders, her father and mother slept together. After all, what would the congregation think of a pastor who quarrelled with his wife? What kind of example the church's First Couple would be giving if their exchange of insults was heard outside their home? But they fired abuses at each other in low tones and their voices were never raised to reach the street.

Endurance marvelled at her parents' self-control in bottling up their fracas. While she hated their squabbles, she admired the limits they placed upon themselves. Quarrel, but let no outsider hear of it. Quarrel, but put on a cheerful face for the world to see. Sleep in the same room and the same bed but ignore the other as much as possible for the children not to know that they did not really sleep together. They had to give a good example not only as a good and happy couple but also as good and happy parents.

There were two men in the house at night: her father and her sibling brother. She could not imagine the impossible, that her father or brother could be the one. There were certain things she did not want to think about and suspecting her own father or brother was ruled out. Endurance was at a loss on what to do.

She was twenty-one and had made love several times before. She knew as a pastor's daughter she had to hide to have her fill in this respect. Her mother and father might think she was still a virgin, but she could not afford to let them know any better. Being a pastor's daughter, she had little chance of going out, and no young man had the courage to come to see her in her father's house.

Their five-bedroom mansion stood at one corner of the mission grounds which also held an elementary school and a big church. Painted brown like the school and church buildings, their house was impressive in size. Endurance and her sisters and brother felt fortunate about their home because they could tell from their friends' homes that theirs was indeed a very big house. They have seen their friends live with their parents in one- or two-room apartments.

She made sure that she wore tight underwear to bed, but that did not stop the intruder from entering into her at will. She wore trousers to bed, and yet she woke with a feeling of sticky wetness between her legs.

As a beautiful young woman of twenty-one, she was attracted to some men, but none of them had made any serious effort to win her love. Her fear and frustration had been this secret stealing into her and waking without remembering anything but only to see the wet and sticky mess between her legs. She has had faint recollections of her ecstasy, but there was no face to place on the man who came into her in her dream. She would not mind sleeping with somebody who loved her and whose face and name she recognized. But she hated this robber who secretly took away from her her most private possession.

She was scared for her life. Somebody or spirit was in control of her life and she could become what she had not planned for herself. If some man or spirit made love with her successfully, would she not be pregnant? Will her parents, especially her father, believe her innocence, or will they blow out for being scandalized by their supposedly wayward daughter? After all, he always preached against young girls and boys for not following the ways of Christ and knowing what they should not know before they got married. Will they understand the strange phenomenon? But why not, if they knew of the Virgin Mary? Endurance acknowledged that though she was a pastor's daughter, she did not have the spirituality of the Holy Mother. Strange things could always happen. But she was not a virgin – she lost that in, of all places, the village where she and her sisters had gone to spend a vacation. There she had been as free as air and her grandfather and grandmother had treated them so specially that they would like to live with them all the time. But she was already a grown-up girl who must go to school.

Recently, when her mother and father travelled out of town, she sat in the sitting room and, since she was the eldest child and in control, nobody told her to go to bed. She fell asleep on the couch and woke after another orgasm. Her thighs as usual were sticky with thick wetness.

She thought seriously of buying contraceptives from one of the many pharmacists in the town. She had to protect herself, and she knew all she had to do was to ask for a packet of contraceptive pills with one hand, while handing over the money to the pharmacist with the other. After all, nobody would recognize her since the pharmacists had the habit of not looking their customers in the face. They avoided visual contacts because all they cared for was their money. They did not want to have to do anyone any favour on the basis of facial recognition. So they avoided it.

But Endurance was not a stranger to strange experiences. She had come home from school to solve a problem, only to face a more intractable one. At school she had been helpless before a succubus. That was what they called the invisible person who came to press her while she slept at night. Again, this person was not barred by sealed school doors. Even though she shared a room with four other girls, she was the only one who experienced the incubus or succubus, whatever that oppressive spirit was called.

At first she was quiet over the experience which came at long intervals, but later when the frequency increased she could no longer bear the burden without crying out. She told me as her bosom friend about it, but I did not have much to say then. What does the daughter of a Catholic Head Christian know about spirits pressing people down at night in their sleep? That was before I spent one of the long holidays with my aunt in Benin. Children of Christian parents, we had been discouraged from believing in the supernatural. We grew up to believe that there were Satanic forces, evil spirits, that could be overwhelmed by constant prayers to God.

'In the name of Christ, I stop you. With the blood of Jesus, I overrule you,' Endurance had chanted many times.

However, like the new evil spirit, the incubus persisted and refused to be annihilated by either the name or blood of Christ or Jesus. She lit candles in the room but the incubus bypassed the candles and still stole in to press her. She placed a Bible beneath her pillow, but the incubus was not scared by the Holy Book; it still pressed her while asleep on the bed.

'Why me, God?' Endurance had asked many times.

'Continue to pray for help,' I told her.

I knew that my friend must be going through a very difficult situation but I did not know of any solution. Endurance was getting more distracted than usual and the former bubbling Black Princess, Warri Queen, as she was popularly called, was losing much of her lustre. It has been because of Endurance's case that I know that worries could hurt more than physical sickness. If she had suffered from malaria or something else, the doctor who visited our college twice a week would have cured her. But this was not a case she could bring to the young doctor who chased many female students who visited him to cook and do other things for him.

It was these strange experiences that drove the pastor's daughter, my good friend, to seek help from her friends.

This was her final year in the two-year programme. She decided to go home and tell her parents what was happening to her. She had to tell the matron and the principal why she needed to go home early. The teachers' college encouraged discipline and the principal did not want students to leave for home individually. During vacations, they went home in groups and that was safer than being alone. Of course, while I and mutual friends knew about her condition, she also needed to explain to her other friends what was driving her home so early.

We had always cherished our camaraderie – gossiping about other female students and their teachers and male students, recollecting common adventures and other things that bound us together as young girls.

But Endurance realized that she did not really need to explain her problems to the whole world. She thought that when she was back at home the aura of prayers would drive away the evil spirit that tormented her. So she had to manufacture a reason to the principal and she got her permission to leave.

The boat journey home on the Warri River always frightened her. She did not know how to swim, but she spent ten hours on the wide river that was notorious for crocodiles, sharks and big fishes that wrecked small boats. A few students had been victims of the vast and deep river, which yearly had its casualties. The current was violent in the salt side of the river. The boat was not as packed full as when she travelled with her fellow students. Then the boatmen filled the boats like the slave ships they read about in their history books to make the maximum profit and did not care if the boat sank from overweight. By the time they had come to the fresh water side of the river, she knew she was close to home. The river was narrower, less angry and had more villages on the banks. Endurance's breath became more relaxed and she started planning how she would tell her mother and father about her problem.

At home she could not immediately tell them about it. She was in a dilemma. On one level, her father railed against evil spirits, witches and demons in his sermons. In other words, these wicked forces existed to be fought and defeated. On the other hand, she as a Christian was supposed to believe that none of the wicked forces could have power over her as long as she believed in the power of Christ. She believed in God and Jesus who came to the world to save humankind, but that belief had not driven away the incubus that tormented her nightly. She was not sure of how her father in particular would respond to her talking about being pressed at night and she was afraid of being accused of believing in the power of demons rather than of Christ whose blood could wash away all evils. For these uncertainties she told her parents that she was sick, always dizzy and feeling like fainting.

My friendship with Endurance made me to know the Anglican pastor very well. I saw him frequently and as children of the same street we heard stories about him. People say he had gone to Jerusalem a long time ago. I believe this because Endurance confirmed it and even showed me one of the silver or imitative silver cups he brought from the Holy Land. Some photographs of Christ on the walls of their sitting room were quite unique and could have come only from the Holy Land.

Pastor Efe in many ways had lived up to the expectations of his wealthy name. How could anyone have predicted that the first son of a traditional healer whom the white missionaries had condemned to hell before his death would become the pastor of a major diocese. Pastor Jeremiah Efe had confounded village pundits. Even his own father, who had hoped that the son would take over the healing trade from him just as he had taken it over from his own father, no longer felt betrayed. He did not visit his son on Sundays, but he saw the big church at the other end of the field in the big compound that his son virtually owned in the name of God. Of course, his pastor son had not visited him on *edewor*, the traditional day of worship, when his home was full of patients needing assistance.

Pastor Jeremiah Efe had gone to school and distinguished himself in the old Standard Six, and a series of missionary schools for would-be pastors had made him very learned. From his preachings, one could tell that he knew the Bible very well. He quoted effortlessly from the Old and the New Testaments. He not only knew the verses but also the very page numbers of his quotes from the King James Version that his church used. He told his congregation that, despite being a busy pastor, he read the entire Bible every year, which meant he had read the Bible twenty times or more since he answered the pastoral call.

His congregation loved him, mainly because he was seen as a happily married man of a good family. And he preached very well. He railed against witches, evil-doers and wicked spirits in the strongest of terms. He could move people to tears and laughter with his words. He got possessed once the sermon began and the Holy Spirit spoke through his tongue. He spoke simple Urhobo-laced English, which worked well with most of his congregation, illiterate, semi-literate and highly literate alike. Men and women, young and old, all were solidly attached to his church, and this meant that Sunday worship at St Matthew's was a fulfilling experience to pastor and congregation.

The white Bishop in Benin must have heard many good things said about Pastor Jeremiah Efe, apart from his own favourable impression of the fine young man, so that when the Archbishop of Canterbury created an opportunity for his 'Nigerian brothers' to visit the Holy Land, he was easily picked as one of the native pastors in the contingent.

Pastor Jeremiah Efe visited Jerusalem in 1971. Jerusalem. The Holy Land. The Stone City. The City of Golden Sunset. The Birthplace of Jesus. The experience remained fresh in his mind. The son of an Urhobo traditional healer in the Land of Miracles! He has not forgotten the Wailing Wall, where he put on a Jewish skullcap and scribbled prayers which he tucked into the cracks of the old wall. He wanted to rise to be Bishop. He wanted peace in his home. He wanted his church to grow big and overflow with worshippers. At the Church of the Holy Sepulchre he visited different chapels and saw the unity of all churches. He even went to Asqua Mosque and was overwhelmed by the grandeur of this other religion. He wondered why Christians and Muslims in Nigeria frequently clashed violently when, in fact, they were worshipping the same God. He saw the make-up tomb of Christ. He followed the stations of the Cross. He wished he were there in Roman times to help Christ with the Cross, as did Thaddeus. Imagine if his wife, Rebecca, had like Veronica wiped tears, sweat or blood from Jesus's body. Everything had a certain aura of sacredness.

But years later, it was the Arab market that gave him the memento of his life. He bought five silver-looking cups. In fact, the Arab trader had told him they were silver goblets. He had an obsession for these silver goblets, which he always wanted to display before his visitors.

'Drink with the cup of Christ,' he told his guests once he offered them drinks.

Later, his familiar visitors got so used to being served with the cup of Christ that they asked for it, a request that became a code for drinks.

'Let me drink with one of those cups of Christ,' they would request, smiling.

Of course, his visitors became many and he spent far more than his congregation and mission paid him. Out of modesty and spiritual concerns, he was reluctant to discuss money even though he needed much more than the little he was paid. He employed innuendoes to inform members of his congregations who paid visits that his pay was not enough, but this never sank into their heads. How could anybody leaving the pastor's wealthy-looking house feel that he was close to the proverbial church rat?

'The Anglican Church is not like the Roman Catholic Church which is a state of its own and has gold reserves,' he told his congregation. 'We need to give to strengthen our church and ourselves,' he would also add.

He was not sure whether plain talk about raising his salary would go on well with his adoring congregation. But as a pastor, Jeremiah Efe continued to entertain his church members who frequently came to visit him. It was not that he was obliged to entertain, but those cups of Christ he so much loved exhibiting made him give out drinks with both right and left hands. This was the main cause of the quiet quarrel with his wife.

'What will we use both to clothe and feed the children and also to send them to school?' she frequently asked.

'God that sent me to Jerusalem will provide for them,' he would tell her.

A pastor's wife, Rebecca remained down to earth. She had lost her Ibo name, Ifi, to this Rebecca. Much as she told people she was Ifi, nobody was ready to call her that name. At first she felt the Urhobo did not want her to retain her real name. However, she also noticed that even the few Ibo women around also called her Rebecca or Becky. Rebecca or Ifi Efe, she was Mrs Efe, Pastor's Wife.

I travelled to spend part of my holidays with my senior sister living with her family in Benin and during that period, through my friend, Esther, I first heard of and later met Odele. I saw Pastor Odele and knew immediately he was a strange man, but I also felt that he might be able to help my other friend Endurance to get out of her problems.

Since our parents knew we were friends, it was easy for Endurance to obtain permission from her parents to visit me and spend some time with me and my senior sister, once I sent word that I wanted her to come as soon as possible.

'Pastor Odele,' as he introduced himself, projected himself as a man of piety, a man of God. He always wore a special hat which he had never changed since the many years I knew him. The hat covered his whole head and left a little of the forehead. So, though he was short, you never saw his exposed head or hair. The head might be bald or the hair shaved, but I could not tell. It seemed part of his spirituality had to do with his gentlemanly and fatherly look and covering his hair. There was some power in his head covered by the hat which did not appear to wear out with time.

Pastor Odele also held a small pocket Bible almost all the time. The letters were very tiny and he must be very familiar with its content to read it without glasses. He told Esther and me that the words of the Bible were the words of God with which one could cure the worst of diseases and cast out the most wicked spirits. The combination of the special hat and the small Bible gave a certain mystique to Pastor Odele's personality. When we first came to him, we were scared but soon got used to his strangeness.

Pastor Odele was not young, somebody in his forties, I guess. Still he lived with his mother and did not appear to be married. He had a big room in his mother's house. He told us he had his own house but since we were never taken there, we felt he might be trying to avoid embarrassment for living with his mother at his age. Or he might be trying to be consciously innocuous to us, he being a man of God and we being single girls. Though he called himself a pastor, he would not take us to his church to pray as we initially thought he would do. He pointed at a distant direction where his church was, but for the months and years we would know him, none of us would ever see or enter that church.

The pastor who looked every way like a medicine-man ministered to us and other visitors who trickled into his mother's home. If the pastor's appearance frightened us at first, the inside of his mother's house gave us even a bigger fright. We looked at each other, held the other's hand and knew we could not run anywhere. There was no way, we felt, that Pastor Odele would hurt all three of us together in broad daylight in his mother's home.

Pastor Odele's mother's home was a big shrine decked with mirrors, sculptures of god-like figures, skulls and white and red feathers. He knew we would be too scared to ask him any questions, so he tried to assure us of our safety.

'Everything on earth is made by God,' he said.

We were so engrossed in the different items in the big shrine of a parlour that none of us responded to him.

'We have to fight battles with whatever arms we can muster,' he told us as if he were leading the many figures of ancestors or gods to a battle that needed extraordinary weaponry.

The pastor led the three of us into his vast room which was comfortably furnished. The floor was rugged, and there were two three-seaters and a sofa – all dark blue and matching the interior painting. On the walls were pictures of Christ, *Mamiwata* and *Ukuakpolokpolo*, the ruling Oba of Benin. There was a cupboard at one end of the room.

Pastor Odele asked us to sit down and feel comfortable. After Endurance told him her problems, Pastor Odele said he would take her to Sakpoba River to wash away whatever evil affected her and pray for her so that her problems would be banished for ever.

We followed Pastor Odele out after he had taken whatever he went for in that cupboard. We went a mile or so on Sakpoba Road and turned left where the river crossed the road. We walked about five poles inside from the main road to the river which narrows before entering Benin. At this brush-covered side of the river, Pastor Odele opened one of the books of Moses, chanted in English and Edo incomprehensible lines that were meant to exorcise Endurance of evil spirits. He then asked the three of us to undress, except for our underwear; enter the water, and bathe. Meanwhile he left us alone for ten minutes or thereabouts before returning to say more prayers.

He came back when we were still in the water and did not feel embarrassed looking at our exposed breasts or body. We also felt no embarrassment since there was a purpose for our nakedness.

'Endurance, I have chased out the evil spirits pressing you or sleeping with you at night,' he told a visibly relieved Endurance.

'Are you finished with me?' she asked him.

'I say, in the names of Olokun and Jesus, you have been freed from bondage to evil angels,' he assured her.

He then prophesied to me that my first child would be a girl and that Esther would not marry her current boyfriend. Esther and I knew that he wanted to appear to be fair to all three of us by giving each of us something to be happy about. We were very happy that Endurance had been promised success and would be freed from both the incubus and the secret lover.

Endurance must have told her mother who told Pastor Efe about the man of God in Benin, Pastor Odele, who prayed and chased off evil spirits. As Endurance told us later, her father admitted he had feelings of a past life in which he was a medicine-man. He could smell burnt herbs, he hallucinated on seeing himself shaking rattles and invoking gods and ancestors. He was meant to take over from his father but it was too late. He could not resign from his pastoral flock to go to the village to be a full-time medicine-man.

What Endurance and her mother had thought would be a difficult task persuading Pastor Efe to go to Benin so that Pastor Odele could pray for them thus became so easy.

'Sometimes, the medicine-man cannot heal himself,' he told Rebecca and Endurance.

'Maybe the Benin pastor can help both of us,' Rebecca told him.

'I believe in miracles,' he said.

'Amen,' his wife and daughter replied in unison.

'When do we go then?' he asked.

'Whenever you are ready,' they told him.

'Next Friday,' he suggested.

And so Pastor Efe, his wife and daughter went to see Pastor Odele to pray for them. The pastor warmly received his guests in his room in his mother's house. Pastor Efe did not wear his pastoral collar so that he did not cut the strange figure of a pastor in his gown in a native shrine.

As if he were a diviner, Pastor Odele told Pastor Efe his problems before he mentioned them. And to gain his confidence the more, he told Pastor Efe that he prayed and made *things* for preachers so that they could overwhelm their congregations. Pastor Efe wanted this. He took the Anglican pastor to a corner and told him he would also solve his problem with his wife.

They prayed together noisily and, as was common with Pastor Odele, he invoked Olokun and Jesus Christ to inspire Pastor Efe to preach to move people's hearts. Pastor Odele in his hat was a medicine-man rather than a pastor. He gave Pastor Efe two wrapped things to rub and lick before going to bed and before going to preach. He was to do these things without fail if he really wanted to avoid squabbles with his wife, if he wanted his congregation to lavishly make huge monetary offerings, and if he wished to get promoted in his pastoral mission.

Endurance told me that her parents became closer and had few incidents of quarrels after their trip to Benin. The quarrels had disappeared before Pastor Odele's visit to Warri, as he put it, for a courtesy call on Pastor Efe, a fellow man of God. He had come with his mother in his new pickup van. You could not tell that one was a medicine-woman and the other was not a pastor.

Pastor Efe, of course, wanted to be very hospitable and as usual

brought out his silver goblets from Jerusalem to entertain his guests from
Benin. He reported to his medicine-man, Pastor Odele, that his monthly
salary was recently raised without his asking for it. He also reported about
his congregation increasing, almost overflowing into the street. In
addition, they were now possessed at the time of worship and gave
offerings and gifts with open hands. Things could not be better than they
were then with him, he reported. He thanked Pastor Odele for his prayers
and everything, as he put it.

'Thank my mother,' Pastor Odele told him.

'Thank you two for your prayers,' Pastor Efe told his guests.

'Better things are coming into this house,' Pastor Odele assured him.

'Amen,' chanted Endurance's father and mother.

By the time his guests were gone, three of his silver goblets had
disappeared from the cupboard where they were kept. Pastor Efe had
promised his wife that he would hold back on his entertainment in order
not to dissipate the new blessings of salary increase and huge offerings.
So when the cups could not be found, Pastor Efe made only a feeble
attempt to look for them. Then he put the remaining two in a box in his
bedroom so as not to lose all of them. These will be his lifelong mementos
of the pilgrimage to Jerusalem. If someday anybody doubted whether he
was a J.P., Jerusalem Pilgrim, he would bring them out and show the silver
goblets to certify his experience.

Visitors who came with the hope of being entertained with the cups of
Christ were disappointed. They were asked to join in prayers, because
prayers are the greatest food of a Christian because they nourished the
soul, the pastor told them. The stream of visitors that depleted their
savings dried to a mere trickle and that was good for the man and woman
who lived in the mission compound. That did not affect the record
congregation at Sunday services.

Soon Endurance would need Pastor Odele's services and this time they
would become part of each other's life, for good or bad. If she was no
longer being pressed by the succubus or being raped in a dream, what
else could Endurance have gone to Pastor Odele to ask for? I can only
string together the pieces that my friend told me, but I knew that, friends
as we were, she told me the crux but not the details of what transpired
between them. Sometimes we could hold back particularly embarrassing
parts of a story and would expect the other to figure out the true situation.
How could we at any stage have foreseen that Endurance, that Warri
Queen as she was called at the teachers' college, would make a choice
that most of us were to laugh at?

As Endurance told me, she developed a certain odour which made people to avoid coming close to her. At this time we were waiting for the results of our Teachers' Grade Grade II Certificate examination and I was again spending the free time with my senior sister in Benin. There was nothing to do till after the results when the successful ones among us would be posted to teach in elementary schools. Some of us might go straight to the university or do the National Certificate of Education programme.

I don't know the number of people who convinced Endurance that she had a very bad odour. But she said after many people had told her, she started to smell it herself. She thought it was gas and bought some medications to purge herself of the bad smell. That did not stop it. She went to a pharmacist who sold her antibiotics, terramycin and tetracyclin, but the smell did not go. She felt it came in her breath too and she found it difficult to leave home. Then she thought of Pastor Odele who had helped her before to perform more difficult tasks.

Endurance did not even come to me or Esther before going to Pastor Odele, unlike on all previous occasions when she had seen him either in our company or that of her parents. The next thing we knew was that she had informed her parents of her intention to marry somebody of her choice now that she had finished school. The person she chose to marry was Pastor Odele.

Pastor Odele had assured her that he would drive away the wicked spirits that tormented her with a repulsive body odour. He asked her to spend the night in his room in his mother's house. He would pray and also perform some sacrifices at midnight at a nearby crossroads. Before that night, Endurance told me, she had placed so much trust in Pastor Odele's power. That very night, she found herself in the experience which Pastor Odele was supposed to have cured her from. The only difference was that this time it was real. When it was over, it appeared Pastor Odele was the only one who used to steal into her because it happened in the same manner. She stayed with him in Benin for three weeks without her coming to see me or Esther and while her parents thought she was with me and my sister. Imagine if something worse had happened to her in a city where ritual murderers were many! But we were lucky that bad as things appeared to me and Esther and perhaps her parents, they could have been worse.

Endurance returned to Warri but soon discovered that she was pregnant. That was how Pastor Odele came to marry Endurance, my own friend and daughter of Pastor, rather Bishop, Efe. Pastor Odele still has no church; he still wears his special hat that covers his head, lives with Endurance and their only child in his big room in his mother's house that is partly an Olokun shrine. Endurance found the three silver goblets that were missing from her father's house in Warri, but now owed allegiance to her husband rather than to her father and so did not report. Her father might have been surprised if told the use to which they were put at Pastor Odele's. They became part of the tools in this God's medicine-man's healing business.

But this, like many other things, did not matter now. Her father was now appointed Bishop of Benin-Delta Provinces of the Anglican Mission in Nigeria. The letter came from and was co-signed by both the Archbishop of Canterbury and the Queen and Head of the Church of England, the spiritual and political heads of the Anglican Church.

Bishop Efe moved to Benin and lived in the same town where his eldest daughter was married. They were really not married in the church or in the traditional way, but had become partners in attending to those who came to Pastor Odele or his mother for help. Endurance had become like her mother a pastor's wife, though the mother was now a bishop's wife. The Efes did not resist Endurance's choice since they believed within that Pastor Odele had done them a good turn that deserved reciprocity.

Pastor Odele's prophecies have been fulfilled. Esther broke from her boyfriend and then travelled to marry a man studying in London. We have not heard from her ever since. I have just got my first child, a girl that my husband and I have named Oghenetega. When next I travel to Benin I will visit my old friend and, maybe, both of us would visit her parents at the Bishop's Court.

Kanchana Ugbabe

Exile

Kanchana Ugbabe is an Indian woman married to a Nigerian and long resident in Nigeria; she teaches English at the University of Jos. In 1993 she participated in the University of Iowa's International Writing Programme. She has published a short story on cross-cultural themes in *Kunapipi* (in 1992) and one in *Stand* (Winter 1996), and had others read over the BBC. This is the first appearance of 'Exile', written to be part of a forthcoming collection on the theme of inter-group contacts.

PALMS JOINED TOGETHER I GREETED, hesitant from a safe distance. As a child it was an awkward routine. You got dragged to the living room every time there was a visitor. I joined my palms together tentatively, then went about twisting the curtains that divided the passageway from the living room, or stood on one leg, scratching my left ankle with my right toe until my mother perfunctorily dismissed me from the scene. As a grown woman it was still not easy, a contortion of the limbs that came gracefully to other women, perhaps, but sat uneasily on me. It was drawing attention to oneself. Further, the response could not be predicted. I wasn't much good at the old ritual of prostrating at the feet of elders either. There was the chance, in my case, of clumsily landing at the wrong feet. Moreover, you were never sure who was old enough to merit your going on hands and knees and who wasn't. Never had I been embraced socially though, or attempted an embrace except that once. In my husband's culture, people habitually put their arms around each other spontaneously, long lost relatives, friends and born-again Christian sisters. In slow motion, on mental replay, what happened in Mamma's courtyard was my mistake. I had broken a code, acted out of turn in a gathering of elders, as it were. It was a bit like twisting the curtains and scratching my foot in public, except more serious, given the circumstances.

Mamma needed a very good reason to come to the city. And when she came, she complained bitterly about the lights being too bright in the house and the coffee cups too small. Away from the farm and the neighbourhood chit-chat, she was restless. She would walk around the yard and give us all jobs to do: wash the bitter leaf for the soup, slice the green pawpaws and dry them in the sun, shell and sift the melon seeds, and pack all the empty bottles and plastic containers for her to take back to the village. She didn't approve of anyone staying out late, least of all the young women in our household. A niece got told off that she was a 'taxi without a garage', the kind that sought the shade of any tree on the wayside.

Travelling south to the hometown was not a big deal for my husband. He routinely bought potatoes, onions and 'bar-soap' to distribute to the members of the extended family, and returned with yams, plantain bunches and local chickens spilling out of the trunk of his car. But to take a foreign wife and children who were neither here nor there, on a formal visit, it had to be Christmas or a family wedding. On seeing me, the street urchins called out 'oyibo' and ran after the car. It was a six-hour drive on a road that twisted itself round hilly terrain, unfurled through a teak plantation, dropped into a valley with oil palms on one side and a banana grove on the other, and came out on to flat yam country. We were reminded on every trip that my husband's hometown and the country thereabouts produced enough yams to feed the entire continent! Sure enough, as far as the eye could see, green and succulent yam seedlings sprouted and trailed out of mounds of chocolate-brown earth. All along the road farmers sold yams, arranged in pyramids according to size. It was the king of crops in this part of the world. A major highway stretched from the north of the country to the south, and ran right through the 'hometown'. It seemed like a town of contented people to me, where at midday the women pounded yam in wooden mortars and the men drank freshly tapped palm-wine in open-air bars, and expected nothing from the government. And the cars, buses and lorries thundering past the colonial outpost churned up the fine red dust, splattering the whitewashed houses on either side of the highway, making the town look perpetually red.

Mamma's house was on a little street off the highway, traditional, with a central courtyard and rooms opening into it. If you walked down a lane, on one side of the house, you could enter the courtyard directly. Over the years this had become the centre of social life for the entire extended family and for the neighbourhood as well. Here, Mamma Ochanya on her way home from the market (a single yam stuffed in a plastic handbag and balanced on her head) stopped to greet Mamma and ask if the daughter in Lagos had given birth. Children curtsied and called out a greeting as they rushed past Mamma's courtyard. The village hairdresser, a thin, gaunt woman with her dyes in a basket, wheeled her bicycle past Mamma's courtyard and stopped to ask if Mamma needed 'retouching'. It was here that the village letter-writter had read my husband's letter from overseas, my photograph had been passed around and, amidst muted half tones and whispers, the idea of an 'oyibo' wife had become a reality.

Mamma's bedroom (which also housed a dysfunctional deep freezer and stacks of enamel containers) opened out into the courtyard. Mamma sat at the doorway of her bedroom on a low stool, facing the general entrance. Nothing escaped her eye from this vantage point. Chickens scratched amid the yams and cassava tubers piled in a corner of the courtyard. Was it on that trip that two women were cleaning out fish in huge enamel basins? With the flick of nimble fingers fish guts spilled out – the sliced fish was washed, piece by piece with great economy, in the water in the basin and flung into a basket nearby. Beside the covered well in the courtyard, a young cousin sat rinsing dishes in a tub. Another pounded dried okra and herbs in a little wooden mortar. Over our heads a clothes-line dangled with wrappers and children's underwear.

This courtyard echoes with women's wails as I recall a young brother's tragic death in a motor accident. Wrappers hitched up and hair bundled in nylon scarves, the women at first sat motionless with their backs to the wall, each nursing a private sorrow. Every now and then they went out into the street to blow their noses, before changing places. Then they wept, sang and sermonized in turn, while others fetched water from the well, cooked, cleaned and served the guests. The family remained an inner circle hushed in their grief. We slept on mats in the courtyard that night, guests and family huddled together under the cold and pale stars. The church choir sang and danced; their bodies moved like lightning in the subdued light of the courtyard. Mamma Onyebe, the soothsayer, sat up in the middle of the night, wrestling with spirits in a hoary prophecy of death. There were stirs and murmurs. Her chant grew louder as one by one the women sat up on their mats, misty figures rocking back and forth muttering the name of Jesus. At daybreak, all ghostly presence dispelled, they gathered in groups fondling babies and reminiscing over previous calamities, their pain blunted by the passage of time.

They seemed an impenetrable wall in the courtyard, strong and resilient, vacillating between idle gossip and home grown comfort. The Prayer Warriors from the pentecostal church down the road had taken it upon themselves to use every occasion available for spiritual reinforcement.

'It is like this,' said Aunt Eya. 'When you get on the bus, some people get off at Ikeja, some at Apapa, some at Ilupeju. The boy had reached his destination and he got off. If you stay on the bus beyond your destination, there is problem. I hope you get me . . .' She trailed off.

Another elderly visitor said, 'Sister, I think it's that name you gave your child – Funso, "give me for safekeeping" – that is the problem. Now, the owner has asked for his property back, who are you to say no? That name . . .' And she clicked her tongue.

The place came alive the day of brother Anthony's wedding. Trays of pounded yam and egusi soup went to and fro, to visitors who sat on wooden benches, stools and bamboo recliners all over the courtyard. The music was loud and children chased each other, ducking in between the food carriers. Mamma made sure there was a big barrel of 'kunnu' full to the brim, in the corner of the courtyard. She personally supervised its dispensation, as plastic mugs were dipped into the barrel and jugs refilled for wedding guests. Patience, my 'co-wife', considers herself something of an alien, as well, coming from the eastern part of the country. In her aso-oke heavy as a blanket, and stiffly starched headtie, she herded her children into one of the bedrooms and forced pounded yam into them. She warned them that the wedding would take hours. 'No food there, O!' she said, rolling her eyeballs. Everyone had to be fortified before the church wedding. Patience is the kind who would swear by the Maggi bouillon cube – her soup would not be complete without it. And then this monosodium glutamate had come into the market, wrapped in cellophane and called 'white Maggi' or Ajino moto. 'For cleaning bathrooms,' Patience declared. She wasn't going to touch it. She has been part of this family longer than I have, and is in the habit of soliciting privileged information from dubious sources.

My sisters-in-law looked gorgeous in white lace with orange and gold headties and aso-oke shoulder pieces to match. It was obvious from the way they strutted about that they wanted to be set apart as the 'family'. 'See the uniform?' Patience nudged me with her elbow. 'They didn't tell *you* and *me* about it, did they?' A big-bosomed niece walked past, swinging her hips. 'Three months pregnant, they say,' Patience commented, and then changed the tone to the parable about casting the first stone.

'See that woman in blue?' Patience continued to gripe. 'That is brother Solomon's girlfriend. Married man! Hmm . . . you won't believe it! They say he paid to train her.' (Train her in what? Monkey in the zoo?) She grabbed me by the wrist in the courtyard and dragged me into one of the bedrooms – there was going to be trouble at the wedding, she said, haggling over the bride price. 'You and I,' she breathed a sigh of relief, 'are out of it. We'll just be watching.' Mamma's voice in the courtyard sent us scurrying towards the backyard.

There the cooking stones had been arranged and a wood fire was blazing. I took over the frying of the fish. I had never cooked over a wood stove before; the smoke filled my eyes and hair. Sister Agnes had come to the wedding with her Lagos friends, a bunch of Army wives with permed hair, imported handbags and shoes with platform heels. They decided to make a salad which seemed like something they could manage. Sitting on low stools with chopping boards on their knees, they diced and chopped a mountain of lettuce, carrots and cucumbers which would at the end of the day have Heinz mayonnaise poured over and blended. Everything was done without anyone taking charge of the whole operation; the menu seemed to emerge as we boiled, fried and stewed. No one gave orders, but comments were made with varying degrees of authority. 'Too many cucumbers,' said Patience, whisking past. 'Is there salt in the fish?' asked one of the Lagos ladies through the fish haze, and followed it with, 'Don't "turn" the fish in the oil. Just leave it to go dry, or it will break up.' Before long, putting their salad effort aside, the Army wives retired to a corner of the courtyard for their tea break, with Tetley teabags and Carnation milk which they produced from their handbags.

I remember now – it was neither a wedding, nor a funeral, nor Christmas, that time. We had just returned to the country after two years in Europe and were duty-bound to visit the hometown. The potholes on the highway were worse than before. Purple watercolour mountains loomed in the distance. The yam heaps were there, but fewer, the oil palms and banana groves stood laden with fruit as we had left them. But all along the road, at every village, people had arranged in the place of yams, bundles of firewood, ready to be sold. How long would it be before the encroaching desert reached Mamma's hometown?

We arrived in that little red town, hot and tired. Cars heaved, sighed and spluttered down the streets of the red town, spewing thick black smoke from the exhaust. A gaily painted truck trundled past bearing the sign 'No Brain is Idle'. Everything looked old and worn, coming from the land of overfed people and dogs and cats, lean and emaciated. The butterflies in my stomach started flitting madly as we passed the Community Bank, the post office with its paint peeled off and the railway crossing, and headed for Mamma's house. All along the street, it seemed people sawed off trees wherever they found them and whenever they were in need of firewood. Tender shoots grew out of the amputated limbs of dogon yaro trees. I tried to recall the traditional greeting, the clan-title by which Mamma had to be addressed, the genuflecting, the stock responses. I would have to reacquaint myself with life in the hometown beyond wearing it as a cameo brooch, reflecting myriad colours from afar. Would there be running water in the taps? Coffee?

As we turned into the narrow street I could see children rushing in to announce our arrival. 'Oyibo oyoyo,' they shouted in unison. Mamma, who was on her usual seat in the courtyard, stood up and made her way to the entrance in a stately dance, singing praises to God and clapping. The women around her clapped as well, and joined in the chorus. There was an air of expectancy, a knot at the base of my stomach. Unknowingly, I entered the courtyard first. Mamma looked much older than when we had left her. Without giving it a thought, I went up with my arms outstretched to embrace her.

She continued the dance movements, elbows bent, feet moving to an internal rhythm, but it was as if she didn't see me. As if I didn't exist. Her eyes were fixed in ecstasy, their gaze went past me to her son and grandchildren coming after me. I had barely touched her when, with one strong elbow, following the rhythms of the dance, she forcefully shoved me aside. Still dancing, she went up and embraced her son and grand-children, one by one. There was laughter and joy of reunion. So many voices in breathless spasms – 'My! How he has grown!' 'Do you still remember our language?' 'Doesn't he look exactly like his father?'

When she finally turned to come towards me, I cowered and froze at her touch. My head reeled in the midst of alien voices, gestures and unfamiliar faces. Their resonance reached me deep within a cavern. It all happened so quickly, so naturally. The message was conveyed to me, quick and sharp, a message I was not to forget for life. The festivities in the courtyard had only just begun.

Ben Okri

A Prayer from the Living

Ben Okri, a Nigerian writer born in Minna who, as a student of nineteen in London, wrote and published his first novel (*Flowers and Shadows*, 1980). He has studied at the University of Essex and been a broadcaster with the BBC. There are two collections of his short stories, *Incidents at the Shrine* (1986) and *Stars of the New Curfew* (1988). In 1991 his magical novel, *The Famished Road*, won the Booker Prize for fiction; it was continued in *Songs of Enchantment* in 1993. In September of that year, in response to reports of the Sudanese famine, he published 'A Prayer from the Living' in the *Guardian* in order to generate funds to donate to relief charities.

WE ENTERED THE TOWN of the dying at sunset. We went from house to house. Everything was as expected, run-down, a desert, luminous with death and a hidden life.

The gunrunners were everywhere. The world was now at the perfection of chaos. The little godfathers who controlled everything with guns raided the food brought for us. They raided the airlifts and the relief aid and distributed most of the food among themselves and members of their clan.

We no longer cared. Food no longer mattered. I had done without for three weeks. Now I feed on the air and on the quest.

Every day, as I grow leaner, I see more things around us. I see all the dead around, outnumbering the living; I see the dead, all who had died of starvation. They are more joyful now; they are happier than we are; and they are everywhere, living their luminous lives as if nothing had happened, or as if they were more alive than we are.

The hungrier I became, the more I saw them – my old friends who had died before me, clutching on to flies. Now, they feed on the light of the air. And they look at us – the living – with so much pity and compassion in their eyes.

I suppose this is what the white ones cannot understand when they come with their television cameras and their aid. They expect to see us weeping. Instead they see us staring at them, without begging, and with a bulging placidity in our eyes. Maybe they are secretly horrified that we are not afraid of dying this way.

But after three weeks of hunger the mind no longer notices; you're more dead than alive; and it's the soul wanting to leave that suffers. It suffers because of the tenacity of the body.

Most of us are already in the other world and only the dreadful strength and resilience of life keeps us staring at this world and at flies.

We should have come into the town at dawn. In the town everyone had died. The horses and cows were dying too. The stink in the air was no longer amazing in its horror. I could say that the air stank of death, but that wouldn't be true. It smelled of rancid butter and poisoned heat and bad sewage. There was even the faint irony of flowers.

The only people who weren't dead were the dead. Singing golden songs in chorus, jubilant everywhere, they carried on living their familiar lives. The only others who weren't dead were the soldiers. And they fought among themselves eternally, fighting for the dying flesh of our land.

They had split into innumerable factions. It didn't seem to matter to them how many died. All that mattered was how well they handled the grim mathematics of the wars, that is to say of the dying, so that they could win the most important battle of all, which was for the leadership of the fabulous graveyard of this once beautiful and civilized land.

The soldiers weren't interested in us; and we who were dying weren't interested in them. We had come on a quest. I was searching for my family and my lover. I wanted to know if they had died or not. If I didn't find out I intended to hang on to life by its very last tattered thread. I will not die till I know where my companions are. I will die at peace if I know that they too were dead or safe and no longer needed me.

In this life everything has betrayed us: nation, history, notions of God, the future, food and air. The fabric of life is thinner than we think. And when all is said and done there's not much to distinguish the good and the bad other than the way in which they face death. And even that's not wholly true. But maybe as a people we've become too much at home with death and have forgotten the miracle of life. Or maybe we've forgotten how to love. I don't know how we got around to forgetting, but we did.

*

All my information has led me to this town. Here is where the trail ends: if my lover, my brothers, my family are anywhere, they are here. This is the last town in the world. Beyond its rusted gate, where the vultures of hunger gladly circulate the air, lies the desert. The desert stretches all the way into the past, into history, to the western world, and to the source of all drought and famine – the mighty mountain of lovelessness. From its peaks, at night, the grim spirits of negation chant their awesome soul-shrinking songs. Their songs steal hope from us, and make us yield to the air our energies. Their songs are cool and make us submit to the clarity of dying.

Here is the world's end. Behind us, in the past, before all this came to be, there were all the possibilities in the world, all the potentials for joy, and the building of a new world, and learning to love one another. There were all the opportunities for starting from small things to creating a sweet new history and future, if only we had seen them. But now, ahead, there lie only the songs of the mountain of death, with its spirits of silence. And time's negation.

We wandered about the town at dawn, and wove our ways through the debris of the dead. After a while the geometry of the dead becomes familiar, even quite beautiful, in its simplicity. Everything is clear.

We search for our loved ones mechanically, and with a dryness in our eyes. Our stomachs no longer exist. Nothing exists now except the search. We turn the bodies over, looking for familiar faces. All the faces were familiar; death had made them all my kin.

I search on, without feeling, or hope. I come across an unfamiliar face; it is my brother. I nod. I pour dust on his flesh. Hours later, near a dry well, I come across the other members of my family. My mother holds on tightly to a bone so dry it wouldn't even nourish the flies. I nod twice. I pour dust on their bodies. Feeling my dry eyes sliding off the things of this world, I search on. There is one more face whose beautiful unfamil-iarity will console me. When I have found the face then I will submit myself to the mountain songs of pure negation.

I wandered through the town, dragging my own corpse with me like the ancient hero who was weighed down by his cross. I search every alley. I crawl past the white ones with their equipments. They point their television cameras at me and ask me questions, and I nod three times and try to smile. I crawl on, aware that they must see me as bestial now, and pity me as such, but aware also that if they knew the object of my search they might see me as possibly the last hero in this land of heroes, with all the heroes dead all about, and most of them children. For they died every one of them without howling and wailing and self-pity, and without fear.

It is possible that a land of heroes eventually becomes a land of grave-stones. Maybe the new heroism of the future will have more to do with the courage to lose, in order to win; to give way, in order to gain ground; to be a little weak, in order to be invisibly strong; to live slowly, and with a low but long-lasting fire. Maybe the future heroism will have more to do with these than with this courage of ours which makes us bear and withstand and ultimately be destroyed by too much suffering. We are too strong for our own good. Our resilience has made a fertile graveyard of this earth.

Sunset was approaching when, from an unfinished school building, I heard singing. It was the most magical sound I had ever heard and I thought only those who know how sweet life is can sing like that, can sing as if breathing were a prayer.

I hurried towards the singing, crawling over the bloated sweet-smelling bodies of the dead, climbing over the shrivelled corpses of sweet young children and babies who had died without a curse on their lips and with flies and worms on their legs. Maybe it takes the dying to see the beauty of the dead.

The singing was like the joyous beginning of all Creation, the first chorus of time at its own momentous dawn, the initial amen to the great idea of the universe, the holy yes to the breath and light infusing all things, which makes the water shimmer, the plants sprout, the animals jump and play in the fields, and which makes the men and women look out into the first radiance of colours, the green of plants, the blue of sea, the gold of the air, the silver of the stars. To me the singing was the true end of my quest, the grail I couldn't have known about, the music to crown this treacherous life of mine, the end I couldn't have hoped for, or imagined.

It seemed to take an infinity of time to get to the unfinished school building. I had no strength left, and it was only the song's last echo, resounding through the vast spaces of my hunger, that sustained me. After maybe a century, when history had repeated itself and brought about exactly the same circumstances, because none of us ever learned our lesson, or loved enough to learn from our pain, or took the great scream of history seriously enough, I finally made it to the schoolroom door. But a cow, the only live thing left in the town, went in through the door before I did. It too must have been drawn by the singing. The cow went into the room, and I followed.

Inside, all the available floor space was taken up with the dead. But here the air didn't have death in it. The air had prayer in it. The prayers stank more than the deaths. But all the dead here, in this room, were differently dead from the corpses outside in the town's square and in all the other towns. The dead in this schoolroom were – forgive the paradox – alive. I have no other word to explain the serenity. All I can say was that I felt they had come here, to this room, and had somehow made it holy with the way they had approached their dying. I felt that they had made the room holy because they had, in their last moments, thought not of themselves but of all people who suffer across the length and breadth of the world. I felt myself doing the same thing as I entered the room. I crawled to a corner, sat up against a wall and felt myself praying for the whole human race.

I prayed – knowing full well that prayers are possibly an utter waste of time – but I prayed for everything that lived, for mountains and trees, for animals and streams, and for human beings wherever and whosoever they might be. I felt myself, in that moment, completely at home with the whole of humanity. I heard the great anguished cry of all mankind and heard its great haunting music as well. And I too, without moving my mouth, for I had no energy – I too began to sing in silence. I sang all through the evening. And when I looked at the body next to me and found the luminous unfamiliarity of its face to be that of my lover's – I sang all through the recognition. I sang silently even when a good-hearted white man came into the school building with a television camera, weeping, and recorded the roomful of the dead for the world – and I hoped he recorded my singing too.

It seemed a long time passed in the singing and I weaved in and out of it all. And when I came to briefly I saw, in a radiant astonishment, that the room wasn't full of the dead, but full of the living. The dead were all alive; but they were alive with light, in a way only few of the living are alive – alive with all the shimmering possibilities of life active in their being; alive in such a way that they come close to sublimity.

*

And the dead were all about me, smiling, serene. They didn't urge me on, they didn't insist; they were just quietly and intensely joyful. They did not ask me to hurry to them, but left it to me, left it to my choice. What could I choose?

Human life – full of greed and bitterness, dim, low-oxygenated, without light, judgemental and callous, gentle too, and wonderful as well, but – human life had betrayed me. And besides, there was nothing now left to save in me. Even my soul was dying of starvation.

The song started again. I opened my eyes for the last time. I saw the cameras on us all. To them, we were the dead. As I passed through the agony of the light, I saw them as the dead. I saw them gesticulating out of time, without eternal connection, marooned in a world without pity or love.

As the cow wandered about in the apparent desolation of the room, it must have seemed odd to the people recording it all that I should have made myself so comfortable among the dead. I did. I stretched myself out and held the hand of my lover. With a painful breath and a gasp and a smile, I gently let myself go. The smile must have puzzled the reporters. If they had understood my language, they would have known that it was my way of saying goodbye.

PART THREE

EAST AND CENTRAL

Taban Lo Liyong

The Big Swallow

Taban Lo Liyong was born in 1939 in the land of the Kuku in Southern Sudan, in the village of Kajokaji, but in 1940 he was carried over the border by his mother into Uganda's Acoliland, where he grew up and went to school. He taught at Nairobi University before becoming the first black African at the University of Iowa's Writers' Workshop in 1966. Considered one of the founders of East African literature (together with Ngugi wa Thiong'o), he has been particularly active as an essayist and as a short story writer who uses oral techniques to satirical ends. His *Fixions and Other Stories* of 1969 began a distinguished publishing career in this vein. His most recent volume is *Carrying Knowledge up a Palm Tree* (Africa World Press, 1998). After many years in exile from Uganda, teaching in Juba in the Sudan, he migrated to the University of Venda in South Africa where he is a Professor of Literature. 'The Big Swallow' is from a new collection of tales and has not previously been published.

IF THE STORY I NOW TELL resembles one I have told before, this is because inadequate communication ends either comically, or tragically, or tragicomically. So it is important that we teach our children good grammar: subject, verb, object. Inexactitude may result in misunderstanding, with fatal consequences. Here goes:

In Africa it is famine time. Or rather, it was famine time in Africa. And the Africa we have in mind is our Kuku Africa. Because this story succeeds on the ground of Kuku grammar. And the plant and its fruit are found in Kajokaji, the land of the Kuku. And the other beast in the story, too, is a citizen of Kajokaji. So, it was famine time. There was a woman – where her husband had gone is unclear. But during famines it is mothers who are more dependable, it is mothers to whom children cling. And our woman had a tiny baby, maybe a kwashiorkor sufferer: big stomach, big head, large eyes, tiny hands, tiny legs. But maybe not. I did not see her. I only heard the story.

And a story in our acceptance of the word is a retelling of what once

happened, now given a second or third life. Retelling by those who are
struck by its poetogenicness, its excitement of the intellect: how a con-
jointure of elements goes to compose an event.

(The story is seen from the outside. Or the teller himself relates how
he felt, as the events were evolving: how his heart thought out the
thought that motivated him, and how the other person fended off, gave
in or repulsed him. The psyche did not get in at all. The heart did
everything. The mind or mindlessness was something one did not play
with. For either you have a head or you have none: *wiye pe* in Acoli, *kuwe
'bain* in Kuku. This has to do with respect, with hard-headedness, with
lack of consideration. You will have to find out that 'psychology' of the
heart, or the heart's heartology, in order to know how Africans feel,
behave, react.)

So, it is famine time in Africa. And there is a woman with her child,
kwashiorkor or not. And also an older child who minded that pot-bellied
thing passing for human. We could call it humanoid, childoid. For two
days and two nights now, they have not had a meal. This morning they
got off very early to go to a faraway place – that would be five or six
hours' trekking – to collect shea-butternuts. The juicy outer rind of the
nut is edible. The shea-butter seed is brought home for extracting oil.
And it is this gathering life they now are reduced to. (Not only this single
parent. Everybody is doing this thing everywhere. Rains have failed and
planted crops dried up. So it is only those trees which live for a hundred
years, like the shea-butter tree, that can manage to flower, flourish
and produce fruit and seed despite the drought.) They went and found a
shea-butter tree in full fruiting.

Then the mother put her kwashiorkor child down. And put her
container for the butter-fruit near the child. She told her older child – a
girl, I think – to collect the fruits; she would throw them down from the
branches. And to put them in the wicker container. Then she climbed up
the tree, picked a few and chewed on them before getting down to the
real work. Her daughter, too, looked forward to having some fruit to chew
to blunt the sharp edge of hunger. When the fruits started falling, the
elder girl ran from place to place, picking them up and bringing them to
the wicker container. This went on for some time, the girl moving from
one end of the area covered by the branches of the tree to the other. This
went on and on.

Then, after some prolonged period, the elder girl happened to find the
head of the humanoid was actually no longer there at all. It was disappearing fast. Inside some long, sleek-looking thing like an oiled log. The

elder girl ran to the side where her mother was. She announced, '*Mama, na wiwi!*' (Mother, it is swallowing!)

'What?'

'I said it is swallowing.'

'Well, let it swallow. Yesterday it slept without.'

The elder girl didn't know what to say. She collected more fruit and took it to the wicker container, only to find that the child's head was now all gone. And it was the neck that was disappearing.

She ran again to her mother's side. 'Mother, Mother, I said it is swallowing.'

'But I told you it should swallow, for last night it slept without.'

The elder girl now collected a few more seeds and took these to the wicker container. And now it was the bulging kwashiorkor stomach which was disappearing.

She again ran to her mother. 'Mother, it really is swallowing.'

'Well, what is wrong with you? I *told* you it should, just because it slept without. Are you a fool?'

The girl collected again. This time when she came back she could see only the tiny feet of her sister disappearing inside this long, bulging bag.

She ran to the mother. 'Mother, now it is finished swallowing!'

'That is good, that will keep it alive!'

At long last the mother came down. And could not see her baby. 'Where is Baby?'

'It is inside that thing.'

'What thing?'

The child pointed.

'Why didn't you *tell* me?'

'Mother, I did tell you that it was swallowing. And you said it should swallow for it had slept without.'

The python, which might also have slept without for a long time, was now digesting its newly swallowed food.

So, if parents don't teach their children to make complete reports, and if parents don't investigate their children's ambiguities, they may feed other pythons with those same children.

Peter Nazareth

Moneyman

Peter Nazareth was born in 1940 in Entebbe, Uganda, into the small Goan Indian-Christian, Konkani-speaking community, the literature of which in many languages he has made his speciality. He was educated at Makerere University and at Leeds, and published novels and criticism, notably on the role of the Third World writer, with the East African Literature Bureau. With the Asian expulsion of 1972, he emigrated to the United States, where he has edited several collections of and on African writers – for example, the July-October, 1981, issue of *Pacific Moana Quarterly*. His stories have appeared in *Short Story International* and elsewhere. His exemplary story, 'Moneyman', was first published in *Zuka*, the journal of East African Creative Writing edited by Ngugi wa Thiong'o during the 1970s, and is included in Valerie Kibera's pick of the fruitful decade of the mid-1960s to mid-1970s, *An Anthology of East African Short Stories* (1988). He currently organizes the University of Iowa's International Writing Programme.

MR MANNA LEITAO had joined the civil service at a time when no Goans owned cars. In those days, it was quite normal for him to be seen walking all over the place, holding his umbrella like a walking-stick. But now, decades later, when Goans had passed through the bicycle age and were affluent enough to own cars, it was strange to see him drifting doggedly along the footpaths and by-lanes. He seemed to creep along the edge of one's consciousness, until one suddenly wondered, 'Who is this odd-looking fellow?'

Odd-looking indeed he was. He had a large mouldy face. The hair on his head looked like one of those ferns you see at a swamp – pokers sticking out at the edges and disappearing into a disc at the centre. His ears italicized his head, hairs standing out of them like mini-television antennae. His lips looked sensual, lending credence to the story that he was secretly a satyr, although he had never married. The Goans thought that he had remained single because looking after a wife and children would cost too much.

He often boasted that he was the richest man in the little town of Apana. Incredible, for how could a lowly civil servant who never played the stock market get rich? Well, in two ways. The first was the straight-forward one of usury. There were always other lowly civil servants in Apana, particularly Africans, who were dead broke around the third week of the month. The bankers never lent money to those who really needed it, so this was where The Man stepped in. He would lend money for a maximum period of two weeks at about forty per cent interest. Not per annum but per two weeks.

This is why Manna Leitao came to be known as Money Leitao and, finally, Moneyman.

Then there was the second way he made money. He did not spend any.

Late one evening, Mrs Carmen Dias heard a groaning outside her house. She told her husband and son to investigate. They found Money-man lying in a gutter in their compound, holding his leg in agony. The story went round later that Moneyman was chasing a spry young African miss across the lawns when he fell into the gutter and broke his leg. Yes, he broke his leg, as the Diases discovered eventually. They would have discovered it sooner had they taken him to the Grade A hospital but, despite his pain, he insisted that they take him to Grade B, where the poor were treated free of charge. His leg was put in plaster, and he was put to bed.

The Diases wrote about Moneyman's plight to his only traceable relatives, who lived in a neighbouring country. They arrived post-haste. Moneyman refused to see them. 'They have come here hoping I will die,' he said. 'They only want to get my money. Well, I won't, and they won't. Off with them!' Despite all efforts, the relatives had to give up and return home in disgust.

So Moneyman had to be looked after by the Diases. They felt that he was their responsibility as they had found him on their doorstep, so to speak. Who would look after this stubborn old man if they refused? They even cooked his meals because he said he could not eat African food. Father and son had to take turns cooking the meals because Mrs Dias had already made plans to go to Goa to visit her parents, and Moneyman's leg took a long time to heal. Needless to say, Moneyman did not pay the Diases anything, taking advantage of traditional Goan hospitality. What is more, after he realized that he was assured of regular meals, he started telling father and son what sort of meals to cook!

Moneyman's brush with death must have made him realize what a lonely man a single man is. At any rate, not long after he left the hospital, he gave up his lonely house and moved in with a family, the Fernandeses. The Fernandeses consisted of mother, father and three sons. It was surprising that they should take him in at all. Mother was a hard-headed, tough-hearted woman. Her husband, who owned a printing shop, was an inveterate drunkard and the eldest son was a playboy. The second son was taciturn and determined. Nobody knew what he was determined about, but it looked as though he had secret ambitions. The youngest son was kind-hearted, but he was painfully shy and it was difficult to imagine him breaking out of his shell and making contact with anybody.

Gradually it was noticed in Apana that Mrs Fernandes was running the printing shop. Mr Fernandes could be seen hanging around, cast aside like an empty bottle of liquor. The creditors had been about to foreclose when Mrs Fernandes stepped in. She paid off some of the debts and promised to pay the others in due course. The creditors agreed to wait provided she undertook to run the business herself. She accepted, even though she did not know anything about printing.

One day Moneyman turned up at the house of Mr Pobras D'Mello, one of the elders of the Apana Goan community. Mr D'Mello was puzzled to see him because Moneyman was not a social man, let alone a sociable one. After the formality of informal talk and drinks, Moneyman said, 'I would like your advice, Mr D'Mello.'

Surprised at this request, and secretly a little pleased, Mr D'Mello replied, 'Of course.'

'Please read this letter,' said Moneyman, handing over a sheet of paper.

'Mrs Fernandes,' read Mr D'Mello, 'you have abused my sympathy and my kindly nature . . .' and a few rude words followed. 'When you borrowed four thousand shillings from me in June, you promised to repay it, plus a small lending charge, within three months. But you have not paid anything, and I demand it all back immediately you . . .' and a few obscenities followed.

'Well?' said Moneyman.

'Well?' said Mr D'Mello.

'Don't you think it is a good letter?' said Moneyman.

Mr D'Mello was known for his tact, so instead of answering directly he said, 'Tell me a little more about this matter.'

'Mrs Fernandes was in trouble because of her husband's debts. She begged me to do her a favour and lend her four thousand shillings to pay off the debts. Feeling sorry, I lent her the money. Besides, I had already stood guarantee for her son's purchase of petrol, and the other day I had to pay a bill of nine hundred shillings . . .'

'You mention a service charge in your letter,' said Mr D'Mello. 'What is this?'

'Well, you know,' said Moneyman, 'I lost interest by drawing my money from my savings account at the bank, so it is but fair that I should be compensated . . .'

'How much?' said Mr D'Mello.

'I . . . er . . . er,' said Moneyman.

'How much?' said Mr D'Mello, a little sharply. 'How much is the service charge?'

'Er . . . one . . . two thousand shillings . . .'

'Per annum?' asked Mr D'Mello, amazed.

'No, to be paid as soon as the money was due.'

'Well, do you want to know what I think?' said Mr D'Mello. 'I think you are a mean, miserable skinflint. However, you have asked for my advice in respect of this . . . this letter, and I shall give it. The letter is extremely rude and offensive and, if you send it, Mrs Fernandes can use it to take legal action against you. Besides, from what you say, I don't think you have it in writing that you gave her the loan—'

'I already gave her the letter this morning,' said Moneyman.

'Then I will ask you to kindly leave my house,' said Mr D'Mello.

Moneyman got back home in time for dinner. He sat at the dinner table, where the atmosphere was decidedly frosty. Finally, he said in Konkani, '*Udoi coddi*,' which should mean 'pass the curry' but, if translated literally, means 'throw the curry'. And the second son did just that. He picked up the dish of curry and threw it at Moneyman.

'You bastard,' he yelled at him. 'You have been staying with us, no? Do the few shillings you have lent us make up for the inconvenience? But you have the cheek to write an insulting letter to my mother! I'll teach you!' And he began beating up the old man.

The eldest and the youngest sons pulled the second son back, but not before Moneyman had had his other leg broken. The eldest son had to take him to the Grade B hospital. After all, the car contained Moneyman's petrol.

Moneyman was abandoned at Grade B. He sent word to the Diases, who found this time that they could leave a stubborn old man to his distress without any qualms of conscience. When Moneyman was finally discharged, he did not press charges. He had nothing in writing, while the Fernandeses had. Besides, the lawyer would cost too much.

But Manna Leitao has benefited from his experience; he has learnt his lesson. He does not trust people any more; people are not as dependable as money. He can still be seen walking around Apana, shabbily dressed and with his ubiquitous umbrella; and whenever he passes the thriving Fernandes Press, he mutters to himself and tightens his grip on his umbrella, as though it is a bankroll from which he does not wish to be parted.

Ngugi wa Thiong'o

Minutes of Glory

Ngugi wa Thiong'o was born into a Gikuyu speaking family in 1938 in Limuru, Kenya, and studied English at Makerere University and Leeds. His novel, *Weep Not Child* of 1964, is considered the founding work of East African literature in English. He has, after censorship problems, since 1970 worked in London and held various teaching posts in the United States. He is widely known for his advocacy of writing in indigenous African languages: indeed, his latest novel, *Matigari* (1987), a powerful satire on post-independent mores, appears translated into English from the Gikuyu. His now classic collection of short stories, *Secret Lives* of 1975, from which the long story 'Minutes of Glory' comes, is still in print in the Heinemann African Writers Series.

HER NAME WAS WANJIRU. But she liked better her Christian one, Beatrice. It sounded more pure and more beautiful. Not that she was ugly; but she could not be called beautiful either. Her body, dark and full fleshed, had the form, yes, but it was as if it waited to be filled by the spirit. She worked in beer halls where sons of women came to drown their inner lives in beer cans and froth. Nobody seemed to notice her. Except, perhaps, when a proprietor or an impatient customer called out her name, Beatrice; then other customers would raise their heads briefly, a few seconds, as if to behold the bearer of such a beautiful name, but not finding anybody there, they would resume their drinking, their ribald jokes, their laughter and play with the other serving girls. She was like a wounded bird in flight: a forced landing now and then but nevertheless wobbling from place to place so that she would variously be found in Alaska, Paradise, The Modern, Thome and other beer halls all over Limuru. Sometimes it was because an irate proprietor found she was not attracting enough customers; he would sack her without notice and without a salary. She would wobble to the next bar. But sometimes she was simply tired of nesting in one place, a daily witness of familiar scenes; girls even more decidedly ugly than she were fought over by numerous claimants at closing time. What do they have that I don't have? she would ask herself, depressed. She longed for a bar-kingdom where she would be at least one of the rulers, where petitioners would bring their gifts of beer, frustrated smiles and often curses that hid more lust and love than hate.

She left Limuru town proper and tried the mushrooming townlets around. She worked at Ngarariga, Kamiritho, Rironi and even Tiekunu and everywhere the story was the same. Oh yes, occasionally she would get a client; but none cared for her as she would have liked, none really wanted her enough to fight over her. She was always a hard-up customer's last resort. No make-believe even, not for her that sweet pretence that men indulged in after their fifth bottle of Tusker. The following night or during a pay-day, the same client would pretend not to know her; he would be trying his money-power over girls who already had more than a fair share of admirers.

She resented this. She saw in every girl a rival and adopted a sullen attitude. Nyagūthiī especially was the thorn that always pricked her wounded flesh. Nyagūthiī, arrogant and aloof, but men always in her courtyard; Nyagūthiī, fighting with men, and to her they would bring propitiating gifts which she accepted as of right. Nyagūthiī could look bored, impatient or downright contemptuous and still men would cling to her as if they enjoyed being whipped with biting words, curled lips and the indifferent eyes of a free woman. Nyagūthiī was also a bird in flight, never really able to settle in one place, but in her case it was because she hungered for change and excitement: new faces and new territories for her conquest. Beatrice resented her very shadow. She saw in her the girl she would have liked to be, a girl who was both totally immersed in and yet completely above the underworld of bar violence and sex. Wherever Beatrice went the long shadow of Nyagūthiī would sooner or later follow her.

She fled Limuru for Ilmorog in Chiri District. Ilmorog had once been a ghost village, but had been resurrected to life by that legendary woman, Nyang'endo, to whom every pop group had paid their tribute. It was of her that the young dancing Muthuu and Muchun g' wa sang:

> When I left Nairobi for Ilmorog
> Never did I know
> I would bear this wonder-child mine
> Nyang'endo.

As a result, Ilmorog was always seen as a town of hope where the weary and the down-trodden would find their rest and fresh water. But again Nyagūthiī followed her.

She found that Ilmorog, despite the legend, despite the songs and dances, was not different from Limuru. She tried various tricks. Clothes? But even here she never earned enough to buy herself glittering robes. What was seventy-five shillings a month without house allowance, posho, without salaried boyfriends? By that time Ambi had reached Ilmorog, and Beatrice thought that this would be the answer. Had she not, in Limuru, seen girls blacker than herself transformed overnight from ugly sins into white stars by a touch of skin-lightening creams? And men would ogle them, would even talk with exaggerated pride of their newborn girlfriends. Men were strange creatures, Beatrice thought in moments of searching analysis. They talked heatedly against Ambi, Butone, Firesnow, Moonsnow, wigs, straightened hair, but they always went for a girl with an Ambi-lightened skin and head covered with a wig made in imitation of European or Indian hair. Beatrice never tried to find the root cause of this black self-hatred, she simply accepted the contradiction and applied herself to Ambi with a vengeance. She had to rub out her black shame. But even Ambi she could not afford in abundance; she could only apply it to her face and to her arms so that her legs and her neck retained their blackness. Besides there were parts of her face she could not readily reach – behind the ears and above the eyelashes, for instance – and these were a constant source of shame and irritation to her Ambi-self.

She would always remember this Ambi period as one of her deepest humiliation before her later minutes of glory. She worked in Ilmorog Starlight Bar and Lodging. Nyagūthiī, with her bangled hands, her huge earrings, served behind the counter. The owner was a good Christian soul who regularly went to church and paid all his dues to Harambee projects. Pot-belly. Grey hairs. Soft-spoken. A respectable family man, well-known in Ilmorog. Hardworking even, for he would not leave the bar until the closing hours, or more precisely, until Nyagūthiī left. He had no eyes for any other girl; he hung around her, and surreptitiously brought her gifts of clothes without receiving gratitude in kind. Only the promise. Only the hope for tomorrow. Other girls he gave eighty shillings a month. Nyagūthiī had a room to herself. Nyagūthiī woke up whenever she liked to take the stock. But Beatrice and the other girls had to wake up at five or so, make tea for the lodgers, clean up the bar and wash dishes and glasses. Then they would hang around the bar in shifts until two o'clock when they would go for a small break. At five o'clock they had to be in again, ready for customers whom they would now serve with frothy beers and smiles until twelve o'clock or for as long as there were customers thirsty for more Tuskers and Pilsners. What often galled Beatrice, although in her case it did not matter one way or another, was the owner's insistence that the girls should sleep in Starlight. They would otherwise be late for work, he said. But what he really wanted was for the girls to use their bodies to attract more lodgers in Starlight. Most of the girls, led by Nyagũthiĩ, defied the rule and bribed the watchman to let them out and in. They wanted to meet their regular or one-night boyfriends in places where they would be free and where they would be treated as not just barmaids. Beatrice always slept in. Her occasional one-night patrons wanted to spend the minimum. Came a night when the owner, refused by Nyagũthiĩ, approached her. He started by finding fault with her work; he called her names, then as suddenly he started praising her, although in a grudging, almost contemptuous manner. He grabbed her, struggled with her, pot-belly, grey hairs and everything. Beatrice felt an unusual revulsion for the man. She could not, she would not bring herself to accept that which had so recently been cast aside by Nyagũthiĩ. My God, she wept inside, what does Nyagũthiĩ have that I don't have? The man now humiliated himself before her. He implored. He promised her gifts. But she would not yield. That night she too defied the rule. She jumped through a window; she sought a bed in another bar and only came back at six. The proprietor called her in front of all the others and dismissed her. But Beatrice was rather surprised at herself.

She stayed a month without a job. She lived from room to room at the capricious mercy of the other girls. She did not have the heart to leave Ilmorog and start all over again in a new town. The wound hurt. She was tired of wandering. She stopped using Ambi. No money. She looked at herself in the mirror. She had so aged, hardly a year after she had fallen from grace. Why then was she scrupulous, she would ask herself. But somehow she had a horror of soliciting lovers or directly bartering her body for hard cash. What she wanted was decent work and a man or several men who cared for her. Perhaps she took that need for a man, for a home and for a child with her to bed. Perhaps it was this genuine need that scared off men who wanted other things from barmaids. She wept late at nights and remembered home. At such moments, her mother's village in Nyeri seemed the sweetest place on God's earth. She would invest the life of her peasant mother and father with romantic illusions of immeasurable peace and harmony. She longed to go back home to see them. But how could she go back with empty hands? In any case the place was now a distant landscape in the memory. Her life was here in the bar among this crowd of lost strangers. Fallen from grace, fallen from grace. She was part of a generation which would never again be one with the soil, the crops, the wind and the moon. Not for them that whispering in dark hedges, not for her that dance and love-making under the glare of the moon, with the hills of TumuTumu rising to touch the sky. She remembered that girl from her home village who, despite a life of apparent glamour being the kept mistress of one rich man after another in Limuru, had gassed herself to death. This generation was not awed by the mystery of death, just as it was callous to the mystery of life; for how many unmarried mothers had thrown their babies into latrines rather than lose that glamour? The girl's death became the subject of jokes. She had gone metric – without pains, they said. Thereafter, for a week, Beatrice thought of going metric. But she could not bring herself to do it.

She wanted love; she wanted life.

A new bar was opened in Ilmorog. Treetop Bar, Lodging and Restaurant. Why Treetop, Beatrice could not understand unless because it was a storeyed building: tea shop on the ground floor and beer shop in a room at the top. The rest were rooms for five-minute or one-night lodgers. The owner was a retired civil servant but one who still played at politics. He was enormously wealthy with business sites and enterprises in every major town in Kenya. Big shots from all over the country came to his bar. Big men in Mercedes. Big men in their Bentleys. Big men in their Jaguars and Daimlers. Big men with uniformed chauffeurs drowsing with boredom in cars waiting outside. There were others not so big who came to pay respects to the great. They talked politics mostly. And about their work. Gossip was rife. Didn't you know? Indeed so and so has been promoted. Really? And so and so has been sacked. Embezzlement of public funds. So foolish you know. Not clever about it at all. They argued, they quarrelled, sometimes they fought it out with fists, especially during the elections campaign. The only point on which they were all agreed was that the Luo community was the root cause of all the trouble in Kenya; that intellectuals and university students were living in an ivory tower of privilege and arrogance; that Kiambu had more than a lion's share of developments; that men from Nyeri and Muranga had acquired all the big business in Nairobi and were even encroaching on Chiri District; that African workers, especially those on the farms, were lazy and jealous of 'us' who had sweated ourselves to sudden prosperity. Otherwise each would hymn his own praises or return compliments. Occasionally in moments of drunken ebullience and self-praise, one would order two rounds of beer for each man present in the bar. Even the poor from Ilmorog would come to Treetop to dine at the gates of the nouveaux riches.

Here Beatrice got a job as a sweeper and bedmaker. Here for a few weeks she felt closer to greatness. Now she made beds for men she had previously known as names. She watched how even the poor tried to drink and act big in front of the big. But soon fate caught up with her. Girls flocked to Treetop from other bars. Girls she had known at Limuru, girls she had known at Ilmorog. And most had attached themselves to one or several big men, often playing a hide-and-not-to-be-found game with their numerous lovers. And Nyagūthiī was there behind the counter, with the eyes of the rich and the poor fixed on her. And she, with her big eyes, bangled hands and earrings maintained the same air of bored indifference. Beatrice as a sweeper and bedmaker became even more invisible. Girls who had fallen into good fortune looked down upon her.

She fought life with dreams. In between putting clean sheets on beds that had just witnessed a five-minute struggle that ended in a half-strangled cry and a pool, she would stand by the window and watch the cars and the chauffeurs, so that soon she knew all the owners by the number plates of their cars and the uniforms of their chauffeurs. She dreamt of lovers who would come for her in sleek Mercedes sports cars made for two. She saw herself linking hands with such a lover, walking in the streets of Nairobi and Mombasa, tapping the ground with high heels, quick, quick short steps. And suddenly she would stop in front of a display glass window, exclaiming at the same time: Oh darling, won't you buy me those ... ? Those what, he would ask, affecting anger. Those stockings, darling. It was as an owner of several stockings, ladderless and holeless, that she thought of her wellbeing. Never again would she mend torn things. Never, never, never. Do you understand? Never. She was next the proud owner of different coloured wigs, blonde wigs, brunette wigs, redhead wigs, Afro wigs, wigs, wigs, all the wigs in the world. Only then would the whole earth sing hallelujah to the one Beatrice. At such moments, she would feel exalted, lifted out of her murky self, no longer a floor sweeper and bedmaker for a five-minute instant love, but Beatrice, descendant of Wangu Makeri who made men tremble with desire at her naked body bathed in moonlight, daughter of Nyang'endo, the founder of modern Ilmorog, of whom they often sang that she had worked several lovers into impotence.

Then she noticed him and he was the opposite of the lover of her dreams. He came one Saturday afternoon driving a big five-ton lorry. He carefully parked it beside the Benzes, the Jaguars and the Daimlers, not as a lorry, but as one of those sleek cream-bodied frames, so proud of it he seemed to be. He dressed in a baggy grey suit over which he wore a heavy khaki military overcoat. He removed the overcoat, folded it with care and put it on the front seat. He locked all the doors, dusted himself a little, then walked round the lorry as if inspecting it for damage. A few steps before he entered Treetop, he turned round for a final glance at his lorry dwarfing the other things. At Treetop he sat in a corner and, with a rather loud defiant voice, ordered a Kenya one. He drank it with relish, looking around at the same time for a face he might recognize. He indeed did recognize one of the big ones and he immediately ordered for him a quarter bottle of Vat 69. This was accepted with a bare nod of the head and a patronizing smile; but when he tried to follow his generosity with a conversation, he was firmly ignored. He froze, sank into his Muratina. But only for a time. He tried again: he was met with frowning faces. More pathetic were his attempts to join in jokes; he would laugh rather too loudly, which would make the big ones stop, leaving him in the air alone. Later in the evening he stood up, counted several crisp hundred-shilling notes and handed them to Nyagũthiĩ behind the counter ostensibly for safekeeping. People whispered; murmured; a few laughed, rather derisively, though they were rather impressed. But this act did not win him immediate recognition. He staggered towards room number 7 which he had hired. Beatrice brought him the keys. He glanced at her, briefly, then lost all interest.

Thereafter he came every Saturday. At five when most of the big shots were already seated. He repeated the same ritual, except the money act, and always met with defeat. He nearly always sat in the same corner and always rented room 7. Beatrice grew to anticipate his visits and, without being conscious of it, kept the room ready for him. Often after he had been badly humiliated by the big company, he would detain Beatrice and talk to her, or rather he talked to himself in her presence. For him, it had been a life of struggles. He had never been to school although getting an education had been his ambition. He never had a chance. His father was a squatter in the European settled area in the Rift Valley. That meant a lot in those colonial days. It meant among other things a man and his children were doomed to a future of sweat and toil for the white devils and their children. He had joined the freedom struggle and like the others had been sent to detention. He came from detention the same as his mother had brought him to this world. Nothing. With independence he found he did not possess the kind of education which would have placed him in one of the vacancies at the top. He started as a charcoal burner, then a butcher, gradually working his own way to become a big transporter of vegetables and potatoes from the Rift Valley and Chiri districts to Nairobi. He was proud of his achievement. But he resented that others, who had climbed to their present wealth through loans and a subsidized education, would not recognize his like. He would rumble on like this, dwelling on education he would never have, and talking of better chances for his children. Then he would carefully count the money, put it under the pillow and then dismiss Beatrice. Occasionally he would buy her a beer but he was clearly suspicious of women whom he saw as money-eaters of men. He had not yet married.

One night he slept with her. In the morning he scratched for a twenty-shilling note and gave it to her. She accepted the money with an odd feeling of guilt. He did this for several weeks. She did not mind the money. It was useful. But he paid for her body as he would pay for a bag of potatoes or a sack of cabbages. With the one pound, he had paid for her services as a listener, a vessel of his complaints against those above, and as a one-night receptacle of his man's burden. She was becoming bored with his ego, with his stories that never varied in content, but somehow, in him, deep inside, she felt that something had been there, a fire, a seed, a flower which was being smothered. In him she saw a fellow victim and looked forward to his visits. She too longed to talk to someone. She too longed to confide in a human being who would understand.

And she did it one Saturday night, suddenly interrupting the story of his difficult climb to the top. She did not know why she did it. Maybe it was the rain outside. It was softly drumming the corrugated iron sheets, bringing with the drumming a warm and drowsy indifference. He would listen. He had to listen. She came from Karatina in Nyeri. Her two brothers had been gunned down by the British soldiers. Another one had died in detention. She was, so to speak, an only child. Her parents were poor. But they worked hard on their bare strip of land and managed to pay her fees in primary school. For the first six years she had worked hard. In the seventh year, she must have relaxed a little. She did not pass with a good grade. Of course she knew many with similar grades who had been called to good government secondary schools. She knew a few others with lesser grades who had gone to very top schools on the strength of their connections. But she was not called to any high school with reasonable fees. Her parents could not afford fees in a Harambee school. And she would not hear of repeating Standard Seven. She stayed at home with her parents. Occasionally she would help them in the shamba and with house chores. But imagine: for the past six years she had led a life with a different rhythm from that of her parents. Life in the village was dull. She would often go to Karatina and to Nyeri in search of work. In every office they would ask her the same questions: what work do you want? What do you know? Can you type? Can you take shorthand? She was desperate. It was in Nyeri, drinking Fanta in a shop, tears in her eyes, that she met a young man in a dark suit and sunglasses. He saw her plight and talked to her. He came from Nairobi. Looking for work? That's easy; in a big city there would be no difficulty with jobs. He would certainly help. Transport? He had a car – a cream-white Peugeot. Heaven. It was a beautiful ride, with the promise of dawn. Nairobi. He drove her to Terrace Bar. They drank beer and talked about Nairobi. Through the window she could see the neon-lit city and knew that here was hope. That night she gave herself to him, with the promise of dawn making her feel light and gay. She had a very deep sleep. When she woke in the morning, the man in the cream-white Peugeot was not there. She never saw him again. That's how she had started the life of a barmaid. And for one and a half years now she had not been once to see her parents. Beatrice started weeping. Huge sobs of self-pity. Her humiliation and constant flight were fresh in her mind. She had never been able to take to bar culture, she always thought that something better would come her way. But she was trapped, it was the only life she now knew, although she had never really learnt all its laws and norms. Again she heaved out and in, tears tossing out with every sob. Then suddenly she froze. Her sobbing was arrested in the air. The man had long covered himself. His snores were huge and unmistakable.

She felt a strange hollowness. Then a bile of bitterness spilt inside her. She wanted to cry at her new failure. She had met several men who had treated her cruelly, who had laughed at her scruples, at what they thought was an ill-disguised attempt at innocence. She had accepted. But not this, Lord, not this. Was this man not a fellow victim? Had he not, Saturday after Saturday, unburdened himself to her? He had paid for her human services; he had paid away his responsibility with his bottles of Tusker and hard cash in the morning. Her innermost turmoil had been his lullaby. And suddenly something in her snapped. All the anger of a year and a half, all the bitterness against her humiliation were now directed at this man.

What she did later had the mechanical precision of an experienced hand.

She touched his eyes. He was sound asleep. She raised his head. She let it fall. Her tearless eyes were now cold and set. She removed the pillow from under him. She rummaged through it. She took out his money. She counted five crisp pink notes. She put the money inside her brassiere.

She went out of room number 7. Outside it was still raining. She did not want to go to her usual place. She could not now stand the tiny cupboard room or the superior chatter of her room-mate. She walked through mud and rain. She found herself walking towards Nyagūthiĩ's room. She knocked at the door. At first she had no response. Then she heard Nyagūthiĩ's sleepy voice above the drumming rain.

'Who is that?'

'It is me. Please open.'

'Who?'

'Beatrice.'

'At this hour of the night?'

'Please.'

Lights were put on. Bolts unfastened. The door opened. Beatrice stepped inside. She and Nyagūthiĩ stood there face to face. Nyagūthiĩ was in a see-through nightdress: on her shoulders she had a green pullover.

'Beatrice, is there anything wrong?' she at last asked, a note of concern in her voice.

'Can I rest here for a while? I am tired. And I want to talk to you.' Beatrice's voice carried assurance and power.

'But what has happened?'

'I only want to ask you a question, Nyagūthiĩ.'

They were still standing. Then, without a word, they both sat on the bed.

'Why did you leave home, Nyagūthiĩ?' Beatrice asked. Another silent moment. Nyagūthiĩ seemed to be thinking about the question. Beatrice waited. Nyagūthiĩ's voice when at last it came was slightly tremulous, unsteady.

'It is a long story, Beatrice. My father and mother were fairly wealthy. They were also good Christians. We lived under regulations. You must never walk with the heathen. You must not attend their pagan customs – dances and circumcision rites, for instance. There were rules about what, how and when to eat. You must even walk like a Christian lady. You must never be seen with boys. Rules, rules all the way. One day instead of returning home from school, I and another girl from a similar home ran away to Eastleigh. I have never been home once this last four years. That's all.'

Another silence. Then they looked at one another in mutual recognition.

'One more question, Nyagūthiĩ. You need not answer it. But I have always thought that you hated me, you despised me.'

'No, no, Beatrice, I have never hated you. I have never hated anybody. It is just that nothing interests me. Even men do not move me now. Yet I want, I need instant excitement. I need the attention of those false flattering eyes to make me feel myself, myself. But you, you seemed above all this – somehow you had something inside you that I did not have.'

Beatrice tried to hold her tears with difficulty.

Early the next day, she boarded a bus bound for Nairobi. She walked down Bazaar Street looking at the shops. Then down Government Road, right into Kenyatta Avenue and Kimathi Street. She went into a shop near Hussein Suleman's street and bought several stockings. She put on a pair. She next bought herself a new dress. Again she changed into it. In a Bata Shoeshop she bought high-heeled shoes, put them on and discarded her old flat ones. On to an Akamba kiosk, and she fitted herself with earrings. She went to a mirror and looked at her new self. Suddenly she felt enormous hunger as if she had been hungry all her life. She hesitated in front of Moti Mahal. Then she walked on, eventually entering Fransae. There was a glint in her eyes that made men's eyes turn to her. This thrilled her. She chose a table in a corner and ordered Indian curry. A man left his table and joined her. She looked at him. Her eyes were merry. He was dressed in a dark suit and his eyes spoke of lust. He bought her a drink. He tried to engage her in conversation. But she ate in silence. He put his hand under the table and felt her knees. She let him do it. The hand went up and up her thigh. Then suddenly she left her unfinished food and her untouched drink and walked out. She felt good. He followed her. She knew this without once turning her eyes. He walked beside her for a few yards. She smiled at herself but did not look at him. He lost his confidence. She left him standing sheepishly looking at a glass window outside Gino's. In the bus back to Ilmorog, men gave her seats. She accepted this as of right. At Treetop Bar she went straight to the counter. The usual crowd of big men was there. Their conversations stopped for a few seconds at her entry. Their lascivious eyes were turned to her. The girls stared at her. Even Nyagũthiĩ could not maintain her bored indifference. Beatrice bought them drinks. The manager came to her, rather unsure. He tried a conversation. Why had she left work? Where had she been? Would she like to work in the bar, helping Nyagũthiĩ behind the counter? Now and then? A barmaid brought her a note. A certain big shot wanted to know if she would join their table. More notes came from different big quarters with the one question: would she be free tonight? A trip to Nairobi even. She did not leave her place at the counter. But she accepted their drinks as of right. She felt a new power, confidence even.

She took out a shilling, put it in the slot and the jukebox boomed with

the voice of Robinson Mwangi singing Hūnyū wa Mashambani. He
sang of those despised girls who worked on farms and contrasted them
with urban girls. Then she played a Kamaru and a D. K. Men wanted to
dance with her. She ignored them, but enjoyed their flutter around
her. She twisted her hips to the sound of yet another D. K. Her body was
free. She was free. She sucked in the excitement and tension in the air.

Then suddenly at around six the man with the five-ton lorry stormed
into the bar. This time he had on his military overcoat. Behind him was a
policeman. He looked around. Everybody's eyes were raised to him. But
Beatrice went on swaying her hips. At first he could not recognize Beatrice
in the girl celebrating her few minutes of glory by the jukebox. Then he
shouted in triumph: 'That is the girl! Thief! Thief!'

People melted back to their seats. The policeman went and handcuffed
her. She did not resist. Only at the door she turned her head and spat.
Then she went out followed by the policeman.

In the bar the stunned silence broke into hilarious laughter when
someone made a joke about sweetened robbery without violence. They
discussed her. Some said she should have been beaten. Others talked
contemptuously about 'these bar girls'. Yet others talked with a concern
noticeable in unbelieving shakes of their heads about the rising rate of
crime. Shouldn't the Hanging Bill be extended to all thefts of property?
And without anybody being aware of it the man with the five-ton lorry
had become a hero. They now surrounded him with questions and
demanded the whole story. Some even bought him drinks. More remarkable, they listened, their attentive silence punctuated by appreciative
laughter. The averted threat to property had temporarily knitted them
into one family. And the man, accepted for the first time, told the story
with relish.

But behind the counter Nyagūthiī wept.

M. G. Vassanji

Breaking Loose

Moyez G. Vassanji was born in Nairobi in 1950, but he was brought up and educated in Dar es Salaam, Tanzania, the setting of his collection of stories of 1991, *Uhuru Street* ('Breaking Loose' is from that work). His highly successful novel, *The Book of Secrets* (Picador, 1996), is a family saga also set there, depicting in rich detail the history of the coastal Asian-African community from the Great War through Independence and into the 1980s. He lives in Toronto where he edits the *Toronto Review of Contemporary Writing Abroad.*

THE ROCK BAND IBLIS was playing. The lead guitarist and singer was a local heart-throb, a young Asian with fairly long hair and bell-bottom trousers now in the midst of another brisk number from the foreign pop-charts. Close to the stage danced a group of modish, brightly dressed girls, proclaiming by their various excesses their closeness with the four band members.

Yasmin was at the far end of the dance floor with her girlfriends. Three of them occupied the table with the only chairs available, Yasmin and the other two stood around. Occasionally she would look up to take in the dance scene, the band, the modish girls, hoping to catch a vacated chair she could bring over. The band was loud, the room hot and stuffy, and the men were drenched with sweat and the girls fanning themselves with handkerchiefs or anything else they could find. A well-dressed black man, somewhat odd in a grey suit, his necktie rakishly loosened, emerged from the throng of dancing couples and went up to her requesting the dance. She went.

Of all the girls here, why me? I don't want *to dance. I can't dance.* From the centre of the dance floor where he'd taken her she threw a longing glance at her gang chatting away in the distance.

'I'm sorry,' he smiled. 'I took you away from your friends...'

'It's okay ... only for a few minutes—' she began and blushed, realizing that unwittingly she'd agreed. After all it's an honour, she thought. He's a professor.

It was a dance that did not require closeness or touching – and she was grateful for that mercy.

'Daniel Akoto. That's my name.'

'I know ... I'm Yasmin Rajan.'

It's all so unnecessary. I'm not the type. He should have tried one of those cheeky ones dancing barefoot. Now that would have drawn some fun.

She looked at her partner. He was graceful, much more – she was certain – than she.

She was a head shorter than him. Her long hair was combed back straight and supported with a red band, in the manner favoured by schoolgirls, and she wore a simple dress. This was the middle of her second year at the University.

'Good music,' he said.

'Yes, isn't it? I know the lead guitarist ...'

'But too Western, don't you think?'

'I don't know ...'

She felt oppressed by the ordeal, and the heat, and the smoke, the vapours of sweat, beer and perfume. There was the little worry too – why had he picked her and would he pursue her. He was looking at her. He was offended by her attitude and going on about Asians.

'... truly colonized ... mesmerized ... more so than the African I dare say.'

She didn't reply, trying her best to give a semblance of grace to her movements – feeling guilty, wholly inadequate and terribly embarrassed.

Just when she thought the rest of the dance would proceed smoothly – the music was steady and there was a kind of lull in the noise level – the leader of the band let out a whoop from the stage. There were whoops of rejoinder, followed by renewed energy on the dance floor. Akoto shook his head, and Yasmin watched him with dread.

'Look at that. Beatniks. Simply aping the Europeans ... not a gesture you'll find original. Your kinsmen, I presume?'

She forced a smile. *I hope he doesn't raise a scene.*

'There are African bands too, you know,' she said.

'But the *beat*, my dear, the *music*. Now take that song. Rolling Stones. What do you call *Indian* in that ... for instance?' he persisted. 'Perhaps I'm missing something.'

Oh why doesn't he stop, for God's sake.

'What do you mean we're colonized?' she said, exasperated. 'Of course we have our own culture. Come to our functions and see. We have centuries-old traditions ...'

She had stopped dancing and there were tears in her eyes. She felt trapped and under attack in the middle of the couple of hundred people twisting and shaking around her. She could feel curious eyes burning upon her, watching her embarrassment.

She left Akoto in the middle of the dance floor and walked stiffly to her friends.

*

The next day she waited for the axe to fall. A call to the Vice Chancellor's office, a reprimand for publicly insulting a distinguished professor, a visitor from another African country. Perhaps she would just be black-listed: a rude Asian girl, who doesn't know her place.

During lunch in the refectory one of her friends pointed him out to her. He was standing at the door, throwing sweeping looks across the hall searching for someone. She drew a deep breath and waited. His eyes found her and he hurried forward between tables, pushing aside chairs, grinning, answering courtesies on the way with waves and shouts. When he arrived, a place was made for him at the table at which he sank comfortably, putting both his hands in front of him. He looked at her.

'About last night . . .' he began. The other girls picked up their trays and left.

She laughed. 'You pushed them out,' she said. 'They'll hate you for that.'

Where had she found her confidence? He was in a red T-shirt – expensive, she thought. He looked handsome – and harmless.

'But not for long, I hope,' he began. His grin widened as he looked at her. 'Again I've removed you from your friends – but this time I've come to apologize. I'm sorry about last night. I asked you for a dance and then played a tiresome little radical.'

'It's okay. I'm at fault too. You see . . .'

'I know, I know. An innocent Indian girl in a den of wolves. But tell me – surely you expect men to come and ask you to dance in such a situation?'

She smiled, a little embarrassed. 'Usually the presence of girlfriends is enough to deter men one doesn't know . . .'

'Trust a foreigner not to know the rules.' He smiled ruefully. 'You came to have a good time with your friends and I spoilt it for you. Honestly I'm sorry. Look: let me make up for it. I'll take you for a drink. How about that?'

'But I don't drink . . . alcohol, I mean.'

'Tut-tut! We'll find something for you.'

He should not, of course, have pressed. But, as he said, he didn't know the rules. That's what she told herself when she found that she had accepted his invitation without any qualms.

'I'll take you to The Matumbi,' he said when they met later that afternoon. The Matumbi was a tea shop under a tree, half a mile from the campus. It had a thatched roof that only partly shaded it, and no walls. She went in hesitantly, feeling a little shy and out of place. But apparently Akoto was one of the regulars. He motioned to the owner who came up and wiped a sticky table for them, and then he pulled up a rickety chair for her, dusting it with a clean handkerchief.

'Are you hungry?' he asked.

'No. I will just have tea . . . perhaps a small cake . . .'

'Righto! Two teas, one cake and one sikisti!' he called out.

She raised an eyebrow when the sikisti arrived. It was an egg omelette between two inch-thick slices of bread.

'It's called sikisti because of its price. Sixty cents!'

She laughed.

'That's the truth, believe me!'

Akoto was a professor of sociology, on loan from the government of Ghana.

'What is your major?' he asked her after some time. 'What subject are you taking?'

'Literature.'

'Literature?'

'Yes.' *Now he thinks we are all shopkeepers.*

'Tell me: any African writers?'

'Yes. Soyinka . . . Achebe . . .'

'Things fall apart . . .'

'The centre cannot hold.'

He laughed. 'Ngugi? Palangyo? Omari?'

She shook her head. She hadn't heard of them.

'Local writers. Budding. You should read Omari. Nuru Omari. She writes about the Coast – your territory. *Wait for Me*; that's her first book. I could lend it to you if you want.'

'It's okay . . . I'll borrow it from the library.'

He looked astonished. 'But it will take time before the library acquires it.'

'I'll wait . . . I don't have much time right now.'

'All right.' He was miffed.

'Now that I have made up for my rudeness,' he said at last, seeing her a little restless, 'I hope – having apologized and so on – perhaps we can go.'

I am studying literature and I have no time to read the most recent books. She felt guilty.

*

When she saw him again it was after several days and he did not appear to notice her. He's got my message, she thought. I am not interested. Why did I go to the tea shop with him, then? . . . Because he's so different. What confidence, what grace . . . so civilized, such a gentleman! That's it! she thought. He said we Asians are so Westernized . . . aping the Europeans . . . mesmerized . . . what about him? All that external polish: he was a proper English gentleman himself! She would tell him so!

'Dear Professor Akoto,' she wrote, 'I wanted to tell you something. I thought I should tell it to you before I forget it completely. You called us Asians colonized. We are mesmerized with the West, you said. Well, have you observed yourself carefully lately? All those European mannerisms, language, clothes – suits even in hot weather: you are so much the English gentleman yourself! Yours sincerely, Yasmin Rajan. P.S. Could I borrow Omari's *Wait for Me* from you after all? Thanx.' She slipped the note under his office door.

He repeated his previous performance at lunch-time the next day, edging out her friends from the table.

'Your point is well taken,' he said. 'Touché and so on. But I thought we had forgiven all that. Still, I don't quite agree with you. And the reason is this: I know my situation. I struggle. In any case . . . Let's not argue. Let me show you my library. You can borrow any book you like.'

'You have your own library?' she murmured.

When she saw it she was dazzled. Three walls were covered with books. She had never before seen so many books belonging to one person – in a sitting room, part of the furniture as it were.

'You've read all these books?' she asked.

'Well . . . I wouldn't . . .'

'I envy you. You must be so knowledgeable.'

'Let's not get carried away now.'

'Do you also write?'

'Yes. But nothing out yet.'

He had a theory about African literature. 'It is at present digging up the roots,' he said. And that's what he was trying to do. Dig. 'So you can understand my obsession with authenticity. Even my name is a burden, an imposition.'

At The Matumbi where they went that evening, she had her first sikisti. She talked about her background.

'My father was a pawnbroker,' she said, 'but pawnshops are no longer allowed, so now he has a tailoring shop. Hardly a Westernized background . . .'

He smiled. 'Aren't you ever going to forgive me?'

'Tell me, do you think pawnshops are exploitative?' she asked him.

'Well, they tempt the poor and they do charge awfully high interest.'

'Yes, but where else can the poor get loans? Would the banks give them? And as for the high interest – do you know the kind of things they bring to pawn off? Old watches, broken bicycles, clothes sometimes. We have three unclaimed antique gramophones at home that we can't sell.'

'Is that right? Can I look at them? I might buy one. I like old things that are out of fashion.'

'Sure you can.'

He played badminton with the Asian girls one day, bringing along a shy young man from Norway. It was at a time (though they did not tell him) when they usually went to the mosque. After the game there was a heated discussion about China. And they arranged to play the next time a little later in the evening.

One afternoon, as agreed previously, Yasmin took him to her father's shop to show him the antique gramophones. They went in his car and he dropped her off outside the shop and went to park.

When he entered the shop her father met him.

'Come in, Bwana. What can I get for you?'

He was a short thin man with green eyes, wearing a long white shirt over his striped pyjamas.

'I came with Yasmin,' Akoto explained in his broken Swahili.

'Yes? You want to buy something?'

'I came for a gramophone—'

'Ah, yes! The professor! Sit, sit.'

Akoto sat on the bench uncomfortably and waited, looking around inside the shop. The shelves lining the walls were filled with suiting, the glass showcases displayed shirts. Yasmin's father went about his work. The girl soon arrived from the back door carrying an old gramophone. Behind her was a servant carrying two, one on top of the other, and behind the servant followed a tall thin woman: Yasmin's mother. While her father showed Akoto the gramophones, Yasmin and her mother went back inside.

'How can you bring him here like this?' said her mother angrily. 'What will the neighbours think? And the servants? It's shameful!'

'But Mummy, he is a professor!'

'I don't care if he's a professor's father!'

When they went back to the store the purchase was completed, Akoto and her father were chatting amiably about politics. Akoto was grinning, carrying a gramophone in his arms. He looked enquiringly at her.

Outside the store a few boys and girls from the neighbourhood walked by, throwing quick curious glances inside at the guest.

'Yasmin will stay with us tonight,' said her mother a little too loudly from the back doorway where she stood. 'She'll come back tomorrow. But she won't miss her classes – I hope that is all right.'

'Don't worry, Mama. It's perfectly all right.'

It was more than a week before they met again, briefly, in a corridor.

'Where do you eat lunch these days? You're the perfect salesman,' he said in good humour. 'You sell me an old gramophone and disappear. You afraid I'll return it?' She gave some excuse.

Later she returned the books she had borrowed from him and declined an invitation to The Matumbi.

The sight of Akoto in her shop that day had driven her mother into a fit. By the time he had left the shop hugging the gramophone she was raging with fury. 'There are no friendships with men – not with men we don't know . . .' she said to Yasmin.

'The world is not ready for it,' her father said quietly.

'You stay out of it!' screamed his wife. 'This is between us two.'

He remained quiet but stayed within hearing distance, measuring out cloth for his tailors. If Yasmin expected any understanding, or even a reasoned discussion with an adult, experienced voice, it was from her father. But ever since she could remember she had been her mother's business. And her mother, she believed, hated her for this, for being a girl. Yasmin was not the only child; there were three brothers. But ever since she could remember her mother was always admonishing, chiding, warning her – as if believing her capable of the worst. Now it seemed that all the horrors she had imagined possible from her daughter – against her, against the name and dignity of the family – were on the verge of coming true.

'What do you know of him?' She had been uncontrollable, obsessive, had gone on and on until she was hoarse and breathless. 'With an Asian man, even if he's evil, you know what to expect. But with *him*?'

At the end of the day the girl felt as if her bones had been picked dry.

Yasmin did not go to the end-of-year dance on campus. From her friends she heard of the one notable event that took place there. Professor Akoto, after sitting at a table all alone for some time and apparently after a little too much to drink, had got into a brawl with Mr Sharp of the Boys' School, calling him a CIA agent. Then he'd staggered out.

*

India was not just the past, or the community, or even the jealous Indian communities of Dar. India was a continent, a civilization, a political entity in the world. Only recently it had emerged from a long struggle for independence.

During the holidays Yasmin discovered her world. She read avidly about India, quizzed her father about it. India came as a revelation. Here in Africa she was an Asian, an Indian. Yet she had been a stranger to even the most recent Indian history. All she had received from her people about India were ancient customs, unchanged for generations, remotely related to the world around her. At first her acknowledgement of her origins seemed to her a reaction against Akoto, the African; yet it seemed to be harking back to the authenticity he had been talking about. In a strange and diabolical way it seemed to be bringing her closer to the man, as if what she was discovering was at his bidding, as if she had to go and discuss her findings with him, answer his challenges.

The world seemed a smaller place when she went back to the University. Smaller but exciting; teeming with people struggling, fighting, loving: surviving. And she was one of those people. People, bound by their own histories and traditions, seemed to her like puppets tied to strings: but then a new mutant broke loose, an event occurred, and lives changed, the world changed. She was, she decided, a new mutant.

Yasmin's father collapsed with a heart attack under the weight of two bolts of suiting in his shop, one month after the University reopened. A servant was dispatched to fetch a doctor, who arrived an hour and a half later. By that time the former pawnbroker had died.

Daniel Akoto attended the funeral. He sat among the men, initially on the ground, trying to fold his legs, sweating profusely, pressed from all sides. A black face in a sea of patient brown Asian faces. He was not wearing a suit, just a very clean white shirt, but this time some of the other men were in jackets. A servant saw the discomfited man and placed a chair for him against the wall adjacent to the door. Now Akoto could see clearly across the room. The body was lying on a low table behind which two men sat on the floor administering the last rites to the dead. The widow sat beside the dead man, sobbing, comforted by her daughter, occasionally breaking into a wail and joined by other women. Mrs Rajan looked away from Akoto when their eyes first met. She moaned and started weeping. She saw him again through a film of tears, lost control and gave a loud wail.

'You!' she screamed, 'what are you doing here? What kind of man are you, who comes to take away my daughter even in my grief ... Who asked you to come? Go away!' she wept.

Akoto, understanding only partly her speech but fully the intent, tried to smile apologetically at the men and women now turning to stare at him.

'Go!' said the distraught woman, pointing a finger at the door beside him.

No one else said a word. Akoto stood up, gave a respectful bow towards the dead man and left.

A week later Yasmin knocked on his door late in the evening and caught him in.

'Come in,' he said, putting away his pipe.

'I've come to apologize about that day.'

'It's all right. A funeral is not exactly where people are at their best ... perhaps they are more honest though.' He eyed her.

'You could have us arrested! You could ...'

'Don't be silly! Take a hold of yourself. What do you think I am anyway – the secret police?'

'You must despise us,' she said more quietly. 'You are educated, learned ... your government has loaned you to us ... You are a great man ...'

'No, I don't despise you. And don't call me great, for God's sake.'

She began to laugh, a little hysterically. They both laughed.

'And you, I respect you.' He spoke calmly. 'You are brave. You left that gang of girls that day at the dance and since then you've done it again and again. It takes courage, what you've done, trying to break away from tribalism – that's all it is ultimately ... Even coming here like this. I realize that and I like you.'

'Well, I like you too!' she said, too quickly. There was a silence between them. 'You know, it's not going to be easy ... with my father dead, this will be the greatest shock to my mother ... it will kill her, it will ...'

'Now, now.' He went up to her, put her wet face on his shirt. 'We'll have to do the best we can, won't we?'

Fatmata Conteth

Letter to my Sisters

Fatmata A. Conteth's 'Letter to my Sisters' was on a shortlist of seventeen finalists (out of a total of eight hundred) in a short story competition for the women writers of Ethiopia, Kenya, Tanzania, Zambia, Zimbabwe and Botswana, organized to celebrate the occasion of the United Nations End of Decade Conference on Women, held in Nairobi in July 1985. The resultant anthology – *Whispering Land* (1985) – was published by the Swedish Independent Development Authority's Office of Women in Development in Stockholm.

MY DEAR SISTER,

When you read this unusual letter, the news of my death will have saturated the atmosphere in our community, Fullah Town. As I write, I can imagine how the news of my death will be received. I can imagine so many things while I am alive and writing. I won't be able to imagine anything when I am dead, because I don't know whether dead people are capable of imagination, though our religion teaches us that there is life after death. I know too that the moment my death is discovered, the Muslim Jamma will be summoned and they will hasten to bury me, not bothering to find out whether I am really dead or only unconscious. Our religion does not allow people to feign death, to faint or fall into a trance. They will bury you as soon as they suspect you are not breathing properly. I can assure you, however, that in my case I will have really died.

I do know as I write these last words in my life that my death will cause a great commotion. As usual, I know how mother will wail. She will beat her flabby breasts. Breasts that have suckled eleven children. She will undo her long, beautiful hair and pull it apart. She will shout and ask what she has done to God that she should deserve such punishment. She will call my name countless times and she will ask why God should deprive her of her eldest daughter and the fifth of her eleven children, why only nine are alive. She will run about, crying and shouting, and many women will chase her and try to console her. Some will say that it is the wish of God, Allah, the Almighty, that I die. She will never believe that I took my own life voluntarily. No, she will never believe it because suicide is uncommon in our community. Poor mother, I know how she will feel.

As for Baba (father), one can never be sure how he will react. In our society men are not supposed to weep. It is a sign of weakness. In any case, none of us ever saw Baba cry. He is such a hard-hearted man. He will feel sad, very sad. Then I know he will grab his prayer beads and start his TASBIH. He will then say, 'SUBHANALLAH' thirty-three times, 'AL HAMDU LILLAH' thirty-three times, 'ALLAHU-AKBAR (ALLAH IS THE GREATEST)' thirty-four times. Indeed, Baba will say, 'Allahu-Akbar, Allahu Akbar, Allah is the Greatest, Allah is the Greatest,' many times. And his peers, some of the neighbours will come and sit by him and say exactly what Baba is saying. But Baba will not weep. He believes so much in his manhood, his religion and God and the total submission of women to men and their parents. He will say I died because it is the will of Allah, the Greatest. He will tell people to hurry and bury me before it is too late. So the whole community will be busy. People will assemble in and around our house, talking about me and my accomplishments. Many will not accept my death as a finality.

My aunts will be full of grief. They are so proud of me. They will curse the day I was born. They will swear I never killed myself. Some will want to accuse some of my stepmothers, especially Mama Janeba who never really liked me that much. They will make all sorts of innuendos against Mama Janeba, poor her. I wish I had a way to defend her. But that is the price she will have to pay for disliking me.

As for my uncles, they will behave like Baba. They will be sad, but will not cry. Everything will be attributed to Allah. They will pray and feel justified that they had opposed our going to acquire Western education. They will tell Baba how mistaken he was in allowing us to go to school. Islamic education was enough for us as they had advocated.

I know how you my sisters will react to the news of my death. You will cry like Mama. Your eyes will be red and they will bulge. I know how Intuma will sing while weeping. She will say she has lost her eldest sister. She will clap her hands, put her hands on her head and run around. She will say she would like to accompany me. Her world, she will say, has come to an end. She will ask who killed our sister. She will talk about her sister who was the first female Muslim girl to get a university education and then to have gone to the white man's country to become the first female medical doctor in the Fullah Town community.

As for Amina, she will just gnash her teeth. She will probably go into a trance. It will take her a long time to believe. She will believe days later, after my funeral, otherwise she will think I will come back to life.

After a while, she will say to herself that she must stop crying. That it is God's will. Isha will take over from her. She will say that someone killed her sister. She will say that she knows the person. But she will never call names of suspects. She will cry for a long time. In the end, she will lose her voice and her speech will be incomprehensible for some time. As for Ajaratu, she will leave the compound and run towards the stream. Then people will chase her for fear she might drown herself or do some other harm to herself. After a while they will bring her back, sandwiched in the arms of people. People will crowd around to console her. I know how all of you, my sisters, will react, but I cannot name all seventeen of you in this short letter.

As for our brothers, they are no different from Baba and all our uncles. But I think that the little boys will cry. They will all cry because they will remember what I used to do for all of them at the end of Ramadan month and on Christmas. They will miss the presents that I used to work so hard to get for them just to make them happy. The older brothers will probably hate me for killing myself. They will never stop to think, to understand and appreciate why I did what I did. But that is their business, they are all just like Baba, full of their manhood.

The dailies will have various captions. I can imagine such headlines as, 'Dr Dao commits suicide', 'Fullah Town has lost its first female doctor.' Some will say, 'Suicide, Dr Dao dead.' Some papers will suspect foul play until the facts are known. But that is what should be expected. It is normal.

In the hospital where I work, my colleagues and my patients will react likewise. Many of my colleagues have always said that I am too reserved for their comfort. Some think it is because I am a Muslim. Some think that it is because I am in a profession which is traditionally male. I never told them the reason for my apparent reserve. My patients would be shocked and baffled. I can imagine how Ya-Yanoh will feel. Remember sisters, I always tell you about Ya-Yanoh, the woman with a big ulcer on her left thigh. In her village they say that her ulcer is incurable because she is said to be a witch. She also believes that and has become very miserable. She is insulted by all and sundry and her situation is made worse by the fact that she is childless. When I admitted her, she narrated her ordeal to me and I told her I would help her to get well. She could not believe it. At the time of writing this letter, she is in the process of getting discharged. Her sore is healed, completely. I remember when I used to go on my rounds in the wards. She was my favourite patient. I treated her like our mother. She told me I had restored her dignity and respect. So when she returns to her village, walking straight and confident, people will regard her as a human being. Before that she was treated with contempt and opprobrium.

Sometimes, after listening to her stories, I felt like crying. She is a nice woman after all. One thing I remember about her is her teeth. They are very clean and almost intact. Because of this also, she said people accused her of witchcraft. According to people in her village, she said, a woman of her age ought to have few teeth. So her life was one full of torment. How she will cry when news of my death reaches her.

Amina and Ajara will recall the lady who said that I am the only female doctor she ever knew and how happy that made her. She used to say that even if she died, she would have had the satisfaction of having known a female doctor. She was joking, of course. I like her all the same. She is one of my favourites. She appreciates the fact that we work hard and make lots of sacrifices, especially those who have night duty. But then she would say that had she been a doctor she would not have liked night duty because she wants to be with her husband. Then she would laugh and the other patients would join in her laughter. She is such fun. She too will cry and feel very sad.

My dear sisters, I know that you will want to know why I took my life. Well, it is a long story. Partly, I am doing it for your sakes. I did it so that you can get freedom. For this, I have to sacrifice my life to set you free, you and your daughters and your daughters' daughters.

You may not understand now. However, as you read along, as you get to the end of this letter, I am sure you will understand and appreciate my action. You may not approve of this method of helping you to be free, to be women of dignity, pride and self-esteem. I have taken what I consider a courageous course of action to assert my dignity and yours too. I am writing this unusual letter to justify my action to be free. I hope I am also helping women of my community. If I fail to tell you the reason for my action, some of you will never forgive me. This is why I am writing the story of my life to you, my younger sisters. I owe it to you as a moral duty, to tell you the truth, nothing but the truth.

From the time I was a little child, Baba was always concerned about upholding the family name of the Daos. The upholding of the family name transcends everything in Baba's life. The respectability and reverence which the name Dao enjoys should never be allowed to diminish. But from the time I can remember things correctly, it had appeared that the upholding of the family name was the sole responsibility of us girls. The fact that our great grandfather was among the few Imams of the mosque of Fullah Town has served to enslave us rather than make us free people. You know how people talk about us. We should not say certain things because we are of the Dao family. The things that normal people do we cannot do. We are a very religious family. But above all we are women; so we hold the family name in trust.

As you know, we went to the Koranic school at an early age and finished in record time, before our brothers – both the elder and the younger ones. We always did better than they did. Baba, as you all know, was against our going to school to get Western education. He was more inclined to allow the boys rather than us. His argument was the usual and familiar one, to which our uncles, apart from one, also subscribe. Girls should get married and have children. Western education, he had observed, bred immorality, disrespect for elders and for tradition. That he finally allowed us to go to school was due to the influence of one of our uncles, Uncle Bubu. But that is not surprising. Uncle Bubu is the most educated and enlightened of them all. That he went to school was an accident of history. So he knows what education means. We all thanked him for what he did for us. But that was a long time ago.

In school we did better than all our brothers. Even the eldest never reached my standard. We all know how Nkodo Shaifu, from our own point of view, brought dishonour to this family. He had had children out of wedlock. Baba was not offended. He was happy he had grandchildren. Worst of all, Nkodo had had these children while still at school. He could not pass his examinations to go to college. That, to me, is a shame. Baba never thought it was dishonourable. It was Uncle Bardara who felt somewhat embarrassed by the incident.

Do you still recall our big secret? No one, as far as I know, can forget that incident. I am referring to the time Ajara almost died while trying to induce abortion. We had all been so terrified that if it became known that one of us had been made pregnant out of wedlock, it would have brought dishonour to the Dao family. Ajara almost lost her life. I hope all of you are beginning to understand what I am trying to point out to you.

Have we not lamented many times that we are not allowed out of the house except when accompanied by several of our younger brothers and sisters? You know that we must always come home much earlier than even our younger brothers. You also know how we are watched. Our friends are even chosen for us. That applied to me too as an elder sister. That was how I found myself the centre of ridicule, because by the time

I went to college I did not know how to dance. I found it difficult to socialize. My friends used to say I had two left feet. I learned to dance much later in life when I was in England studying medicine. I was afraid of men, because I was afraid they would ask me out to parties. I must confess that I was miserable.

Have you girls noticed how our younger brothers can dance to all sorts of music? Baba would only say with delight that they are men.

You all remember the incident when Baba threatened to disown me. I am referring to the day I wore trousers. I had just come from England and thought I had grown out of that type of family control. Baba said it was a big shame, a dishonour to the family for a girl, his daughter, to put on trousers. 'This was why I said that Western education breeds immorality. You have come here now to teach your own younger sisters bad manners. God have mercy on you. I tell you, hell fire will consume you for this!' He had even scolded mother. It was mother who had given birth to somebody like me. Hell fire, he said, will also consume mother. According to him, hell was not comparable to anything we knew of on earth. He always threatened us with hell fire. That day, Baba was very angry with me. He even threatened to set fire to me if he ever saw me in trousers again. I always damn that day when I think of it. It was a terrible day. Mother wept later for me. Poor mother, she weeps for everything. I felt guilty as though I had committed a crime.

I always thought women could wear trousers in Islamic countries. Baba said I was to dress like a woman. He meant perhaps for me to tie a wrappa. To tie a wrappa, and to do work, I thought. Whenever I looked into my wardrobe and glanced at my beautiful trousers, I felt pain in my stomach. The thought that I could never put them on while I was under the regime of Baba made me feel sick.

Home has become hell for me. No boyfriend would dare call me or come to our house. When I had intimated to Baba that the government had provided me with a house, he told me I would leave his house only on my way to my matrimonial home. I wept bitterly. Mother wept too. For Baba, unmarried girls should not live by themselves. It is immoral. But it is all right for our brothers to live by themselves. That would not bring dishonour to the family. My God! So I accepted in disbelief.

'Why then did I have to spend so much of my time going to college?' I asked myself. I would have been like our mother. Mama accepted and believed that she was born to serve Baba or any man that would have her as a wife. Mama could never question anything Baba said to her, good or bad. Mama, whose once seductive figure had now become lost in fat, because Baba had scolded her that she was giving him a bad name by staying slim. Baba likes fat women. So Mama became fat. I once told her that from a professional point of view her fat would kill her. I meant it. She laughed and ignored me. 'If you disobey your husband, you will not go to heaven.' She was sure and very serious about it. I laughed and Mama thought I was stupid.

You all remember when we wanted to talk to Uncle Bardara. We wanted to talk to him so that he could talk to his brother to allow us freedom of movement, speech and association. We hesitated. It was difficult to trust Uncle Bardara also. We saw him beat his wives very often for minor offences. One day he beat one of his wives until the woman vomited. Her crime had been that she had gone to watch masquerade devils. For Uncle Bardara, it was the devil that had induced his wife. So he had decided to beat the hell out of her, as our people would say. In many ways, Uncle Bardara is like Baba. Many people also like Baba because he is said to be very religious. He knows the Koran and quotes from it with ease, which has earned him the envy of his peers. He has visited the Holy City of Mecca several times and this also adds to the reverence people have for him. He looks like someone incapable of hurting a fly. His countenance is deceptive, very deceptive.

We could not appeal to Baba's best friend. He is a lamentably dull man who cannot offer Baba the intellectual stimulation Baba always seeks from his colleagues.

My world then became a prison, a closed world. Sometimes I feel guilty even just talking to men. I feel my father's curse will affect me. I have contemplated rebellion many times. But again, I have been taught that an outright act of rebellion against any of one's parents is sinful. I am afraid.

Do you remember when our elder brother searched my wardrobe after money and inadvertently came across a letter from a boyfriend of mine? You remember how he read my letter and reported the matter to Baba? You know that his emphasis was on these sentences: 'I got attracted to you because of your brown eyes, beautifully framed features and exquisitely contoured body which makes men stare at you when you walk. You are also as brilliant as you are beautiful.' He was vexed. He had already assumed the role of Baba. Can all of you imagine? Our lives would be regimented from morning to evening. I know as well as you do that Nkodo will be a worse tyrant than Baba. Most tyrants in history are mediocres. They are also either of average height or below. Well, look at Baba and Nkodo, they are of the same height, barely five feet five inches tall.

What then is our future? Amina, that question is for you. Of all my sisters, it is you who will say that, despite my feelings, I should not have taken the action I have taken. Maybe you are right. Well, wait until you get to be my age. Wait until you qualify. I hope, however, that by the time you finish reading this letter, your view will support mine. I really hope so. I do not want to feel that the action I am taking will have been in vain. I hope you feel that life is worth living and not something you should endure.

As the Christians rightly pointed out, Jesus died to make us free. You can only be of use to yourself and to mankind if you are free. I mean if you are free to move, to associate, to talk, to feel inner harmony and a sense of worth. That is exactly what we have not been able to achieve.

Exactly five days ago, a meeting was held. Baba had summoned many elders and family members. Unknown to me, they agreed that I should marry the son of Alhaji Hamsu. The decision was final. You all know Alhaji Hamsu's son, the head teacher at the Islamic school. You remember how we used to make fun of him. His head, we would say, when shaved, looked like a mango seed. Then all of us would laugh. He is even older than our elder brother. He has two wives. I am supposed to be wife number three, because we are all Muslims. Baba said he comes from a noble family. Their great grandfather was also among the few who became Imam of Fullah Town Mosque. These are all the considerations. Mama unfortunately is in favour, because she has no choice.

Yes, I am to marry to Alhaji Hamsu's son, the fat man. As fat as a bundle. Fat and clumsy. He has created around him an aura of innocent vulnerability. Perhaps that is why Baba likes him as a husband for me. But despite this deception, like our Uncle Bardara, he beats his wives and children with efficient brutality.

I know that Amina and Aisha would laugh at this. You will think it is a big joke. We are so incompatible that I find it difficult to believe that Baba did this without consulting me. So I asked myself whether I was born never to make a choice, never to enjoy freedom, never to be happy.

Now I am to move to another house of exile, to serve a worse master, to be enslaved again. To say no would be to bring dishonour to the family. To accept is to compromise my freedom. So what is my choice? If I had told mother that I would not accept such a proposal, she would have ordered me to repeat 'ASTERFULAI', seven times, because I am not supposed to refuse whatever my father proposes or wishes, even as an adult. I do not know what is good for me. Women do not know what is good for them. Imagine any of you, my sisters, being a wife of Alhaji Hamsu's eldest son. Our mother married Baba because, in their time, their own concept of marriage was different from ours. Things have changed, you know. We should not be standing still while others are moving. Everybody has a right to be happy, to be free, to love someone of his or her choice, irrespective of family name or religion. It is because of these considerations that I have decided not to enter into such a relationship, organized by Baba and others. I have decided not to move from one prison house into another for the rest of my life. If this act of defiance robs me of the Kingdom of Heaven, I am prepared to explain myself to Allah the Greatest. I am sure there is justice and freedom in Heaven.

The time I have set for myself is near, the time for my departure. I know that death is painful. Many have died before me in this world because they believed in a cause. Many more will die for ideas and principles they believe in. Many have died, indeed, because they want society to unchain its victims. It is honourable to die because of such convictions. It is by the death of such people that society will be free.

As you know, sisters, for me the world has been a rugged terrain for most of my life. I hope that as a result of my action you will in time enjoy the softer terrain of this world. Do not despair, but do not be complacent either.

The moment is coming nearer. The minutes are moving faster. I am now coming to the end of my letter. The room is hot. There is a breeze but not enough to make the place cool. As usual, I can smell some of the concoctions in Baba's room. He is probably awake, making all sorts of things for his numerous clients. Or maybe he is awake, praying. He could also be just reading his Koran. The smell from his room is very fresh.

Mother is fast asleep. I am sure she hopes to see me in the morning. She will come to wake me up. She will come to say, 'N'damba my daughter, are you not going to work today?' Then I will reply, 'No, Mama, today is my day off.' Then she will go and prepare breakfast. Breakfast that is always like a feast in this house.

I am now looking at my wardrobe. It is full of all sorts of clothes. Clothes that all of you have always admired and wished to have and wear. But where do you wear them to? To the office? I look at my many trousers and shoes. They are so nice. But of what use are they if they cannot be worn in freedom? I cannot wear them in Baba's house. It would have been worse at Alhaji Hamsu's son's house. Now, as I look at them, I feel happy, I enjoy them, I enjoy the feeling of possession. It is a wonderful feeling.

Finally, my dear sisters, it is said in the Koran that there is life after death. I am not sure about that. Let us hope it is true. If it is true, then we shall meet again. It will be a wonderful reunion. I will be eager to hear the stories of your lives, to know if they were different from mine. Then we shall make merry eternally and live for ever after.

So Goodbye
N'damba

Nuruddin Farah

The Affair

Nuruddin Farah, hailed in 1999 by the *New York Review of Books* as 'the most important African novelist to emerge in the last twenty-five years', was born in 1945 in Baidoa in the Italian-administered south of Somaliland, which would be united with the British north at independence in 1960. In the 1970s he produced the first novel ever written in Somali, before going into exile (in 1974). He has lived in many other African countries where in English he has produced eight novels, beginning with *From a Crooked Rib* in 1970; *Maps* (1986) was published by Picador. His recent novel, *Secrets*, was published in 1998 and won that year's Neustadt International Prize for Literature. The first draft of his story, 'The Affair', appeared as 'The Green of my I-Ps' in *Bananas*, London, in August 1980, but it has been revised for inclusion in this anthology. He is at present based in Cape Town.

WE HAD KNOWN EACH OTHER for years, she and I. Or did we?

I would call her whenever I was in London, to give her my latest news. She talked invariably of a husband I had never met, she spoke of a daughter who had embarked on her monthly interruptions, or alluded to a teenage son who had broken an arm, or been up to some mischief. I would tell her whatever I had done since our last telephone conversation. Before I rang off, for it was always I who originated the calls, we would arrange to meet. We knew nothing would come of these arrangements, even though for some seven years we went through the motions of fixing appointments neither of us kept. Maybe arranging to meet gave our telephone conversations a meaning, I have no idea. Even so, neither reminded the other that we had met only once and that, too, so very long ago. We might have forgotten both the date and occasion of our encounter if a brochure prepared for my lecture which I delivered that evening had not existed. She had offered me a lift to my hotel, and we talked in the car until it was too late for her to come up to my room for a nightcap. At some point she referred to a husband waiting impatiently for her return. I promised I would get in touch with her again when I was in

London. The following morning I left for another city, I forget which now, and before the month ended I wrote her a postcard, with no address on it. I was transiting through Rome's Fiumicino, but didn't give her any details. However, I promised I would call her up for a chat when I was in England.

Of one thing I was certain: she was older than I. I was in my early thirties, she in her middle forties. She had a daughter who had begun to think of herself as a young woman and behaved as such, and a boy who was taking his A-levels. There may have been a third child, but I am not sure. Her husband, I now recall, had been the principal of a college she had taught at. I also remember being invited by her to their home so I could meet her entire family. But I was averse to the idea and so declined the invitation, preferring to keeping a secret line of communication open between her and myself. I feared I might not want to continue nurturing our furtive contact if I had met her husband and children. Mark you, I was not always clear in my mind if I wished to sleep with her, no. As a general rule, I avoid married women. Moreover, I sleep with women either on our second or third encounter, or I never sleep with them at all. So whenever she invited me to her home, I kept declining. Likewise, she would promise to meet me alone in London, but somehow this did not appear to happen.

Now and then I dreamt lovingly about her, many of my dreams ending in dampness. But I never told her about my dreams when we spoke on the telephone. Nor did I tell her how much I wished she and I would have a meal alone by candlelight, as I watched her hazel eyes in the dimly lit hotel room, my foot teasing her stockinged leg. I imagined a rushed scene of love-making, imagined her consulting her watch frequently, and speaking of her husband or children needing her to look after them. I hoped that, upon leaving me, she would ache for me as she swung corners, reached the blind curves, which she took in her embrace, and she would longingly think about me and of the brief love we had shared. My name, I hoped, would for ever remain an initial in her diary, a mysterious letter never to grow the flesh one associates with a name consisting of vowels and consonants and of the physicalness of a pronounceable name.

Let me add this: I have a weakness. I respond positively to women older, and in their own way, wiser than I. I think it wonderful to have a female companion capable of filling my days with stimulating discussions. Encountering these women produces in me such lusty feelings that, having been turned on, I then try to make an earthy contact of a corporeal kind.

*

I do not recall her name. But then I seldom needed to call her by name. After all, she knew my voice, which, as she put it, had in it a touch of sand, maybe because I come from the semi-arid northern reaches of the Somali peninsula. Besides, I called her when her husband was at work and her son and daughter were likely to be away from home. Only once did the husband answer. I cut off the communication, explaining, 'Wrong number, sorry!' and hung up. As for her when she picked it up, she was quick enough to sense the earthy huskiness of my voice: and she would take over and speak and speak and speak. Then she would fall silent abruptly, put a few questions to me and give me a couple of minutes to deal with them while she waited impatiently to talk. I would tell her my latest news, where I had been, what I had done with my time. I loved to hear her voice, loved to listen to her theories, of which she had legion. I believed that her head burst with the wealthy propensity of so many first-time-heard theories, and that I was of some service to her, she who was as capable of arguing about a philosophical point as she was of wiping away the drool on a teething baby's chin, but who hadn't a husband loving enough to listen to her. In the Africa you come from, she would say, paraphrasing Saint-Exupéry, '... intellectuals are kept in reserve on the shelves of the Ministry of Propaganda, like pots of jam to be eaten when the famine is over'. One day I lost my reserve and made a flippant remark: how women like her ought not to mind pots and babies, but should attend to the turn of the wind in their minds, or should follow the mirage of their elusive selves. 'You ought to be free,' I concluded, 'to breed thoughts, not only babies.' Vexed, I had no idea why, she hung up on me.

I called her up the following morning. And neither alluded to what transpired between us the day before. As though emboldened by this, I suggested that she and I spend a few days together in total isolation, 'days whose suns might brighten the smile in her eyes, and nights whose moon might moisten the runny darkness of her mascara'. She was discomfited by the changes in my attitude towards our relationship, making it clear that she didn't like the direction I was headed. I remarked a change in us both. I hung up, a little vexed, without promising to ring her up during my next visit to London. She did not augur me well in my travels, a departure from her usual farewell warm wishes. Something had taken place, but what?

When next in London I called her from Heathrow to inform her that I was going to be in the city for a week. Did she have the time to meet up? I had never known her to speak briefly and to the point, but that was what she did. I should've prepared myself for more surprises in store for me, but I didn't. Saying that her husband and children had gone off for a few days to Wales, she wondered would we have a candlelit dinner as I had often intimated? I gave her the address of where I was putting up.

*

You would think she had been starved, the clumsy way she ate fast, breathing, panting as she took mouthfuls of the food, on occasion knocking the candles over. You would think she was insane, the inordinate noises she emitted when we made love. Why was she in such haste? Was she getting things out of the way? Why couldn't she wait for me, a slow eater, to finish my meal? Why did she not show the slightest interest in talking the excitingly intelligent way she had often talked to me on the phone? I had looked forward to her coming, and had asked for room service, no expenses spared. There was a bouquet of roses, there was my gift to her too. I am inclined to be romantic and like being seduced first by the forcefulness of the woman's intelligence before I am gradually persuaded by the eloquence of a shared emotion. But that was not to be.

Her clumsiness knew no bounds, her noise recognized no limits! I wondered if anyone in the corridor might hear us. She was mechanical, she was methodical in the manner of air hostesses, too forward and too brusque for my taste. In a matter of some ten minutes, we made love twice. The first time I pretended as if I enjoyed every instant, but couldn't help betraying my unease when she went down for a second go soon after the first disaster. I caught her looking up at me, as though her hazel eyes were questioning my slackness. I chose to ignore the questions now invading my mind, and decided to shut these self-queries off in the same way as you shut off a terrible *colpo d'aria*.

Undeterred in her desire to please, she suggested we run a bath, soap each other's back, play footsie and see. I consented. Once in the bathtub together, I kept changing the subject, leading our conversation back to a real talk between two intelligent persons. I lay back in the tub, across from where she was, and was as formal as a Chinaman. For a while I thought she had regained the grace I associated with her in my mind when she spoke of the war. She had been in her teens then, and had taken an aversion to a brand of chocolate available in England in those days. Presently she stood up and, not bothering to explain, stepped out of the bath. I followed suit.

When next I stood close to her, she smelt of some French perfume sprayed as though at the wake of a disastrous moment. She sat in one of the chairs nearer the bed, looking uncomfortable. She smiled awkwardly, her eyes betraying a certain antagonism. Neither of us spoke for a quarter of an hour.

'You think I've been cheap, don't you?' she said.

I didn't speak, but waited uncomfortably, considering the implications of her remark.

'You think I've been as cheap as a whore, don't you?' she charged.

I didn't know what to say. No, let me rephrase it: I didn't know how to express the sad thoughts which had come to my mind. Fearful that she might accuse me of imposing my will upon her, I recoiled, recalling how often women were heard to advise that before engaging in love, it was best that the couple knew each other better. Men were supposed to be impatient, when it came to love-making, because they grew lustily hot where women remained cool and placid. No doubt things do not make sense when spoken in the heat of coupling, when one is wet in the groin, when one might tell any lie to arrive at a sexual truth. Before today, I had believed that women's self-restraint was greater than a man's, that they were ultimately more capable of touching the origin of their own otherness: men, who blew hot where women blew cold! In short, I was taken aback by her total abandonment of sexual protocol.

'What does that make you, if you think that I am as cheap as a whore!' she said.

I went closer to her, toweringly tall, my posture suggestive of a man unprepared to be judged by a self-condemned woman. One of her knees was now touching the floor, the other was detained in the knot the edge of the towel had rolled itself into. I had no idea what I was doing, but I extended my hand, maybe in a gesture to make peace. When it became obvious to me that she didn't want us to touch, I said, 'It takes two to make love.'

I had expected her to point out to me that I was a man, to wit a woman's imagined nightmare, the consequences of her measled fevers. This was how she put it when, within the first week of our meeting, she spoke of her husband, whom she likened to a zebra. Take away the stripes, and a zebra is but a donkey! I doubt that I understood what she had meant, only there was something highly imaginative about the way she said these things. Quite often I had replayed portions of our telephone conversations in my mind. Was this to be no more?

Now we were purposelessly silent. To alter our mood, I helped her get to her feet. Whereupon both our towels dropped to the floor. Naked, we held hands for a moment or two, kissed and touched each other here and there. In a moment, and to my relief, I was a rising fibre of muscles, and was overwhelmed with heated lust; she was warm, she was moist. We kissed a little more passionately, her eyes runny with tears, my cheeks stained with their dampness. I dragged her to bed, maybe because I believed we might make things better by overriding the disastrous consequences of the previous few minutes.

She said, 'I hardly know you.'

'Nonsense!' I said.

'And you hardly know me!'

I insisted, 'But I do.'

We made love, as though the future of our relationship depended on it. I kissed away her tears, she kissed away the unspoken dots of my misgivings. There was no need for me to worry about her untoward noises, for she made none until the end as she arrived. I stopped her mouth with my hand and she bit deeply into it.

*

I could not sleep!

She lay on her back, like an upturned wagon, her legs moving every now and then as if they were the wheels of a vehicle someone had jerked into motion. Her snore reminded me of the laboured noise a car makes when its battery is low. I got out of bed, and switched on the lights, maybe because I hoped this would wake her up. I needed a minute or two to fall asleep before she resumed her heavy snoring. No such thing. She lay on her back, dead to my awoken worries. I poked her in the ribs hard and called to her until she was awake. She sat up, startled. She squinted, the bright light hurting her eyes. 'What's the matter?' she said.

I said, 'You're snoring!'

'Snoring?' she asked, as if she didn't know the meaning of the word. 'Me, snoring?'

I nodded my head.

'But I never do,' she said. 'My husband does. I don't!'

Not knowing what to say to this, I fell silent. Then she apologized: maybe her inner worries were making unprecedented demands on her unconscious. I suggested she give me time to fall asleep myself. She acceded to my request. But no sooner had she turned her back on me than she dropped into her deeply disturbed sleep, still snoring.

The lights off, I moved about the room and busied myself with other thoughts, other errands. I gathered the food plates and left them outside the door for the hotel staff to find them there in the morning. I hung the hotel's Do-not-disturb sign on the door, rummaged in the cupboards for a blanket and a pillow and lay down on the carpeted floor, in the furthest corner from her. I could hear the orchestra of her nostrils, the A- and B-majors in her sinuses.

Now it was she towering above me, and telling me to please wake up.

I did so, wondering if I too had snored.

'I am going,' she announced. She was already dressed and ready to leave.

'What time is it?' I asked.

'My husband will be ringing,' she told me, 'and I want to be home when he does.'

From here on the uncertainties begin. Did I fall asleep after she left because I didn't wake up until after midday, on the bed, even though I had no idea how I got there? But then why did it feel as though I had slept alone all along in my hotel bed, there being no tell-tale signs of a female companion having shared the bed with me! I've often wondered if I had dreamt it all. Could it be that *she* and I never met a second time, that I had dreamed the love we made, the quarrel we had, the room service meal we ate together? Perhaps I had dreamt about her in the same way I dreamt about her for a very long time, dreams in which we made love. Presently I thought about some psycho-jargons, something to do with epiphanies, with the revenge of the unconscious on the conscious. As I once again drifted into sleep, I heard her voice insisting that I hardly knew her.

Abdourahman Waberi

The Dasbiou Mystery

Translated from the French by Anne Fuchs

Abdourahman A. Waberi was born in the former French Somaliland, Djibouti, in 1965 and, after passing his Baccalauréat, in 1985 left the miniature republic for France, where he lives in Normandy and has written a dissertation on the work of Nuruddin Farah. His first collection of short stories, *Le Pays sans Ombre* (Le Serpent à Plumes, 1994), included several spirited sketches and tales of the Horn of Africa; his contribution here is from that volume. It was followed by a further collection, his *Cahier Nomade* of 1996. When he won the Grand Prix Littéraire de l'Afrique Noire in 1997, issue number 27 of *Sépia* was dedicated to his work; in the same year he published his first novel, *Balbala*. Apart from some excerpts from his stories in *Revue Noire*, Paris (in number 4 of 1992 and numbers 23 and 24 of 1997), none of them has previously appeared in English; Anne Fuchs has translated 'The Dasbiou Mystery' especially for this book.

'All men are born mad and some remain so.'
– Samuel Beckett

AN INCREDIBLE STORY is being circulated all over the country. At Dasbiou, a quiet little village and modest railway station on the Djibouti–Addis Abeba line, the sky is always blue – it's perpetual summer, yet the inhabitants can talk of nothing but this. The stately elders who chat quietly outside the Goffané Café on the Station Square no longer know which saint (or which sayyid) to swear by. And the Dasbiou schoolboys, previously so fearless, no longer dare play football on the balding field right next to the Residency, with its sparkling colours of yellowy brown, saffron and vermilion, and the giant euphorbia trees of the Assistant Commissioner. Usually so keen on gossip, even the housewives are unforthcoming. From time to time one of them raises her arms heaven-wards, invoking I don't know which of the gods. Nobody risks speaking in public about the source of the trouble, tongues hardly wag even within the family or between friends.

Rayaleh Abaneh, the chief elder of Dasbiou, who isn't a poet, can't get over it. He could be dreaming. It's unthinkable. What an extraordinary story! In the heart of the Issa country nothing like it has ever been seen before! Ever since the train appeared, things have been happening, mon-strous things. So Rayaleh Abaneh decided to call a meeting of the Wise Men for Friday, that is exactly a week to the day after the beginning.

'According to tradition when something so untoward happens, we must gather together the forty-four wisest men. They must come from all over the country, from between the two seas, they must all come! Oh, and don't forget to mention it to His Majesty the Ogass, may God protect his venerable person.'

This is how, for the last two days, Chief Rayaleh Abaneh had been giving firm orders to his young lieutenants: Dirir the schoolteacher, Saad the postmaster and Guedid the khat salesman. The latter, as a great traveller, had been entrusted with informing the Wise Men inhabiting the west of the country. He was to take the first train and would stop off only where one of the forty-four Wise Men lived, in the towns or villages such as Aïchaa, Hadagalla, Harawa, Milleh, Chinileh, Awash, Hourso ... and Dire-Dawa itself, the residence of His Majesty the Ogass.

The two friends, Dirir and Saad, had the easiest job. Their mission was to travel round the Republic of Djibouti and its main towns: Ali-Sabieh, Dikhil, Tadjourah, Obock, Arta, Ouéah and finally the capital, Djibouti itself.

Have I already said that the whole country had its eyes fixed on Dasbiou, and that one of the repercussions was a renewal of interest in the place?

'Dasbiou! Dasbiou! What a pretty name!' murmured with delight the citizens of the capital, most of whom had ignored the very existence of this hamlet, as isolated before as an Arabian douar, or as a pebble on the moon.

As foreseen, on the Friday the forty-four Wise Men were all present for this much awaited meeting. They all expressed the desire to get on with the most serious business. Enough of 'salamalec' greetings, they had to get down to their task! Many arrived on the train and others by buses specially chartered for the event. Two or three arrived as in the past, leading their caravans. For others it was a case of improvisation, which meant they had to come on foot. Finally one of them, a former immigrant worker from the Gulf, now the businessman in a hurry that he was, disembarked from his private helicopter. Most of the forty-four Wise Men sported fine beards, reddish because of the henna (which is no longer associated only with women), were well over sixty and distinguished themselves through their infinite knowledge of custom and usage. They venerated, so it was said, the secular harmony between the visible world and that other one, invisible, unknown or simply forgotten by mortal men. Thus the forty-four Wise Men met the okal, the village elder of Dasbiou, the much respected and no less wise Rayaleh Abaneh, and held their council under that famous tree of Galilee, an acacia. After a long formal speech interspersed with greetings and handshakes, Rayaleh Abaneh as master of ceremonies revealed what could only be called the mystery of Dasbiou.

'Alhamdoullilleh! I shall begin at the beginning as our very holy Koran requires of us, so most Wise Men, lend me your ears and hold your breath, for up until now you have never heard such a story, you may take my word for it . . . (silence) . . . But you will have to judge for yourselves.'

Upon these words one of the Wise Men, Awaleh Absieh from Holl-Holl, I think, made this clever remark which has since been elevated to the rank of proverb: 'Honourable Wise Man,' said he to Rayaleh Abaneh, 'if we are all assembled under the tree of Galilee, it is because there is seldom rain without clouds.'

'Yes, there is indeed a viper in the bushes,' the Chief agreed calmly, before immediately continuing: 'Make of it what you will. Here is the story exactly as God willed it to happen right in front of my door, in the very heart of Dasbiou and not far from the mosque . . . Soubhan' Allah, isn't that already a sign in itself?' He raised his arms to indicate his helplessness.

Straining their ears and fixing their eyes on the horizon, the Wise Men kept listening to Rayaleh Abaneh, who was indeed a fine storyteller.

'A young Bedouin clansman of mine, Jilaal Okieh, came to Dasbiou to see his brother Assoweh, a civil servant who was said to be a man of integrity, and an important person in the town; so far there is nothing strange, as Jilaal is a young man as straightforward as you and me, a bachelor and a God-fearing camel driver. He led a wandering life following his herd of dromedaries, certainly a life of poverty, but also full of poetry and freedom . . .'

Rayaleh Abaneh cleared his throat and went on: 'Jilaal was a courageous camel driver, a soldier of valour, happy to be leading an ascetic life like that of our ancestors...'

He paused, pretended to be at a loss for words, and after a short interval began again with relish: 'Only once he set foot in our peaceful town, he was never the same again; Jilaal was betwitched by a djinn and, can you believe it, he had the same symptoms as Aïdid Sanbour, the one who died of suffocation. He had hardly begun to look for his brother when, so they say, he felt signs of weariness and irritability, as well as the signs of suffocation. He told himself he could snatch some sleep, if only for a few seconds, under the old laurel tree in front of the station. After a refreshing nap, he would go off to see his brother Assouweh, his sister-in-law Ambaro and their last-born, Diraneh.'

A bit further on, a few yards away from the gathering, the young village lads were playing at policemen and robbers. The former, holding in their hands sheep's jawbones to imitate pistols, were running after the others and shouting: 'Stop! Stop! Put your hands up!'

At this same moment, Rayaleh Abaneh was holding the Wise Men spellbound: 'Just try and imagine what followed ... No, no, don't say anything because you are not going to believe me ... Well, here goes. When Jilaal woke up, he no longer knew a single word of his own language. Don't you find that strange?' Here and there whispers could be heard. The audience was visibly troubled. Many of them, not able to follow the thread of the story related by the okal, were turning over a string of questions.

'Do you mean to say that he had lost the use of his tongue?' ventured the Wise Man with the peppercorn hair, the one who had been an infantryman during the last colonial war.

'Honourable Wise Man, I never said that: it's only that Jilaal no longer speaks the same language as all of us, but otherwise, as far as talking goes, he talks all right – but very strangely indeed!'

In the living memory of the Issa patriarchs there had never been such a complete mystery. Who had ever heard of a Bedouin old enough to get married being suddenly struck down with an illness so incredible that he forgot his mother tongue? The only one he knew. And what the deuce of a language does he replace it with? He who'd never been to school, not even to the Koranic one!

'By Almighty Allah, what on earth is this language that has bewitched him?' shouted a Wise Man, stiffly clad in a red-wine-coloured caftan.

And Rayaleh Abaneh had to admit his ignorance. 'In Dasbiou nobody can understand his gobbledygook, not even Dirir, the schoolteacher.'

Another Wise Man, who until then had been muttering Paternosters with his rosary in his right hand, threw himself into the discussion, which had now become quite heated: 'Sallawaad, it's a sign from the Spirits! By Abdelkadir Jilani, we mustn't take these things lightly! This man is possessed, and my words are those of a believer who says his prayers five times a day!'

A grumbling undercurrent ran through the assembly, murmurs rising to the heavens. Rayaleh Abaneh seemed to have lost some of his loquaciousness. None the less, the village lads continued with their games.

After the meeting of the Wise Men, the Assistant Commissioner of Dasbiou asked for the help of a few friends to investigate this affair which was tormenting the villagers. An inspector from the Crime Squad, who had been rushed in, found at least part of the key to the mystery. This civil servant, a former ethnology student at the Catholic University of Ghent in Belgium, managed to find out where Jilaal's new language came from. For the inspector there was no doubt at all: this man was speaking in French Creole. How could this possibly be? And while he was at it, why not in Afar, in Amharic or Arabic? And it was quite unbelievable, as Jilaal had never even set foot in a big town, Creole or not.

The Assistant Commissioner, always very active when he could turn public affairs to his advantage, had all the volunteers who could speak Creole come in from the capital. A schoolteacher who was a Freemason, originally from Fort-de-France in Martinique; a physiotherapist from Guyana; a cook from the island of Réunion who was probably of Tamil origin; a diplomat from Haiti, mad about Césaire's poetry and married to a local girl; a soldier from Guadeloupe, a fine figure of a man, native of Gosier; and finally a few young men who shyly admitted that their knowledge of the matter was rather limited.

The diagnosis was as dry as a weather bulletin: Jilaal spoke perfect Creole; a rich and colourful Creole, neither too technical, nor too abstract. They were, however, able to trace a few archaic and even anachronistic expressions.

'Ici mêm cé komun Vauclin' – those were Jilaal's first words.

All excited, Wenceslas, the native of Martinique, was overjoyed to translate: 'It's unbelievable! He claims he comes from Vauclin – a tiny district in Martinique,' he added with precision.

The crowd were turned to stone.

Rayaleh Abaneh, his eyes all bloodshot, suddenly started threatening him: 'JI-LAAL O-KIEH, when are you going to decide to talk like everybody else?'

The poor person so addressed, who was neither a prophet nor a poet, kept silent.

To make quite sure, the native of Martinique posed one last question: '*Sa ou fé?*'

'*Moin la ka bé.*'

'He says he is quite well,' said the enthusiastic translator.

'*Mwâ-ikô shuval, la ka galopé, mwâ veni la Matinik,*' hummed Jilaal to himself.

'I come from Martinique, I have galloped like a horse.'

Without listening to Wenceslas's wonderful translations any longer, Rayaleh, in a dreadful rage, spat on the ground and concluded acrimoniously: 'This man is mad!'

'Mad! Mad!' chorused the Wise Men, who were not all without guile.

'Mad! Mad!' repeated the crowd.

The person concerned, who hadn't picked up a single word of their conclusions, went on singing:

> *Shuval la ka galopé*
> *Shuval la ka kuri*
> *Shuval la ka volé*
> *Mwâ shapé adâ soleye*
> *Mwâ volé â la nuit...*

The council of Wise Men no longer served any purpose. The patriarchs returned each to his own business. The Assistant Commissioner invited the Creole community to his own house. During the meal only Wenceslas appeared to be deep in his linguistic dreams. After a brief exchange of courtesies, they left as quietly as they had arrived only five hours earlier.

At Dasbiou life went back to normal. Except that on the Station Square, in front of the Goffané Café, Jilaal Okieh hums his perpetual refrain:

> *Lagié mwé, lagié mwé,*
> *Vauclin sa paï*
> *Matinik sa paï mwâ*
> *Mwâ chéché soleye...*

> (Let me be, let me be
> Vauclin is my home
> Martinique is my country
> I'm looking for the sun...)

Idris Youssouf Elmi

He Has Come Back

Translated from the French by Chris Dunton

Idris Youssouf Elmi was born in Djibouti in 1961, self-taught to become a student in Montpellier; he has been an educator in his home country and presently teaches French in a secondary school in Paris. With L'Harmattan there he has published poems and a first collection of some fifteen sketches and short stories, *La Galaxie de l'Absurde* (1997), from which 'He Has Come Back' is taken.

Chris Dunton, himself a short story writer, is Head of English at the National University of Lesotho in Roma, and undertook this translation for the purposes of this collection.

> Look at this landscape carefully, so as to be sure to recognize it, in case some day you travel to Africa, into the desert. And if you happen to pass by here, I beg you, don't hurry on, but wait a little while, just under the star. Then if a little man appears, one who laughs, who has golden hair, who doesn't answer your questions, you will know exactly who he is. And then, be so kind as to comfort me: write to me quickly, that he has come back...
>
> Antoine de Saint-Exupéry, *The Little Prince* (1944)

SO HOW DO THINGS STAND NOWADAYS? We have come to a point where our planet, the seventh, looks as if it were number eight. The earth is simply unrecognizable to the eyes of the Little Prince.

He has come back, by the way. Once more he meets our kings, geographers, businessmen, the drunks and the conceited ones – in other words, any number of grown-ups. But since his last visit the number of these grown-ups has tripled. With the result that the Little Prince no longer recognizes the earth. Only the face of the desert is unchanged, he thinks to himself.

The Little Prince has come back. Even if the grown-ups don't believe me, even if they take up all that room, even if they see themselves as being so important, even if they visit my place without wishing to take account of the mood I'm in, even if they decide on my behalf what rain and what fine weather I'm going to get, I know how to tame their behaviour, not just because they're grown-up, but because, seeing that they are handicapped by their size, I'm able to describe the contours of their navels.

A faint smile on the lips of the Little Prince says to me: 'Hey, nomad, you are used to endurance, take heed of the strength and the message of that little sand-coloured beast, the fox – so lean, and hungrier than a louse on a bald pate.'

The desert fox holds a secret unknown to the grown-ups hereabouts and elsewhere. See with the heart. 'What is essential is invisible,' says the fox.

'Now tell me why the planet earth has changed its appearance,' asks the Little Prince.

'I think the earth is still the planet of all those people who think they're grown-up, who imagine they alone are in possession of the Universal Truth.'

But as the Little Prince never lets pass a question he has asked, he raises it once again.

'I don't know,' I tell him.

'Well then, why should you seem distressed and bad-tempered?' the Little Prince asks me.

'Well, I'm fed-up because at least you've made the acquaintance of a king, a conceited man, a drunkard, a businessman. Myself, I'm close to becoming just a hopeless, cack-handed fiddle-faddler, in spite of myself. So I keep quiet. I watch, I take note. Sprung from parents – "the one a painter of seascapes by vocation, the other, through dereliction, a drinker of wind" – you could say I live on my own planet P. Beyond that, to me everything else is just nothingness and desert.'

'Desert,' says the Little Prince.

'Yes, nothingness and this desert.'

'But what do you have against the desert?' the Little Prince responds, astonished.

'Nothing,' I say. 'Only, how can I think of remaking the world from here?'

'Then you must be a grown-up.'

'Yes, a grown-up, just like those you've met since you set out on your journey. I am he who doesn't know that in this nothingness, faced with this desert and such unhappiness, he who strikes the wind with the waves of the sea and doesn't know that people who live round about here are proud of very little, of nothing, of the void, and that his planet P, lacking all modesty and even honesty, doesn't interest them at all. Enthroned on his planet, he just thinks of ordering "a general to flit from one flower to another like a butterfly, or to write a tragedy, or to change into a sea-bird."'

'And if that general weren't to obey a given order, what would you do?' asks the Little Prince, still astonished, thinking of that planet inhab-ited by the king who, for his part, knew perfectly well that authority rests first and foremost on reason . . .

'He's never put that question to himself,' I tell him.

'Don't you think perhaps he might be right? And what if he departed from the principle, like king, like people,' the Little Prince retorts.

I open my mouth, but find nothing with which to reply.

My Ego rises before me. The more headway I make, the more complex the Little Prince becomes. *Dico ergo sum.* I am about to seek notes of music in a place I have never been, his eyes are an air from the *Qaaci*, an aria drawn from the lute, his mouth a Sudanese flute. I blend all the phrases and all modes, and I let other tempi and other sounds wind like a creeper around my violins.

But I shall tell you what my imagination suggests to me. It's possible that those men have taken fright. You see, the Road to Gaza is a danger-ous one.

'What happens to me now hardly matters. We have difficult journeys before us, Little Prince. But it matters little what happens to me now. I have reached the height of absurdity. And I am no longer so anxious. Like everyone, I should like to live a long time. Without a plan. Without assistance. I should like to touch the depths of profundity. I should like to draw the threads of my life together, to gather stone after stone to fill the void, to rise up once again on my own to the plane of human dignity. Longevity has its price. The inhabitant of planet P forgets the General George C. Marshall plan. Let him know it's hardly a matter of concern to me now. The truth is within my grasp. I want only that Allah's will be done: He who has already bestowed on me the heart of a human being. And I looked around me. And on my mother's back I learnt not to fawn and flatter, in case I lost my honour in the eyes of men. I am not troubled by anything. Well yes, by one thing. By the future of the occupant of planet P. What is such a demagogy worth?'

Understanding not one word of all this, the Little Prince says to me: 'Could you rather tell me a story, please.'

'With pleasure,' I say.

*

Long ago, a long, long time ago, a big mango tree – a very big one – towered over the region of my schizophrenia. People could only gaze at its fully ripened fruits. Children sang under the tree. One day a stranger arrived in the land, claiming to be steeped in knowledge.

Among the young men a thrilling desire for consciousness was born. Not a trace of those steps, forward, backwards, so often taken by their forefathers. The stranger proposed to lead them in the direction proper to the human condition.

Some months afterwards, sensing his powers slipping away from him, this expert stranger insisted upon a great effort of thinking and its meticulous application, the implications of which I did not really grasp at all.

He demanded, then, that everyone come in under the big mango tree and pile one on top of the other, so as to be able to pluck those so coveted delights. One above the other and himself at the very top. And then the way to the secret danced in the heat. But suddenly one man among the heap of men resisted and pulled out. Our usual Third World, hands and mouths so nearly filled with the so long forbidden fruit, crashed to the ground.

*

'But tell me the fate of the man who pulled out?' the Little Prince interrupts. 'Was he a martyr?'

'In your opinion, Little Prince, can that be what martyrs strive for? And does greatness really lie in failing to do your duty?'

'I don't know, I really don't know,' repeats the Little Prince.

He has come back, but now he is sad to see that humans remain such great weighty beings, whether they are kings or conceited men, drunkards, businessmen, party leaders or geographers or self-serving strategists.

He has come back, but he will leave again without notice.

Francis Bebey

If Only the Gauls

Translated from the French by Norman Strike

Francis Bebey, poet and traditional musician, was born in 1929 in Douala, Cameroon – the country that joins West Africa to Central Africa – in the French-speaking part of the republic, united with the English-speaking part since 1972. He has worked for UNESCO in Paris as a broadcaster and head of musical programmes. One of his several novels is *The Ashanti Doll*, first published in Yaoundé in 1973, a classic about African family tensions. In his collection of some thirty short fictional pieces, *La Lune dans un Seau Tout Rouge* (Hatier, 1989), he draws a distinction between 'dicontes' (tales derived from the oral tradition, delivered orally) and 'diracontes' (stories written by particular authors which may later be read out aloud). His sketch, 'If Only the Gauls', is a witty confounding of the differences between the two modes.

Norman Strike was educated at the University of Aix-en-Provence and has been head of the Department of Romance Languages at UNISA in Pretoria, South Africa, where he also taught French translation. His version of Bebey, and the following one of Dongala, were undertaken especially for this collection.

AT SCHOOL THAT DAY our teacher had spent the morning telling us of a most interesting episode in the life of what our history book called 'our ancestors the Gauls'. A treat!

The Gallic tribe, led by Vercingetorix, lived on the plain. A few miles further on stood the village of the Romans. Its chief, Caesar, possessed a magic telescope in which he could see the entire world. Herveus the ambitious, thinking it was a television camera, went and stood in front of it, to be seen.

'Get out of the way, you fool!' cried Caesar, who was scanning the horizon. 'I want to know if those damned Gauls are still there.'

*

If the Gauls had only known
They wouldn't have stayed on the plain
If our blond ancestors the Gauls
Had been smart like us ...

*

Caesar is looking through his telescope. And what does he see? Over there, in the distance, Vercingetorix and all his men are holding a tribal palaver.

'The Gauls are still on the plain,' says Caesar with a smile. 'Today's the day we're going to capture them.'

And the whole Roman tribe approves. 'Yes, Caesar! Ave, Caesar!'

The crowd was shouting for joy.

*

Now, the Gauls don't know that Caesar can see them in his magic telescope, right? They calmly carry on cooking up their little plot against the Romans. Seeing the danger they're in, and carried away by the teacher's story, I shout to the Gauls: 'For God's sake! What's wrong with you, staying there on the plain! Run for your lives, get out at once! The Romans are coming to get you!'

I yelled so loud that our teacher punished me for uncontrolled babbling during his class. Too bad, because I just kept on thinking that ...

*

If the Gauls had only known
They wouldn't have stayed on the plain
If our blond ancestors the Gauls
Had been smart like us
They'd have rented an aeroplane
– With a credit card it's easy –
They'd have beat it to Africa
– Ah yes, now that's a great idea –
Hidden in the forest like Tarzan
Bet Caesar would never have spotted them there.

*

Caesar and his men arrived like a tornado in the rainy season and they captured the Gauls, every last one of them. But I had warned them, right?

'Right.'

They led off the whole Gallic tribe in chains to another village. You should have seen it! Vercingetorix taken prisoner with all his dignitaries: Grumpix, Patientix, Sleepix, Optimix, Negatorix, Pessimix and many others.

'Hey! D'you hear that?'

That was the day the whole sky came down on their heads. Dear oh dear!...

'Dear oh dear!...'

*

> If the Gauls had only known
> They wouldn't have stayed on the plain
> If our blond ancestors the Gauls
> Had been smart like us
> They'd have rented an aeroplane
> – The Swiss could easily have lent them the cash! –
> They'd have beat it to Africa
> – With Air Belgix of course –
> Hidden in the forest like Tarzan
> Bet Caesar would never have spotted them there.
>
> If the Gauls had only known
> They wouldn't have stayed on the plain
>
> But what the hell were they doing on the plain
> Those wretched Gauls?
> Instead of rushing off to hide in Afrix!

*

Laughter.

The end.

Emmanuel Dongala

The Ceremony

Translated from the French by Norman Strike

Emmanuel Boundzéki Dongala was born in 1941, with a Congolese father and a mother from the Central African Republic. He was brought up in the (former French) Congo, went to study science in France and the United States. His reputation as one of Africa's leading satirists began with his debut novel in French (in 1973), but for English-language readers it was his story, 'Jazz and Palm Wine' (first published in *Présence Africaine* in 1970), that first made his mark (in Willfried Feuser's anthology of Francophone work, published by Longman in 1981, which used the same title, *Jazz and Palm Wine*). Another noted story of his, 'The Man', has been translated by Clive Wake (for Chinua Achebe and C. L. Innes's *The Heinemann Book of Contemporary African Short Stories*, 1992). From *Jazz et Vin de Palme et Autres Nouvelles* (Hatier, 1982) also comes 'The Ceremony', his withering report on the People's Republic of the Congo's twenty years of socialist rule – and one of the major pieces in this collection, not previously published in English. His latest novel was put out by Le Serpent à Plumes in 1998.

YOU MUST UNDERSTAND I'm a modest militant and, I could even add – if it's not contradicting the quality I have just mentioned – a model militant, in both my public and my private life. The ceremony was to commence at nine o'clock sharp, but I was already there at seven thirty. Of course I'm not saying I would have minded if the Secretary General of our sole trade union had noticed that I was there before anyone else, ready to give a hand here and there, to straighten up the staff of the red flag, or dust off the portrait of our great immortal leader so ignominiously assassinated by the forces of evil, namely imperialism and its lackeys, or even just to help spruce up the red upholstered chair upon which the Chairman of the Central Committee of our sole party – who is also the President of the Republic, the Head of State, the Leader of the Cabinet, the Chief of the

Armed Forces, the close companion and worthy successor of our founding leader now immortalized since his cowardly assassination – was to put his revolutionary backside. No, I wouldn't have minded; but, well, I was there early just because I am a sincere militant applying for Party membership. Needless to say, I agree entirely with the radio communiqué which reported that the ceremony would be a political event. Ah, but I see I haven't yet told you about that historic event. Damn, I'll never manage to organize my thoughts scientifically the way we're supposed to, according to our revolution in its dialectic. I'll get to it now.

You know that, in order to combat international imperialism and its lackeys, we need self-managed, self-centred development (I learnt all these terms by heart because to get into the Party we are asked loads of questions about those things so that they can see if we are real communists and know our Marxism-Leninism); now, to achieve this self-contented – I mean self-centred – development, we have to combat the democratic – sorry, bureaucratic – bourgeoisie (excuse me, I've learnt so many things in such a short time that sometimes it all gets mixed up in my head). To that end, competent red workers must be appointed to manage our factories. In all modesty, I believe that I am competent because I have been a watchman at our factory for more than ten years, even though after all these years I earn only fifteen thousand CFA francs a month. And in all those ten years no theft with breaking and entering was ever committed, by day or by night. Obviously there was some misappropriation of funds and once the factory was even closed down for a whole year because the former manager, a member of the autocratic – sorry, bureaucratic – bourgeoisie had stolen two million three hundred thousand francs and seventy centimes reserved for the purchase of new machines and spare parts for the factory. He had built himself a seaside villa. But our avant-garde Party, in its vigilance, took harsh measures: he is no longer our manager here, he is now only the manager of a sub-branch somewhere, although, for humanitarian reasons, his villa was not seized (he has ten children, poor man, and is the Under-Secretary General of our sole trade union). My honesty compels me to be frank with you and tell you that I too, in a moment of counter-revolutionary weakness, embezzled national property; but today my conscience is clear for I have paid my debt to society and the Party. Indeed, after a year in prison and after paying back the three tins of sardines, one of which had gone off, that I had 'borrowed' one day when there was nothing in the house for the kids to eat, I was granted amnesty on the day of the inauguration of our new President who re-established democracy and at the same time freed several political prisoners arrested at the time of the last attempted coup d'état, the one before the successful coup which brought our Leader to power. But I digress. I was saying that I had been a watchman for ten years without a single case of theft with breaking and entering. To my mind, that was proof enough: I was competent. All I still needed to be was red.

In the beginning, when they asked us to be red, I didn't know whether they meant the colour of our clothes or our skin. You know, I left school after the second grade and I don't always understand the niceties of political language all that well. Nevertheless, through scientific reasoning, I ended up eliminating skin colour for, as I learnt in the evening classes I attended to improve my chances of being appointed manager, only Indians, the Amerindians, not to be confused with the Indians of India, have red skin, and those creatures do not occur in our part of the world; so it had to mean the colour of our clothing. Moreover you will recall that if those people are called Indians, it is due to the Eurocentric ignorance of Christopher Columbus who, having sailed westward to discover India so as to increase the capitalist and monopolist profits of the bureaucratic bourgeoisie, landed on America and its Indians. But let me continue. So they meant the colour of our clothing, and anyway it would have been racist to consider an individual's skin colour or tribal origin for admission to the Party.

For a month I wore only red. I came to work in a red shirt, red trousers, a red scarf; only my shoes were brown because I couldn't find red ones. When the Secretary General of our trade union, who is a member of the Central Committee of the Party, visited the factory, I always made a point of blowing my nose with a scarlet handkerchief to show him that all my clothing was red. In our country the Security Services, that is to say our CIA and our KGB, often use women of somewhat doubtful morals to extract information from persons under surveillance; well, every time I discovered that one of them was a State spy, I would do my best to sleep with her, always taking care to undress with the light on so that she would see my underpants were red! I wasn't cheating on my wife out of debauchery or immorality but as a sacrifice to further the cause and redness of the revolution. I once even managed to have red eyes after drinking a few glasses of red wine and exposing my eyes to cigarette smoke. So everything about me was red. I even had my bike painted red.

To tell the truth, I didn't know why they attached so much importance to the colour red. Personally, I prefer the restful green of our forests, or

the turquoise blue of the sky which soothes body and mind after the
agitation before the storm. Sure, I like the bright red of the flamboyants
when their flowers suddenly burst forth at the end of the dry season, or
rather at the beginning of the rainy season; but those flowers are beautiful
because they break the dull evergreen monotony of the rain forests and
also because they only last for a short time. But let's leave aside the
subjunctive – I mean the subjective – let's stick to being objective; it was
worthwhile liking red, since if I were identified with that colour, in
addition to my competence, I would be appointed manager of the factory
and, just think of it, my salary would go up from fifteen thousand francs
a month to three hundred thousand! Oh, but I'll tell you straight away
that the money side of it didn't interest me in the least, for I am a modest
militant, exemplary and sincere.

During the month when I was red, or at least thought I was, I noticed
a few discreet smiles whenever I passed, an occasional mocking wink
heavy with innuendo, bizarre questions and riddles like 'What has red
eyes and rides a red bicycle?', as though they were making fun of me.
They *were* making fun of me! I saw red when I finally realized that being
red had nothing to do with the colour of your clothes, but that it was in
your heart you were supposed to be red. And all that time that I had been
going to such insanely crimson expense they had left me in my ignorance!
They were jealous of me, of course; but, I said to myself, I'll get them back
one day when, proven red and competent, I'm their boss.

So you were supposed to be red in your heart; that seemed idiotic to
me, as everybody's heart is red and we all have red blood, even inver-
tebrate – sorry, inveterate – reactionaries who are all theocratic, no,
autocratic, no, bureaucratic bourgeois (excuse me, really, I'm tired and
I'm confusing everything after this sleepless night). Finally, after several
inquiries and much investigation – President Mao said that he who is
denied speech has no right to an inquiry – I understood that to be red
meant to be a good militant, a good Marxist-Leninist communist. You
understand, I didn't want the position of manager to slip through my
fingers on account of something so trivial. To go up from fifteen thousand
francs a month to three hundred thousand was not to be scoffed at: the
good life, women, the car I've always dreamed of, a two-seater Triumph
convertible like that of the comrade Minister of Propaganda and Ideology;
of course, I hasten to add at once, being the good, honest, modest and
model militant that I am, the money and material possessions were not
my main motive.

I tell you in all militant simplicity, and you can check this out with my fellow workers at the factory, I was a true defender of the faith, I mean of the right line. In our country, there are evil beings that we call sorcerers; they travel by night disguised as birds such as owls or nightjars or as weird animals like chameleons and tortoises to go and kill people by 'eating' their souls. To protect ourselves against these evil spirits, we cover ourselves with powerful fetishes such as panthers' teeth, leopards' claws or charms sold by Senegalese hawkers. This we call being armoured. As for me, let me assure you at once that since some members of the Party were expelled for occult practices and fetishism I am against God, for religion is the whisky ... the hemp ... the podium ... the opinion ... the odium of the masses. It was hard losing the faith, for God had helped me a lot in the difficult times of my life but, well, I had to choose and choose I did. So, to be armoured, I remained faithful to the symbols of the Party; on my red shirt I had stapled a medallion bearing the effigy of the founder of our Party; on the front mudguard of my red bike I had stuck a full-length colour portrait of the present Leader of our revolution, and on the rear mudguard the coat of arms of our historic Party composed of a crossed hoe and machete, garlanded with palm fronds on a yellow background. With that protection, with such a talisman, I couldn't see how the reactionist demons could succeed in tempting me. My zeal was genuine, believe me when I tell you that money and other material possessions were not my main motive.

I then decided to study the word of Marxengels and apply for Party membership. All modesty aside, I have to admit to being gifted with a slightly above-average intelligence for, in spite of my limited education, I succeeded in mastering the Party terminology in one week: every day I listened to the journalists on radio and television because in our country, as the comrade Minister of Information and Agitation has so ably explained, journalists were not there to inform us and analyse events as they perceived them, they were mere propagandists of the right line, that is to say Party parrots. I learned everything by heart including the slogans which papered our walls, such as 'Life is productivity', 'Censorship of certain ideas is essential to the survival of our revolution.' What was important was not really to understand what it all meant, but to come out with one of those ready-made phrases at the right moment, either to get yourself noticed or to confound a contradictor. You need only say to him, for example: 'Comrade, your attitude is that of a counter-revolutionary saboteur' and you'll see him tremble, because he is already imagining the State Security agents hot on his heels.

I also learned many new terms and believe me it wasn't always easy to understand what they meant. For instance, it took me a while to fathom what a member of the bureaucratic bourgeoisie was. At first I thought it was a good thing, you had to be one to live well; they said on the radio that a bureaucratic bourgeois was an individual who drove luxury cars, owned at least one beautiful villa, had lots of money, etc., etc. What fooled me was that, looking around me, I saw that all our ministers, our political big shots, the members of the Central Committee of our glorious Party, all of them had air-conditioned luxury cars, their wives and children did not bake in the sun waiting for some unpredictable bus in order to get to market or to school. Their celebrations were awash with champagne, they preferred imported drinks to the local ones, etc. So I thought all our revolutionary leaders were members of the bureaucratic bourgeoisie and naturally I wished to become part of them.

It was only later that someone explained to me that to be a bureau-cratic bourgeois was a bad thing. Finally, thanks to my intelligence, which I mentioned to you earlier, I found an easy solution to this thorny problem. If you have in front of you two people who both own luxury cars, sumptuous villas, have champagne dinners, etc., this is the infallible method: the one who is a member of our sole and historic avant-garde Party is a 'top-ranking' revolutionary and everything he possesses is but the material base essential to his task; the one who does not belong to the Party is, on the other hand, a bureaucratic bourgeois, a comprador and exploiter of the people from whom he has stolen everything he possesses.

From time to time, as you have no doubt realized, all these phrases, all these slogans, these terms learnt all at once, cause a bottleneck in my brain, but when all is said and done, a bottleneck followed by a slight headache is better than missing a promotion from fifteen thousand to three hundred thousand francs a month, isn't it?

But – surprise! surprise! – the new manager of the factory was appointed, and it was not me! It was not even someone from inside our company! They really take us for fools, I tell you. After drumming it into us for months that the new manager would be a worker from our factory, someone red and competent, they go and catapult an outsider into the manager's post, an individual who is a proletarian, they say, because he is from the country and a member of the Party. Shit! I'm also from the country! In Africa we are all farmers' children or grandchildren! But wait a minute, don't go thinking I was jealous because I hadn't been appointed, no, I am honest and after my brief disappointment, I analysed the situation and saw that the Party was right, the man was competent: not only was he a chap that the President knew well, but he also came from the same ethnic group. Thus he could be nothing but competent. And so it was that, to prove my revolutionary sincerity and that I harboured no ill feelings, I was there at seven thirty to attend his inauguration ceremony, which was only due to begin at nine.

But I see that if I have been speaking at great length about myself, I have not yet told you about the ceremony. It was an historic event for, to inaugurate the new manager's taking office and to show how much importance the revolution attached to the smooth running of our factories, the President of the Republic, who is also Chairman of the Central Committee of the Party, Leader of the Cabinet, Chief of the Armed Forces, etc., insisted on attending in person, in front of the assembled lifeblood of the nation.

The first to arrive were the professors. I don't know whether they are part of the bourgeois commodores, I mean compradors, but they were all there in their blue and wine-red togas. The professors were people I had always admired. Now I admire them less since the day they allowed themselves to be publicly insulted by a student representative who, at a formal academic opening ceremony, had referred to them in his official speech as a class sympathetic to reactionary bourgeois ideas and activities. None of them had dared to respond. Our professors have become like everybody else, militarized and officious, repeating the same slogans as us, the workers and farmers; they too hang on to their bread and butter. Mind you, I judge them less severely now that I'm about to be red, as today I understand that, to succeed in climbing the steep paths to redness, you must first drain your personality of all colour.

And so the professors stood there in their robes and headgear in the hot tropical sun; there were no chairs for them, there were only a few chairs in the shade for the invited VIPs. Next, the workers arrived in buses provided for them by the State, as it was they who were the lifeblood of the nation, the proletarian revolution-makers, and I hasten to point out, lest there be any misunderstanding, that I consider myself one of them. Then came the women and their revolutionary movement, the funeral undertakers and their association of revolutionary funeral parlours ... in a word, all those who make up the lifeblood of the nation.

By this time it was already ten fifteen. The ceremony was supposed to have started at nine o'clock sharp, but you know in Africa time is always fast; hurry as we may, time is always ahead of us. The workers, who were getting tired, had spread themselves out on the grass, in the shade of the palms and ravenalas adorning the square; the revolutionary and funereal undertakers had taken refuge inside their black van. Everybody had found some or other form of temporary relief from the heat of the sun and the cramps in their weary legs ... except the professors who, mindful of the dignity expected of intellectuals and the nation's elite, remained standing in the scorching equatorial sun, sweating profusely under the heavy cloth of their medieval togas. As for me, I slipped into the shade of the shelter reserved for the VIPs, pretending to straighten a chair here, a flag there, and making myself sort of indispensable.

At ten forty-five the car of the comrade Secretary General of the sole trade union appeared, led in by two motorcycles. I can tell you in all sincerity that I was the one who started clapping; the others, including the new manager for whom this event had been organized, only started well after me. Better still, with the advantage of my ten years as a watchman and knowing my way perfectly around the premises, I was the first to reach his car. I opened the door for him, he shook my hand before any others and so thoroughly that the photographer of our Party's revolutionary newspaper in which only the truth is printed, in his surprise, thinking I was a VIP, took several shots.

Perhaps I unintentionally held the comrade Secretary's hand a little longer than necessary, long enough for the photographer to frame his shot properly; but you can take the word of a sincere, honest and modest militant: I did not do it for myself but in the interest of the revolution, so that it would be clear to all that our comrade Secretary General, although very high up in the country's political hierarchy, did not hesitate to rub shoulders, converse and live with the masses, even with the most obscure little proletarian worker.

He went and took his seat; everything was ready, we were only still waiting for the Leader of our revolution.

All of a sudden we heard the sirens. The Leader was arriving. Much fuss and commotion. People applauded as they rushed towards the avenue from which he would emerge. As for me, as a dignified and competent militant, I stayed where I was, for I had managed to get myself put in charge of the microphone, that is to say I was the man who had to raise or lower it according to the height of the speaker. They had first wanted to entrust this task to a State Security agent, that is the secret police, but I finally convinced the factory supervisor of the ceremony that this job should be given to an insider, a longstanding model worker in the company, so as to respect the spirit of the occasion. I had no trouble persuading him for he was a reasonable man although, in the end, seeing his hesitation, I had to slip him a thousand franc note, not to grease his palm, but simply to thank him for giving up his time; besides, I had often noticed that here, in our revolutionary country, for some reason people were much more diligent when you slipped them a little something. You are wondering why holding the mike was so important? Well, because when you're in charge of the mike, you go up before each speaker, you raise, you lower the mike and, if necessary, test it. Suppose it's the President of the Republic himself: if you're smart about it, you can see that you get photographed with him. Just think of it, being in the same photo as the Supreme Comrade! You tell me a better way to get noticed! This is not opportunism or an anarcho-exploito-bureaucrato-situationist attitude. Put yourself in my place: I was competent, I was red, all I still needed was to be noticed. But how? By being a militant, naturally. Well, raising and lowering the Republican President's microphone was one way of being a militant!

So it was all sirens and motorbikes. Then armed soldiers, in front, behind, on all sides. Oh, he's very well loved, our President, you know. He feels at one with the people, according to the phrase of President Mao Zedong, like a fisherman in water, no, a hook in the fish, no, like water in a fish – well, something like that. Armed soldiers? To prevent the merce-naries recruited by the pluto-anarchical bourgeoisie and who hide on the other side of the river and the forest from coming with their remote-controlled missiles and their neutron bombs – capitalist, anarchistic devices – to attack the Leader of our revolution; that is the only reason why his every movement is accompanied by this cohort armed to the teeth. Of course there is the odd unfortunate mistake! Like that buddy of mine who, carried away by his enthusiasm during a visit to our firm by the Leader of the revolution, raised his arms to acclaim him, but a little too quickly: he was shot down on the spot. They thought he wanted to kill the Leader. But one must forgive our great historic army these unfortunate slip-ups for, tell me, where in the world is there a country whose army or police don't make mistakes?

The Leader was arriving. The Leader arrived. Jubilant cheering. I stayed close to the microphone, straight as a palm tree in the sun, chest out, ready for the revolution. The Leader alighted from his six-door white Mercedes. Tall, dark, good-looking, with a thin moustache, martial gait and praetorian bearing, a man of the people, a man of the State, a man of the Party, a man of the masses, the revolution incarnate, Chairman of the Central Committee of the Party, President of the Republic, Head of State, Leader of the Cabinet, Supreme Chief of the Armed Forces, Marshal for life! The twentieth century would never be complete without such a man!

Ours is perhaps a small country, but it was led by a great man! One cannot speak of France without speaking of Napoleon, of the Soviet Union without Lenin, of China without Mao; similarly it will no longer be possible to speak of Africa without speaking of our supreme guide, who was there in the flesh before my very eyes. In my mind I could see again the giant posters of our Leader, his chest emerging from a sea of hands stretched out towards him, his inspired gaze fixed upon a distant red star, guiding our people to a radiant future ... Ah! tears of emotion and revolutionary fervour streamed down my cheeks! He advanced with slow measured steps to his place, through the ovation and hymns of praise, delicately seated his Leninist posterior on the red-upholstered chair and crossed his legs. The ceremony could begin. It was eleven thirty.

The Secretary General of our sole trade union came forward; I rushed up and lowered the mike one notch, tested it with a flick of my finger which resounded in the loudspeakers, then stepped aside.

He started his speech by saying that we should combat tribalism. That tickled me because all three of them, the General Secretary of the trade union, the new manager and the President of the Republic, all came from the same clan. And I'm not sure I wouldn't have been the manager of this plant today with three hundred thousand francs in my pocket if I had come from their part of the country. Now wait, this is not an attack; it is normal for the leadership of the country to be dominated by people from the President's region and ethnic group for, like in a garden, certain patches produce better fruits and vegetables than others. Once, when a chap from my region was President, most of the political and administrative functions were filled by people from my ethnic group; now it's the other way round. It's normal.

In Africa, you know, competence, like genius, has a way of suddenly blossoming in the region or in the ethnic group of the man in power. I have experienced cases where model revolutionaries turned into inveterate reactionaries and vice versa within a few hours after a coup d'état. But I'm getting off the point again, let's return to the ceremony. The Secretary of our sole trade union had already come to the end of his speech; he concluded, shouting at the top of his voice: 'Long live the Chairman of the Central Committee of our Party, who will be our President for life until his death!'

Naturally, full of zeal, as always and taking advantage of the fact that my voice could reach the mike, I enthusiastically yelled the Secretary's slogan: 'Until death our President, to the death of the President, President to death ... to death the President ...'

And the crowd took up the slogan and started chanting, with particular fervour from the quarter of the very funereal undertakers. 'Death to the President, death to the President, death to the President . . .'

I noticed that the professors were not crying out, possibly jealous that it was I, a person of limited education and a mere worker at that, who had launched the slogan. Anyway, they looked perplexed, as though they could not understand what was going on.

Whatever the case, I know that those professors have always been against me. And the proof? During a poetry competition at the factory, for which we had been asked to celebrate the pious memory of our late founding President, I wrote, and I say so in all modesty, the best poem of the lot. Here are a few lines:

> O Immortally dead
> fallen beneath the mortal blows
> of the imperialist-capitalists
>
> Our cell number 5, a district
> red and revolutionary
> will for a hundred years support
> your three-year plan
> for self-centred economic development . . .

Admire the imagery, the allegories, the movement of the word 'Immortally' which, in long strides, embraces and stifles the word 'mortal' as though to negate it in a dialectic correlation! Ah well, all of that went completely over the heads of the eminent professors of the jury and my poem was rejected. So their lack of appreciation now for the slogan I launched hardly came as a surprise to me. However, what I did not understand was why the comrade General Secretary was darting angry glances at me; yet all I had done was to take up his slogan. He grabbed the microphone, clutching it in his fist and shouting so loud that for a moment I thought the speakers would blow up: 'President for life, long life to the President, for life . . .'

That is when I understood my blunder. Immediately I took up the refrain with redoubled zeal to obliterate my faux pas: 'For life our President, for eternity our President, immortal our President.'

Finally the comrade Secretary stood back and forced a tight little smile in my direction. Phew! it had been a narrow escape. Which goes to show that, in all matters, one should moderate one's zeal.

Next came the new manager. He praised the revolution and its Leader;

he exhorted the workers, telling them that they should put in eight hours *of* work and not eight hours *at* work, because those who had not worked had no right to a salary. Inside I was saying to myself, Sure, mate, me too, I would also have paid homage to the revolution, just like you, if, like you, I had been pitchforked into the position of manager out of the blue; and you can ramble on all you like, my boy, what do you say when our salaries have not been paid for two or three months, does that mean that even those who *have* worked have no right to a salary? In any case, with your three hundred thousand francs a month, not counting allowances, you wouldn't feel a few months' delay, while the rest of us with our fifteen thousand a month and our six children! ... Obviously I hasten to say that that is not what I really thought, I was just trying to imagine what a reactionary toady of cock-eyed animist imperialism might think of the comrade manager's speech; for as Comrade Lenin said, applying Marxengels's scientific discovery, one must combat erroneous ideas before you even know what they are. That is why I agree with the banning of newspapers which do not think like we want them to, I agree with the Party when its censorship committee prohibits poets and writers from writing unauthorized verses and sentences. The comrade general manager finally concluded his speech by reciting the usual slogans against imperialism, the acrobatic bourgeoisie and the state of prime evil chaos prevailing in the management of State affairs.

And now, at last, let me tell you about the climax of the occasion – and how I got nailed, so to speak.

The Leader of the revolution, the man of the people, the African Lenin, approached the platform; I lurched forward to raise the microphone. I flicked it with my finger, the noise resounded in the loudspeakers, everything was okay, so I made way for him to pass – slowly enough, I admit, for me to be caught in a photo or two. It was just as I was about to step down from the platform, at the precise moment my right foot touched the top step, that the explosion occurred ...

In spite of my limited education, I am not entirely without culture, so I can tell you that I still see exactly what happened as if it were in 'slow motion', as the film-makers call it, that is, in English – I have a smattering of that language – 'flickback ... backflick ... backflash': when we heard the explosion, all the soldiers threw themselves down flat on the ground! For once they were not standing in front of poor terrorized civilians, after their habit of arriving in dozens and armed to the teeth to carry out a brutal search in some poor defenceless guy's shack before putting him behind bars; they had lost some of their insolent arrogance. It's not true when they say now that they were 'advancing in a concerted crawl'. They were just plain scared! And as for the professors, the least said about them the better. I saw one of them, a chemistry professor, the one with the round glasses, beard and bushy hair, getting entangled in the folds of his long toga; he fell, tried to get up and fell again, losing his headgear and glasses. When at last he got back on his feet, he pulled up his toga like the priests used to do with their cassocks in the days when they still wore them and started running as if the devil were on his tail. You bet he was scared stiff, him too! But me, what did I do?

You know, at the time when I was trying to become red, I had attended combat and self-defence classes, as my ambition – since abandoned, alas – was to become a Presidential bodyguard; in my short life I have always reached for the heights even though today I am only the watchman at a manure reprocessing plant. So, when I heard the explosion and saw everybody fleeing, my heart just skipped three beats. As a revolutionary, I forgot about my life; as a revolutionary, I forgot about my wife; as a revolutionary, I forgot about my six children, three of whom are still very young: the Leader was there, alone, wide-eyed with panic, hesitating between his dignity as the marshal and Head of State, on the one hand, that is to say between standing straight like de Gaulle in front of the cathedral of Notre-Dame de Paris (I saw a film last week on the liberation of Paris at the French Cultural Centre because there was no revolutionary film on Lenin and the Russian Revolution that week at the Soviet Cultural Centre), and, on the other hand, flinging himself down flat to save his life. I'm telling you, I saw his eyes and believe me, he was terrified out of his wits. I hope that at that moment he experienced the anguish of those poor folk whom he and his kind, seated in the comfort of their air-conditioned offices, send before the firing squad at dawn, accusing them of all sorts of crimes without proof. But if it is true that might is right, you only need the armed forces on your side to be right. Now wait, whatever you do, don't get me wrong. If the Leader was afraid, it was not on his own account, he was afraid for the revolution, for, if he were to disappear, who would lead our revolution, which at that time was flying from victory to victory? The Leader was there, alone. He wanted to shout: 'Help! Guards!' but the guards were advancing in a concerted crawl under the platform or behind the chairs. He should have shouted: 'Help! My people!' and the people would have come running up from the furthest working-class quarters to defend their Leader, alone and panic-stricken on the platform. I was the only 'people' present and I did what my conscience dictated – offer my body as a sacrifice to the revolution: I dived on to

the Leader to shield him. Taken by surprise, he moved back and tried to
pull out his revolver, for he always carried a weapon. But his legs got
caught up in the wires of the microphone, he stumbled, tried to hold on
to the red cloth which covered the platform; the cloth tore and the Leader
fell down, right to the ground, landing first on his revolutionary and I
suppose red Presidential backside. The platform tipped over with me on it
and I fell on top of the Leader. That is what saved me. For, were our two
bodies not so intimately locked together, I the guardian of a manure
factory and he the guardian of a revolution turned towards a radiant
future and promising distant happy tomorrows, the soldiers would not
have hesitated to shoot me; they did not because they were afraid of
hitting the President. Besides, firing was now breaking out on all sides. As
for me, I was battered with rifle butts, boots and goodness knows what
else. With a split eyebrow and two broken ribs, I passed out and only
woke up in the commission of inquiry torture chamber to the electric
shocks being applied to my balls.

At about three in the afternoon I was brought a list of fifteen names
that I was asked to acknowledge as being those of my accomplices. Really,
I had no idea what plot this was supposed to be about, but my physical
suffering had become unbearable; so I acknowledged them all as my
associates. After recordings had been broadcast on the radio in which
they spontaneously confessed to their crimes, they were immediately
shot. After that, I was hung up by my feet, head down, with a radio
blaring in the cell.

Of course, forty-eight hours later, the inquiry revealed that the explosion had been the bursting tyre of a Renault 4 taxi and that it was the
noise of this blow-out that had caused the panic. But, as was brilliantly
demonstrated by the government commissioner presiding over the extraordinary revolutionary court in a declaration read on the radio blaring in
the room where I was being tortured, there is no such thing as fate: who
had asked that taxi to pass by there at the very second that the President
was going up on to the platform? Why did the explosion occur at the
precise instant that that microphone man had begun moving back, if it
had not been a prearranged signal? Better still, how could a nail, an old
rusty nail what's more, an inanimate object, that is to say not endowed
with autonomous will, deliberately move, point first, beneath the left rear
wheel, that is to say the most worn wheel of the vehicle, if someone had
not put it there?

Is it not abundantly clear that the aim of the operation was to take
advantage of the utter confusion caused by that deliberately contrived

explosion to bring down the Leader of the Revolution? And if there were no plot, why then had one of the women travelling in the taxi denied that she had anything to hide when in fact, after stripping her and systematically searching every inch of her body, the Security Services, a living example of revolutionary competence, discovered a large black beauty spot about one sixteenth of an inch across on her right buttock? (I insist on the word *right*, he cried, because that goes to show on what side the political sympathies of these people lie!)

To come back to the role of that manure guard posing as a sound technician: why had he, on his way to the ceremony that morning – *two* hours early! – on his blue-painted bicycle (comrades, blue is the colour of reaction, he screamed, one says 'blue-blooded' when referring to the degenerate nobility of Europe, those neo-feudal exploiters!), why, on that very morning, in the street, had he greeted one of the people whom he spontaneously identified at the interrogation as one of his accomplices and whom we immediately sent before the firing squad, a person whom he claims to have known for some twenty years, were it not an act of collusion? What was a copy of the French Constitution doing among his books, as well as a copy of the Constitution of the United States and, take note, a volume of articles on abominable South African apartheid, if this did not betray a secret and repressed desire to institute those regimes in our country ... etc., etc.? It's getting all mixed up in my head.

I don't know whether I'm coming or going. I'm tired, I'm hungry, my body is chapped and stinging all over from spending the night in a barrel of salted limewater; please, Mister Chairman of the Commission of Inquiry, tell me what I must confess, what you want to hear me say; tell me whom else I must denounce as accomplices. I'll do anything, sign any document. For pity's sake, although I'm a revolutionary – a sincere, honest, model militant – the body does have its limits, I can't take any more!

PART FOUR

INDIAN OCEAN
AFRICAN ISLANDS

Édouard J. Maunick

Kala Who Dreams of Going to the Sea

Translated from the French by Denise Godwin

Éduard J. Maunick was born in 1931 in the village of Flacq on the island of (formerly British) Mauritius, in the circumstances the personal details in his piece here make clear. A prolific Francophone poet, he has been publishing collections in Mauritius since 1954. In 1961 he left for Paris and began publishing there, notably with *Présence Africaine* in its great days through to the 1970s, and he won the Prix Apollinaire for his achievement (in 1971). From 1982 he worked for UNESCO, directing cultural and translation projects, and was a founder in the 1980s of Radio France Internationale's annual short story competition (organized by Michèle Rakotoson). He retired to Pretoria in South Africa in 1995, where this essay-reminiscence was written; it has not previously been published.

Denise Godwin began as a scholar of the seventeenth century, is head of the Department of French at the Rand Afrikaans University, Johannesburg, and has taken up studying Francophone African writers, particularly of the Indian Ocean.

I LEFT MORE THAN thirty years ago. A day at the end of November – at the time when the flame-trees bloom. One of those rituals only the earth understands. Colour – bloody, blazing – rises from the roots, scales the trunks and spreads along the branches until it explodes in petals. That blaze, which neither burns nor consumes. Flame-trees, flowery heralds of a good year. I vowed at a very early age never to indulge in a game that I saw as pointless and cruel: within the flower, the stigma forms a little fragile orb, and children cross two pistils and duel until they break off their adversary's stigma – in other words, a victory by decapitation. How heartless children can be!

I left in the season of the flame-trees and I returned in time for the horse races, held on the Champ-de-Mars, nestled in the embrace of the mountains that guard Port Louis, black-grey ramparts these, streaked with green. Such a miserly coat of green in the cauldron of the capital. I left again in the season of the cyclones, when the island stands alone against God, and returned at Easter. I hope this toing and froing like a pendulum will not cease for a long time, not until I am really too old. As late as possible . . .

This time a painful mission has brought me back from Paris to the cemetery of Saint-Jean, where I have come to bury my mother. We laid her to rest on the hillside, at the entrance of Quatre-Bornes, a few graves beyond where my father lies, deceased four years earlier. So now, Saint-Jean is the home of my dead.

Each time mourning grips me, wherever I am, I feel an urgent need to go and walk among trees: in town along the great streets, in the country in the nearest woodland. To walk for a long time. Rapidly, to think as little as possible. I walk until I am exhausted, until a stitch provokes a pain other than rage or regret. Perhaps it is a way of taking myself out of myself, or of punishing myself for having survived when the other has not, who can really tell? There are lots of superstitions like this that we resort to, hoping to lessen the impact of death, but they are all more or less ineffectual.

My predilection for trees dates back to the majesty of an immense flame-tree growing at the tip of the isosceles triangle made by the courtyard of the house my family lived in when my father was transferred from Flacq in the North, to Port Louis, facing the sea. This yard differed from all the others in the capital. It was an island, the three sides of which were named Milk, Ternay and de Courcy, streets full of subdued noises because a ghost whose legs ended in hoofs like a pony inhabited them. At night it slept in the yard of Mr S–, a ruddy faced neighbour who was very fond of the cheap, bitter wine bottled by La Cloche. These were the haunted surroundings of a tamarisk tree, backed against an outbuilding in Milk Street nicknamed *Casa del demonios*, where much later a crime would be committed under ominous circumstances.

Now, waiting for the departure of the next plane, barely two days ahead, I am determined to use the time remaining and search, among the trees growing in gardens, in public squares, along the roadside, for the island's most handsome lafouche (the common name for the banyan in Mauritius). My quest had already begun on the day a particularly violent cyclone sent a blast that felled the one that once dominated Port Louis. It used to stand at the end of Labourdonnais Street at the foot of Signal

Mountain, a veritable colossus, wound about with creepers that sometimes intertwined, multiplying into secondary growths the instant they
touched the earth. That tree became my flagship. Perched on top of the
highest creeper, I became Errol Flynn as I'd seen him in the films *Captain
Blood* and *The Sea Hawk*, yelling orders at my young brothers duly
transformed into sailors, cabin boys, able seamen and so on ... A little
later, more alone but still roosting in my lafouche, brandishing my
wooden sword, I steered towards unknown lands. I had become Christopher Columbus, Ferdinand Magellan, Amerigo Vespucci, Bartholomew
Diaz, great discoverers of oceans who confronted eternity, and whose
stories I had just learned from our geography teacher, Mr Arékion.
Devoted man, did he ever realize that the urge to travel took possession
of me at those moments, plunging a splinter into my soul that would
pierce more deeply with each passing year? As early as that, the fertile
wounds of exile!

And so, that fateful day of January, an awful wind uprooted my
Flagship Lafouche. I saw it, a pitiful wreck, thrown on to its side in the
middle of a fearsome swirl of thunder, lightning, wind and mud. I saw it
as I was often to see it again in my dreams, during nights when sleep was
disturbed by despair, despair waiting to remind me as soon as I awoke
that, in a country flayed by war, children are murdered by hunger, by fire,
by steel. The inhuman condition, stuff of nightmares ...

I spent most of the time I had left before returning to Paris pursuing
this quest of many years. And I found what I sought. With Gorah, a taxi
driver I've known for more than thirty years, firmest of all my friends
now, we started by exploring all the suburbs of the capital, making sure
we stopped in front of the lafouches in the French East India Company
Garden. The hold Port Louis has on me is such that at least a thousand
years' worth of memories seem to linger here, echoing in my mind. Its
lafouches were indeed handsome, but they struck no answering chord in
my soul, and they failed to charm my eye. Some enchantment was
missing. It was as if they had not been lived in as much as my Flagship
Lafouche; no ghosts haunted their branches. We continued our quest
towards the south, finding nothing surprising by nightfall.

The next day, a little short of time, we headed north very early in the
morning. Around mid-morning we saw it, suddenly, standing on the top
of a gentle incline as if wanting to make it easy for us to spot, just there,
on the left at the edge of the road, rearing up in unashamed lafouchian
pride. Gorah got out of the car and ran to the tree. What if it escaped us,
vanished? I was riveted to the edge of the ditch, not just surprised but

transported. I felt as though I had been plunged into the Indian Ocean, near Poste de Flacq, not far from La Source where I was born. I felt strange ferns, nameless algae surging up and down my body. No, not ferns, not algae, but those creepers. Strong, supple lafouche tendrils everywhere. I was contained, enclosed in my tree. Enfolded in its roots, in its sap, in its bark, but as by a gentle hand, not by a fist. The lafouche possessed me and I was the most willing prisoner who ever lived.

The miracle of it made me thirsty. I went nearer to the tree to lay my hand flat upon it: a gesture I often find myself making in response to some secret ritual inherited with the triple Creole bloodlines of my mixed European, African and Indian heritage ... I really needed a large mouthful of cool water. I left Gorah to his own devices for a while and climbed up the mound that backed on to the tree. From there I could see a woman working in a little vegetable garden on the edge of a vast field of sugar cane, stretching to the horizon. She was wearing a pale linen blouse and a multicoloured skirt with lots of yellow. She was of that indeterminate age that usually characterizes women obliged to labour long and hard in all weathers. She lifted her head, and smiled, greeting me in Hindi: 'Namasté!' There was sweetness in her voice and in her movements. A real sweetness. Our greetings were uttered simultaneously, and a little embarrassed I asked her if I might drink at the tap in the middle of the orchard. Smiling more widely, she came nearer and invited me to her home. I followed her to her little straw house, surrounded by a wall of dried mud and dung half its height.

She led me in, pushing open a plank door, the only access to a biggish single room, with a window opening in the opposite wall. On the brown floor also brushed with dried mud, beside a metal stove, an aluminium kettle and three or four simple utensils, stood a low, single bed made of loose planks covered with a very thin mattress over which an Indian cotton cloth was draped. At the head of the bed was a large, red satin cushion. On the floor two raffia mats added a touch of brightness to the extremely tidy room. However, what drew the eye irresistibly was the television set, placed at an angle on a chest painted in broken white. At some stage I must have vaguely noticed electric wires outside running between the branches of other trees, but without taking it in. My hostess's smile broadened. She took a *lota* made of pale beaten copper and emptied water for me into a tall white metal goblet that echoed as she poured.

When my thirst was quenched, I thanked her, and she spoke, in Creole this time: *'Mo boukou kontan géte télévision...'* (I really like watching television).

I told her I did, too. And with that, she said that after the death of her husband, who had worked for the Department of Public Works at Montagne Longue, she had left her in-laws and come to live alone up the valley of Rivière du Rampart. Here a small planter and former associate of her husband had agreed to rent out a patch of land on the edge of his fields to her for a modest fee. On this she now grows vegetables, and sells what she produces to travelling hawkers from the area. She earns enough to live respectably and can even save a little in good times.

As I listened to her, I savoured the sweetness of her speech. After a while I came back to the presence of the television set. She gave a happy grin and confided that she had already had it for three years, since winning it in a raffle during a great charity fête held in the Pamplemousse Gardens. She had even seen me, once, on the screen. They were showing a film based on a long poem I had written in Creole: *Ki koté la mer?* (Which side is the sea?) She had really liked the story of that man who had been away from his island for long years and then come back to seek and find the sea. She remembered the end of the story: the moment when the young boy playing me as a child was running with me (the adult) and I dropped my bag and all my papers as I reached the beach. Emotion filled my whole being. I had sought a single tree, a lafouche, my flagship, and I had now found the whole ocean. With that, I understood the strange complicity of the woman's grin. She had recognized me immediately. Was it the smiling witchcraft of chance? Magic? A bit shaken, I took her hand in both of mine and asked her name.

'Kala,' she answered.

I repeated her name over and over again in my head. But the surprises weren't finished yet. On the threshold of the house, as I took my leave, she confided the most disconcerting fact I had ever heard from the mouth of someone born and having lived their whole life on such an island. After telling me she often took the bus, and that many of her journeys passed right alongside the shore, she said she had never actually touched the sea. 'One day,' she said in conclusion, recovering her smile, 'I'd like to get off the bus, go down to the beach and plunge my bare feet into the midday sand and then let the sea bathe my feet for a long, long time...'

Michèle Rakotoson

Dolorosa

Translated from the French by John Taylor

Michèle Rakotoson was born in Antananarivo, capital of the great island-state of Madagascar, since 1960 the Malagasy Republic. She began writing in Malagasy and is noted for the plays she devised for her own theatre troupe. Now living in Paris, she has published a novel on traditional themes and, as a journalist, contributes to several reviews on cultural affairs. In an interview on *Notre Librairie* (July–September 1992), she declared her special interest in continuing to write short stories – her 1984 collection with Karthala, *Dadabé et Autres Nouvelles*, contains both autobiographical and erotic pieces. 'Dolorosa' was published in *Revue Noire* (number 13, June–August 1994), with the present facing translation; the issue was devoted to artists' treatments of the AIDS epidemic in Africa. It has also been used as the basis of a dance-drama by the N'Soleh Dance Troupe of Côte d'Ivoire.

John Taylor has translated French-language authors from Algeria, Benin, Rwanda and more for *Revue Noire*, the Paris-based bilingual quarterly devoted to the arts in Africa.

THE BLOOD OOZING from the wound.
  Blood and pus.
  Sweat.

The mother wipes off the sweat.
  They are people who don't talk very much.

'My son came back sick,' she would say, 'my son came back sick. So sick.'

The gasp like a breath, which chokes.

*

'It hurts, Mum.'

'I know. We don't talk about those kinds of things, Son.'

Death has been consented to; the son has been laid down amidst the blood, the sperm, the shit.

The mother has closed the door, the windows.

'No one will see you suffering, no one will hear you screaming. Sleep, Son, sleep. I'm going to tell you about the outside world: the child you never had, the little cat, the pirogue.

'Sleep, Son, sleep. On the sea the waves become mottled and the wind puffs up, from everywhere, from nowhere. The door is closed, the windows locked, the words of the dead man will not cross the threshold. Sleep, Son, sleep.'

The mother puts her hand over the mouth of her son, muffles his cry.

'Men loved you, women loved you. Don't cry, Son, please don't cry. Love is to be sung, not cried over.'

'Then I got sick.'

'I know. Be quiet.'

The mother has got out her white flowered dress and slowly undoes her hair, softly, ever so softly, turning so that she won't see her skinny son, so skinny, his bones burning in his fever. She lets down her hair. In mourning.

'I'm going to take you far from here, to a place where words are no longer heard. Close your lips, don't scream, my son's not one to complain.'

And she has picked up the rag, the rag kept in a corner, the rag with its scents of cinnamon, benjamin and vanilla.

'Don't move. I'm going to wash you.'

The mother rubs her son's body – her adult son. She lets her hand wander over his skin, so warm, lets her fingers roam over his sex, into his anus, her son's virility, which she had never been able to see. The mother anoints her son's body, his body with its ganglions, his body with its pustules bursting underneath her fingertips.

*

The oil spreads over his limbs. The mother slowly massages his sex, ever so softly, her fingers grazing the sex and the curly hairs, cleansing the crack.

'Men liked my sex.'

'Your mother gave you life. Forgive me, Son, forgive my screams and shouts in front of the men you loved. Forgive me, Son, forgive my hate of the women who came to you, forgive . . .'

The mother stops speaking, thinks of the denied grandson, of the grand-daughter she desired, of her son's child, of the child she would have had through her son. Of her womb that gave birth to death. The mother remains silent.

'It hurts, Mum, it hurts. My guts like an open wound, my throat on fire, endless pain. It hurts, Mum, it hurts. Please, Mum.'

The mother raises the head of her son. The mother sits her son upright in the bed, dresses him in a white shirt, so white, in the black pants of his father, and in the coat that had been saved, saved for such a long time.

'My son will not suffer, my son will not suffer.'

A stubborn pain, a quiet pain. The mother lifts her son, her son who now weighs so little.

He screams.

She puts her hand over his mouth.

'Be quiet, my baby boy, be quiet.'

*

On the sea the light diffracts, the waves become mottled. The sea and its breakers.

The mother leads her son onward, softly, slowly.

The water ankle high . . . waist high.

Lukewarm water, soft water.

The water slides over the skin. Lukewarm, soft, so soft.

The son walks. Leaning on his mother. Holding back his screams.

The water like a tongue – walking, wandering.

The wounds burn again. The son wants to scream.

The mother has sat down. The water comes up to her chest.
She has bared her chest.
Slowly she caresses the head of her son, slowly, softly, then presses down on it. Presses it against her chest, just at the level of the water.
She sings, hums a lullaby.
She tells him of the pirogue and balancing poles, the waves that become mottled and the wind that puffs up, from everywhere, from nowhere.
The water slides over the skin of the young man, his breathing quietens down, he has fallen asleep.
The mother spreads her legs. And pushes the head of her son into the water.

Aboubacar Ben Saïd Salim

The Revolt of the Vowels

Translated from the French by Carole Beckett

Aboubacar Ben Saïd Salim (who writes under the pseudonym 'Abou') lives in the three-island Islamic republic of the Comores in the Indian Ocean, equidistant between the African mainland and Madagascar, and independent since 1975. Born in the capital, Moroni, in 1949, he was a student in Grande Comore and completed in France; currently he lives in the islands as an economist, and has published poems in Mauritius. He is the author of several unpublished short stories, one of which appears to mark his debut here.

Carole Beckett is South African-born and completed her education at the University of Aix-en-Provence; she lectures in French at the University of Natal in Pietermaritzburg. In 1995 she edited and published with L'Harmattan the first anthology of Comoran poetry of French expression, in which Abou features centrally.

EVERYTHING IN THE BEDROOM, which was flooded with an almost unreal red light, suddenly seemed to possess a life of its own. On the corner of the bedside table lay a thick school notebook which rustled softly, as though someone were flipping through the pages. In the early dawn the muezzin's cry and the cock's crowing echoed almost in chorus, disturbing the silence interwoven with a multitude of muffled sounds, filling the night that was drawing to a close.

On the other side of town, in a small reed hut, a man turned over in his bed and threw off the sheet, revealing a thin, sunburnt body. His face would have been really handsome were it not for the vacant expression caused by the fact that he had been mute since birth. He sat on the edge of the bed and reached for the carafe which always stood on the three-legged table close at hand. He poured out a whole glass of water, which he drank with obvious pleasure. Then he lit a cigarette and, while inhaling the first puff of the day, he thought of Kamambo, his best friend. He hadn't seen him for three days. The man's name was Kiziou. He and Kamambo had been friends since childhood.

When he had taken the last drag of his cigarette and blown out the smoke with satisfaction, a burning desire to speak took hold of our dumb man. As he was to say later, it was like the need to yawn, tickling at his larynx.

At first he thought that it was the cigarette giving him a bad turn. One day, he said to himself, he would have to give up smoking. This thought expressed itself aloud in his head; the words 'I must stop smoking', clearly and audibly, caressed his ears. It was like the first gush of a spring in the desert.

Stupefied with joy and surprise, Kiziou savoured the miracle. And he started to say aloud the names of the objects which surrounded him: 'table', 'bed', 'chair'. He couldn't restrain himself and shouted out: 'sun ... trees ... sky ... flowers'. Yes, it was really true: Kiziou had discovered the word.

*

In his house along the coast, Kamambo had also woken up. He turned off the bedside lamp and switched on the main light. Then his first action was to pick up the manuscript to finish correcting the passages which he had underlined the previous evening.

At the sight of the first page, his eyes widened and his expression froze in utter surprise and horror. He adjusted his spectacles and drew the pages nearer.

T.R.V.L.T.- laboriously he deciphered what remained where he had written the title of his short story.

Bewildered, he tried to pronounce aloud some of the sentences. But in each of those, too, there was only a series of meaningless consonants, like S.H.T. ... which sounded more like cave-man language than that of the eloquent stylist he had always been.

Kamambo thought that he must have gone mad, that he was suffering from some new, unnamed disease. He rushed into the shower, shaved quickly, slipped on his grey boubou and began to run to town in search of a doctor.

When he reached the small town of Moroni, nothing seemed to have changed. There was the usual air of nonchalance which had always existed in such a place, part African, part Arabic, typical of an island where time seemed to obey the dictates of man.

Except in the streets. Now the passers-by no longer greeted one another with 'Peace be with you' and other lengthy, polite phrases, but rather in the Hindu manner, slightly nodding their heads.

In the district of the Koranic schools, where from the break of day children's voices normally recited the Arabic alphabet, silence also reigned supreme. Kamambo began to be disturbed by this silence which had suddenly enveloped the town.

He lengthened his stride and hurried towards the Masiwa Bookshop in search of the only daily newspaper, so that he could find out what was going on. But there, once again, he was faced with the same problem. The bookshop looked its usual self. Salespeople and clients sauntered, as they always did, from the shelves towards the till, but no one spoke. In addition, as had happened with his manuscript, all the vowels had disappeared – they had disappeared from everything written, making the books and the newspapers equally useless.

*

That same morning, some kilometres further to the north of the town, the telephone rang insistently in the office of the President of the Republic. His Ministers were all gathered there. The President himself had been obliged to search them out, one by one, as he had been unable to send any message, either in writing or by telephone: the vowels had also disappeared from the Presidential end.

When the phone rang the Council was for a moment interrupted, the Ministers' gestures punctuated with s.h.t. and other onomatopoeic sounds. The President lifted the receiver. He said: 'Hl ... hl ... hl.'

At the other end of the line he heard, 'Y.N.C.M.P.T.N.T.F.L.'

You might well be surprised to hear of the 'y' and you will have noticed that I have been able to write it down. The explanation is simple: 'y' had betrayed its fellow vowels. Only part consonant and part vowel, it had opted for the status of a fully fledged consonant. This was possible especially in French, the language in which the vowels' plot to overthrow the world had initially been hatched. But by then the phenomenon had affected all other languages. Whatever the country, whatever the language, as from this Friday in September 199– no more vowels existed.

So everything ground to a halt. No more debates at the United Nations, nor at the OAU, the latter having completely disappeared because of its acronym. The armies of the world became totally immobilized as no orders could be given with the vowels having gone 'awol' – or should I say 'wl'?

The stock exchanges in Paris, New York, Tokyo, etc., ceased to function. The radio stations, 'This is Washington, the Voice of America', 'Radio France Internationale', were silenced. Not one broadcast its insidious propaganda to the countries of the south. It was as though there were a gigantic breakdown of the world's systems of communication, a return to prehistoric times when mankind just grunted instead of using words.

A few days later the situation remained unchanged. Faced with the incomprehensibility of international grunting and the vast expense of attempting to remedy the situation, world leaders and their grand countries launched an appeal for total silence. An appeal which, naturally, was not understood. But none the less that universal silence came into effect by force of circumstance, to the great satisfaction of the White House and the Kremlin, both of which believed that the rest of the world was obeying its orders, and for once without protest marches or strikes (the right to veto had of course also vanished).

During this worldwide general silence everyone started to look more to himself. In certain countries even buildings and skyscrapers were demolished and barbed-wire fences surrounding military camps were torn down, so that there was enough room for everyone to have his own garden. This was the only feasible course to take in a situation of such total confusion.

*

However, in the small town of Moroni, a momentous event was about to take place.

One afternoon Kamambo decided to find his friend Kiziou, to get lessons from him in techniques of practical silence and of meaningful gestures and mimicry. He blessed fate for his deaf and dumb friend, with whom, in the current situation, he would be able to talk and at last make himself understood!

So our stylist went to his friend's home. For the last four days Kiziou had not tired one bit of the wonder of the spoken word. When Kamambo arrived before his friend's house, he saw him walking up and down in the courtyard, proclaiming aloud the names of everything he saw.

At first Kamambo thought that his friend had gone mad. As he had become used to the vast silence, he did not realize that Kiziou was actually talking.

When he approached his friend, managing to tear himself away from his fascination, the two of them looked at one another for a long while without saying anything. And then, suddenly, as though he had been activated by a hidden spring, Kiziou threw his arms around his friend's neck and blurted: 'I can talk, Kamambo! I can talk!'

Kamambo couldn't believe his ears. 'What,' he thought, 'Kiziou is now talking!'

He tried to say something himself, but in vain. As always, there was nothing but a meaningless series of consonants.

'Come on, Kamambo,' said Kiziou, 'speak to me. Stop making fun of me! You can hear that I can talk. It's a real miracle.'

Once again Kamambo tried to say something, but he was no more successful than he had been the first time. The expression on his face told Kiziou that his friend was not joking: in truth, he couldn't utter a single sentence.

*

Meanwhile, in the Western capitals of the world, the people who couldn't resign themselves to the silence were trying to find some way of communicating. They thought of pictures, and so television screens were invaded by deaf and dumb people who attempted, for better or worse, to communicate messages. Special films were also produced and distributed throughout the world. Thus it was that even the Comoros became aware of the appeal launched by the United Nations through the medium of television and film. This appeal stated that, among other things, the person who could inform them of what had happened to the vowels would have his every wish granted.

Back in Kiziou's small hut, once their surprise had passed, Kamambo invited his friend to come with him. Together they went straight to the Presidential palace. There they were taken directly to the Council chamber. At the President's invitation, Kiziou took the stand and told his story.

The upshot was that that afternoon a plane took off for New York with a large delegation aboard, including the only man in the whole world who could still speak.

Using drums and morse code, an extraordinary meeting of all world leaders was called. Kiziou was welcomed like a true hero. No one could do too much for him.

From eight o'clock that morning the main hall of the United Nations was bursting at its seams. The streets adjoining the remaining skyscrapers were black with crowds. At ten o'clock Kiziou took his place behind the speaker's rostrum and began to tell his story in front of a barrage of television cameras and photographers' flashes. He recounted how, deaf and dumb since birth, he had, one fine morning, nevertheless been filled with such a burning desire to talk and how he had pronounced his first sentence. But just before the end of his speech, to the stupefaction of the entire assembly, he suddenly became inarticulate once again.

However, his speech ended with a prosopopoeia, addressing the vowels as people, and a voice which seemed to come from nowhere continued to deliver it. Heads turned in all directions. Finally, on the corner of a table near the rostrum, one of the delegates noticed that it was five superb vowels on a white page holding forth.

The 'A', appearing as a capital letter, spoke first. 'Human beings,' he said, 'for centuries we vowels have been subjected to all your moods expressed in your words and in your writings. We have never been able to have our say other than through you. Today, we have had enough. That is why unanimously – with the exception of the treacherous "Y" – we decided to disappear for a few days and to take refuge in Kiziou's mouth. Why did we do that? Well, we believe that you now recognize our importance, even though we are so few. We have many complaints, but let us start with the most important.

'We are tired of being subjected to the tyrannical laws imposed by the consonants which separate us, one from another. You will observe that I refer to myself in the masculine; you have always incorrectly assumed in French that we vowels are all of the female gender. Well, in our community there are males and females, just as there are in all communities. In our family two of us are male: "I" and your servant "A", myself. Being constantly separated by those consonants has always been very painful for us. One hardly ever encounters an "O", a "U" and an "E" in a diphthong or even a triphthong. Only children seem to care that we be permitted the pleasure of meeting one another, and then you call that spelling mistakes. To be honest, only children really communicate with us and each time we wish to meet up with a fellow or a sister vowel we have had to depend on them making an error. That was the only way we could meet one another without the intervention of interfering consonants.'

When 'A' had finished his speech, 'O' took her turn: 'We have also had enough of being included, against our will, in declarations of war, in iniquitous treaties, in unfair agreements and in all the wrongdoings perpetrated on earth by all the human race.'

Noticing that the assembly was showing a strong desire to express itself, the vowels deliberated for a moment. They decided to observe a truce just long enough for the humans to have their say.

After so many days of enforced silence, mankind had great difficulty in using words once again. Several minutes were needed to master the art of making speeches, even of pronouncing words correctly, but eventually they managed to express themselves.

The Secretary General of the United Nations, who at that time was a Black African, spoke first: 'Ladies and gentlemen, at last we can talk once more. How wonderful it is to be able to speak! Thanks to you vowels, we have rediscovered the joy of speech. We have listened to your demands, which are quite legitimate, but it must be admitted are difficult to meet. On the one hand, being placed next to consonants is part of being a vowel – one might call it an aspect of your "vowelness". On the other hand, the industrialized nations cannot live without unjust treaties – that is to say, treaties which preserve their basic interests according to the famous north/south rule which states that "the giver takes all". This is equally true of all unfair agreements as well as other unjust undertakings, without which equal suffering would characterize the condition of the whole human race and even worse, on a different level, give rise to equal wealth. Poor nations would lose their reason for existence, which resides in a tradition of complaining about richer nations and in feeling sorry for themselves. Nevertheless, in order to safeguard the ability which separates mankind from other species – that is to say, the ability to speak – we are prepared to make certain concessions.'

The vowels returned to the platform. This time it was 'I' who was their spokesperson. 'At last we will be able to dot our "i's", or should I say make things clear to humanity? We demand the right to place ourselves next to the consonant of our choice, and too bad if the word or the sentence doesn't make much sense. Secondly, we appreciate that you have a vital need to speak and to write. But we simply refuse to participate in the apocalyptic chaos which you keep causing. Starting today, we will be boycotting certain words, such as "exploitation", "hate", "violence", "power" and especially "war". That is our final word: take it or leave it.'

Much relieved, mankind accepted the vowels' terms.

Since that day there have never been spelling mistakes in schools and mankind has not been able either to pronounce or to write the words boycotted by the vowels. These words were completely forgotten, as were the concepts to which they used to refer. War, for example, became 'wr', a sound of anger, but one which could no longer tumble armies into hostilities. This was the most important result of the historic revolt of the vowels in the year of grace 199–.

PART FIVE

SOUTHERN

Luís Bernardo Honwana

Rosita, until Death

Translated from the Portuguese by Richard Bartlett

Luís Bernardo Honwana was born of Ronga-speaking parents in 1942 in the former Lourenço Marques, now Maputo, capital of Mozambique; he grew up near the South African border in the town of Moamba, where his father was an interpreter for the administration. In 1967 he won the short story competition, organized by *The Classic* in Johannesburg and judged by William Plomer, James Baldwin and Noni Jabavu, with the English translation by Dorothy Guedes of his 'Papa, Snake and I', since frequently anthologized. This was part of his only collection to date, *We Killed Mangy-Dog* (1969), widely considered the founding work of modern literature in Mozambique. In the 1980s he became Minister of Culture in the Frelimo government, and now is director of the UNESCO mission to Southern Africa. One of his few uncollected stories is 'Rosita, until Death', which first appeared in *Vertice*, Coimbra, in August–September 1971.

Richard Bartlett edited *Short Stories from Mozambique* (COSAW, 1995), which contained several of his own translations from the Portuguese, including an early version of Lília Momplé's 'Celina's Banquet', here considerably revised in collaboration with the author. The English version of Honwana's Rosita story here, also made with the author's assistance, has not been published previously. The original is written in what was once derogatorily called 'Pretoguês', the basic Portuguese spoken by disadvantaged, especially rural dwellers during the colonial period.

Chiguidela, 17 April 1961

MANUEL MY BELOVED:

So how are you? I is good thankyou with my mother which sends greeting, she is sick in her back which hurt at night with the suffer of old age. Your daughter sends also greeting, she is play, is grow, is ask every day where is papa, where is papa, afterwards crys, she doesnt want to play. One day she is big but not go to school, her father doesnt care, doesnt wrote her name in the administration, but God only knows.

Sorita with Matilda with those other sends greeting too, she are good thankyou. They do littel, I know it is like that when a woman has disgrace, a child comes and the man doesnt make lobolo. I not saying anything, God knows.

I meeted mamana Rita in the market, she came cause of the witch-doctor to treat her, she said woman who you runs away with her left you, a nurse stealed her love, now you are suffering, not work, not eat or anything, dont have anyone.

I not forget you dumped me, I sleeped with you, I was a girl – you found it – left me pregnant, runs away with other woman. I not forget but I still not angry or anything, my mother says it is like that, the mens is mad. I didnt go to skool, dont have studying or anything, writing my name was what you taught me. I just know to make machamba, to make food for you, to wash your clothe, to like you. Look after your child too. Ssimilated woman burns the hair, puts shoes with beautiful dress, with the portuguese she speaks you didnt dare dump her. Its her that dumped you. Left you to cry: Oh mother, I'll kill her, I'll kill her! I say: dont kill her. You dumped me she dumped you: you started.

Here at home goat doesnt give birth to five nor give birth to one with two heads. There is no witchcraft. Nor be jealous of the people I has with me didnt do anything. Rain comes. I made big machamba of mealie with beans with peanut, with mapila. There came one day I woke up happy, I sold a sack of peanut, bought beautiful clothe with taralatana petticoat, with red shoe with hat for you daughter! Ermelinda what is her name but I am used to call her Linda, sometime Nyeleti, you like?

When you want you come rest, just rest, know your daughter, eat egg with chicken, with goat if you like, drink ucanhi with the family on the land, swim in the river, dance the xingombela at the house of N'Dlamini, nothing else. You want? you can see the people round here speak like this: Oh! Manuel has this skin like us but now he is white, he bought being white with a paper, he forgots his gogo who died, he forgots his daughter who was born, he forgots his land, forgots everything. I say its lies, Manuel cannot forget, the people laughs, the people says I dont know, the people says perhaps I am police also. Are you? Oh, they say that anyway.

Afterwards you go then when you dont like to stay here to make machamba, to teach the people in the school at night that you has in

Mussa's house. You go, I am not go to catch you, I just go to cry lots. When you go I give sack of peanut which you can be able to carry on the bus, it can be 4, then it can be lots, I is poor but have good hands to work also to give, you go to sell the sack, to eat the money all alone.

When you want to come you write letter, give to driver of Oliveira bus to deliver to shop of Mohano. You say I go to arrive day such and such. I send cart with the childrens to wait for you.

My mouth does not like to speak things which my heart is saying, but my head is going mad when my mouth doesnt say: I like you much. sometime I thinks you went in the witchdoctors to get medicine so that I am liking you. You makes me to suffer, I crys, I angry, I forgetting, i like you again more! You who dont care: you like ssimilado woman who dumps you.

It is me Rosa of your heart who sends this letter to your heart. Chico Mandlate is to write this letter also sends greeting. Chico not say to anyone things which written to you.

Rosita

until death.

Lília Momplé

Celina's Banquet

Translated from the Portuguese by Richard Bartlett

Lília Momplé was born in 1935 on the Island of Mozambique, off the northern coast of that country. She went to secondary school in the old Lourenço Marques and lived and worked in Lisbon, London and in Brazil, before returning to Maputo in 1981. She has since published a collection of short stories, *Ninguem Matou Suhura* (*No One Killed Suhura*), in which the original of 'Celina's Banquet' was included.

Lourenço Marques, April 1950

'IT'S BEAUTIFUL,' sighs Leonor, examining the dress.

Dona Violante de Sousa doesn't respond, but her face shines with pride as she hangs up the masterpiece which is the product of her hands. She has put the finishing touches to the white organza dress which her daughter Celina will wear to the Salazar High School matriculants' banquet. A hem of perfect lace, running between two ruffles, decorates the neckline and the shoulders. An identical hem, just slightly broader, elegantly finishes off the long gown. It is, actually, a beautiful dress in its apparent simplicity.

'How lucky she is, having a dressmaker for a mother! I'm certain that Celina's dress will be one of the most beautiful!' says Dona Celeste.

The three women are talking in Dona Violante's dining room, which also serves as a sewing room. Leonor is a good-looking mulatto with her thirty years, married to a placid worker on the railways. Throughout her entire married life she has deceived her husband and, about two months ago, ended up abandoning him to become the latest lover of old Sales Moreira, a stinking-rich white man, married and with sons already grown up. Dona Violante has known Leonor since before she was married and, to tell the truth, never appreciated her way of living. She considers her as a loose woman and, were she not a customer, would never receive her in the house. Dona Celeste, also a mulatto, is an old friend of Dona Violante. She suffers from a strange illness which the doctors ascribe to the menopause. And because in Iapala, where her husband lives, medical facilities are virtually non-existent, she has come to Lourenço Marques for treatment. Dona Violante, owner of the house, was born on Mozambique Island, and her history is curiously linked to that of the old millionaire Catarino da Silva, head of one of the greatest fortunes of the colony.

When this man, native of Urgeiriça in Portugal, disembarked on Mozambique Island, he brought with him only his 'face and his courage'. But he also brought, well hidden inside, a strong conviction that Africa existed to make the whites richer and, in a special way, him, Catarino da Silva. So, furnished with such a powerful spiritual weapon, he put his hands to work. He began by going to live with a black girl, the gifted Alima, who roasted peanuts perfectly and, as he discovered much later, with the same peanuts baked delicious torritoris caramel sweets. Catarino da Silva spent his time selling roasted peanuts and torritoris, also taking on himself the job of managing the money from the sales. And he managed it so well that in a short time he could join up with another settler, Benjamim Castelo, owner of the only butcher shop on the island. It is very likely that the nickname Silva Porco, by which he is known in Ponta da Ilha to this day, had something to do with that butcher shop. But it is also possible that it had something to do with his somewhat unkempt appearance, before he had turned into a rich man.

The partnership of Catarino da Silva–Benjamim Castelo prospered on all fronts, thanks to cheating and the unchecked exploitation of black workers, forcibly rounded up by the colonial authorities. In this way they prospered so that, within a few years, the two partners were owners of enormous plantations of sisal and cotton, machambas and shops spread over almost all of the north of the colony.

At this point Catarino da Silva understood that the time had come to rid himself of his black girlfriend and to make himself a worthwhile marriage. He then cast his greedy eyes on the young Maria Claudina Bordalo Monteiro, renowned all over the island for her beauty and for having passed the fifth year of high school, a notable achievement for a girl in those days. She was the daughter of the lawyer Bordalo Monteiro, member of a ruined Portuguese noble family who, with grown children, had ended up, at his wife's insistence, leaving Portugal and going to Mozambique Island. Not that she had any desire to live on the Island, which she barely knew anyway. What she desired was to leave Portugal,

a long way behind if possible, finally to get her husband away from the
overbearing influence of his noble parents, confirmed drunkards and
cheats, incapable of benefiting her life. At that time fateful circumstances
helped the whole family to reach the Island. There is no doubt that the
move brought them advantages. In fact, the constant court cases between
the shop owners of the Island, mostly the Indians, were an inexhaustible
manna for Dr Bordalo Monteiro who got what he wanted, defending
causes just and unjust. It is known that he spent a large part of the money
he earned gambling the night away. But he always left enough to support
the family at a level they would never have reached in Portugal.

Maria Claudina was eighteen years old when Catarino da Silva asked
for her hand in marriage. And to everyone's surprise, even slightly to his
own, he was accepted. The girl obviously followed the advice of her
mother who, after having suffered with her husband's noble family,
considered the marriage of her daughter to a man who was simultaneously common and rich beyond measure a true blessing. The wedding was a grand affair. And, equally to everyone's surprise, the couple
suited each other perfectly. From the start Maria Claudina knew that her
husband saw her above all as a trampoline to position himself in society.
For his part Catarino da Silva had no illusions as to the motives which
led the girl to accept him, with his grotesque figure, his hillbilly fashion
sense and rudimentary education. He knew that he only presented her
with the possibility of a future free of economic and emotional pitfalls,
the primary objective in the life of a daughter of a man full of failings.
Such an absence of romanticism in a marriage can only lead to a complete
split or, as happened in this case, a more perfect harmony.

In this way, Catarino da Silva felt fulfilled, as only those who have
been able to give shape to their very deepest desires can be fulfilled.

As he had expected, Africa had turned him into a rich man and,
because of his wealth, he was also a respected man. And the atmosphere
of happiness in which he lived was almost tangible, which did not go by
unnoticed with Benjamim Castelo, his partner.

'Castelo,' said Catarino da Silva provocatively at times, with badly
disguised pride, 'you also ought to get married with a girl like Maria
Claudina. A man needs to have a family. Forget your black girl, that was
only necessary in the beginning.'

'But I have a baby girl, Violante. She's still very small and it'll hurt to
separate her from her mother,' replied the partner.

'Listen, don't separate them. Leave her with her mother, there'll be no
shortage of children . . . and legitimate ones,' insisted the other.

At first the idea of abandoning his girlfriend and daughter disgusted Benjamim Castelo. Without ever having taken notice of the fact, he had become attached to Muaziza, her sweet manners, her unique insight and even the fresh smell of her body. He had also become fond of his daughter, a handful of tenderness and grace, to whom he had given the name Violante in memory of his own mother. But, while feeling sentimental, Benjamim Castelo was also easily influenced. And, little by little, he began to desire next to him the presence of a white woman who could receive his friends with the same openness with which Maria Claudina presided over the get-togethers at his partner's house. Finally, he needed someone whom he could consider as his true wife, giving him legitimate children who could associate with other white children.

Without realizing it, his gentle moods changed to include a growing impatience which Muaziza bore in stoic silence. In the end he appeared at the house at meal times, ate quickly, his brow creased, speaking only to complain if something irritated him. And at night he threw himself into bed and slept until sunrise, a heavy and unkind sleep, like a drunkard. Even the playfulness of little Violante didn't make him happy. And the child became restrained and shy, which irritated him even further.

One day, on arriving at the house for lunch, he could find neither Muaziza nor his daughter. On the laid table there was his lunch, still hot on serving plates.

'They've gone then,' he thought immediately, looking at the plates which, covered like that, seemed an obvious sign of farewell.

He searched for them all over the house, but only the enveloping silence answered, emphasizing the sound of his steps. He realized then that Muaziza had taken the only trunk with all the clothes she and her daughter owned. She left neither a message nor an address with the neighbours. Much later Benjamim Castelo found out that the girl had gone to her mother's house in Mossuril. There she lived with Violante, providing for her from what the old woman's small machamba could produce, sometimes barely enough to eat.

When Catarino da Silva found out about Muaziza's flight, he comforted his partner with great outbursts of joy. 'Hey man, what good luck that she left,' he shouted, dancing with his small skipping steps. 'I'd seen that nothing else could set you free from that black woman. She's left, and good for her. Scoundrel that she is, she ought to have realized that it was high time to become scarce. I've better judgement than you with your silly morals, in longing for her now. And what of the little coloured girl: let her be with her mother. I think it's stupid to go looking for her.'

'But she's my daughter,' interrupted the partner timidly.

'She's your daughter, she's your daughter. I know that, I know she's your daughter,' continued the other. 'And it's only for her own good that I think it's better for her to stay with her mother. Suppose you had married? Where is the woman who would put up with a mulatto step-daughter? And if you had children? What would it be like with the mulatto girl among white brothers and sisters?'

'That's true, she was trouble,' agreed Benjamim Castelo, somewhat perplexed.

'Don't I know she was trouble! No man, don't torment yourself with useless remorse. Forget the little girl, once and for all, it's better for you and for her. If you go looking for her, I guarantee it'll only bring complications in the future,' concluded Catarino da Silva, giving his partner a friendly pat on the back.

This conversation laid Benjamim Castelo's doubts to rest and he began to see Muaziza's flight as a release. And with a free conscience, with the precious help of his partner, he set about finding a bride from among the white girls on the island.

The choice fell on the young Maria Adelaide, only daughter of the admiral of the Port Authority. She wasn't quite as brilliant as the wife of Catarino da Silva. But she was a girl of courteous manners and a wholesome and fresh appearance. At the same time she was pleased with her suitor, not only because of his wealth but also because of his calm and gentle manners, the dark complexion of his skin and, above all, by a certain air of helplessness which really appealed to her maternal instinct. They were married, and neither Benjamim Castelo nor his friends informed the girl of the existence of the little Violante. He for fear of offending her, and the others because they didn't think it worth their while.

The first two years of marriage was a succession of happy days. In this way they never became aware of the illness which surreptitiously was laying waste to Benjamim Castelo's healthy body. When they discovered it, they left immediately for Portugal to get better medical facilities, but still nothing could be done. It was then, on his deathbed, moved by belated remorse, that Benjamim Castelo revealed to his wife the existence of little Violante. And, contrary to what he expected, this revelation became a source of hope and a stimulus for his wife to continue living. In reality, as they had no children, that child arose like an extension of her husband, something of his which survived for her to protect and to love.

After the death of her husband, Maria Adelaide wrote a long letter to

Catarino da Silva. Mainly it was to inform him that she didn't wish to return to Mozambique. She also asked him to arrange for a share of the estate to be received by herself as the widow of Benjamim Castelo. Finally she urged him to get into contact with Violante's mother and inform her that, as was the express desire of Benjamim Castelo before he died, all the necessary legal requirements for the child to come to enjoy the fruits of all her rights as his daughter would be seen to. Maria Adelaide said she would also like to attend to the education of the youngster, with the mother's agreement, as she continued to be the only holder of maternal power.

Catarino da Silva hurried to answer Maria Adelaide's letter. He told her he was in complete agreement with her staying on in Portugal. He promised to take care of the estate quickly, and effectively did so. But, by bribing the legal officers, he succeeded in robbing the widow in any way he could, and in a very crude manner. Regarding the young Muaziza, he was quick to respond that such a daughter did not exist, attributing the declaration of his partner to the hallucinations of a man on his deathbed.

Furious, Maria Adelaide didn't write again, deciding rather to handle the subject of the child through legal channels. In this way Muaziza was called to make a statement in court, as it depended on her to confirm that Violante was the daughter of the late Benjamim Castelo. And, to the surprise of even the judge who knew the case, she declared that the child was the daughter of a white sailor who had stayed over on the Island and had never returned.

In this way Violante lost all the rights as heir left to her by Benjamim Castelo. Maria Adelaide never knew the reasons which brought Muaziza to give false testimony. But Muaziza carried with her until her death the anguished memory of that decisive hour in Violante's destiny.

It was in Catarino da Silva's office where she, standing, heard what this one, sitting at his desk, said to her in his 'black Portuguese'. 'I am calling you to tell that Castelo died,' he began. 'His wife wants to take away your daughter for her. She wants go to court and everything. If you want keep your daughter you must tell the court she is not child of Castelo. If you tell that she is child of Castelo, you will never see her again. I am telling you because I have pity, a child so small without mother, going so far with nobody! It is for this that I am telling you. If the court asks . . .'

And he continued with this advice in a gentle tone, until the words were cast in an obscene mould of complicity.

Muaziza did not stop to wonder at the sudden anxiety on the part of someone who had never wanted to know either her or her child. But she had nobody else who could explain the complicated and terrible laws of the whites. And the panic at losing her daughter for ever led her to follow the advice which Catarino da Silva had given. Only much later did she understand his real intentions.

At that time Violante was eight years old. But she had already experienced the insecurity, the fears, the violent contradictions inherent in her situation as a colonized mulatto. And the suffering which this situation caused her became almost unbearable with the passing of the years. Because of this, when Celina, her only daughter, was born, she promised herself to defend her, at all costs, from the humiliations which lay in wait through the sole fact of being mulatto. And she attempted to keep that promise, adopting a strategy which seemed more than adequate for her intentions. In reality, this strategy was limited to providing her daughter with the best education because, in her opinion, this was the only way of guaranteeing at least acceptance on the part of the masters of the land, in other words, the settlers. How far she could go with such conviction not even she could guess, perhaps from the fact of not knowing a single mulatto with a level of education beyond primary.

Aware that the education of a child is a costly venture, Dona Violante turned her hands to her gift of making clothes, spending nights on end sewing for other people, in the end adding a little money to the meagre salary of her husband. When Celina had reached her seventh year she was enrolled in the Luis de Camoens School, the only one on the Island. From then on, because bad pronunciation of Portuguese was sufficient reason to fail an exam, the child was expressly forbidden by her mother from speaking Macua, a language she had mastered with fluency and love. She also observed a rigorous study timetable. In this way, not being an especially gifted child, thanks to the iron-willed discipline imposed on her, she completed her primary education with some success.

Inspired by the good results achieved by her daughter, and because the only high school in the colony was to be found in Lourenço Marques, Dona Violante persuaded her husband to ask for a transfer so that Celina could continue with her studies. It was not easy for a poor man, a lowly third-class artisan, to obtain the longed for transfer. And so it was granted only after two successive years of whining and humble petitions and requests. The family then did move to Lourenço Marques, and Celina was finally able to enrol at Salazar High School.

Established to serve the interests of the settlers, the high school clearly reflects the racial segregation prevailing in Mozambique. In her final year

Celina and a young Indian are the only students of colour, and in the whole school there is not a single black student. During the first years, in that atmosphere, Celina only wanted to pass by unnoticed. But, just the same, she was often to read in the expressions of most of her colleagues and teachers the interrogation: 'But what is that mulatto girl doing here? Does she not know this isn't her place?'

Meanwhile, the habit of disciplined study weighed in her favour. Actually, despite usually being unjustly criticized as a result of the colour of her skin, Celina has always been a good student. And this fact has won her, little by little, some acceptance on the part of her colleagues. So, inspired by this unexpected gift, today she is capable of laughing, talking and even presenting a façade of being accepted at will in the presence of other students of the high school. Despite this she doesn't ignore the fact that this acceptance which they show has its limits. And it's not possible to step over this limit without a gesture, a word or a sudden silence to remind her of the colour of her skin.

Meanwhile Dona Violante frets on in her happiness, glued day and night to her sewing machine so that there is no shortage of money for fees, books and clothes for her daughter. And when at times Celina laments the contempt or indifference of her fellow students, her mother responds in a voice of unshakable confidence: 'Study, girl! Only education can obliterate our colour. The more you study, the faster you become human!'

And now, looking once again at the gown which Celina will wear to the matric banquet, she sees a partial affirmation of her words. In fact, the matric banquet of Salazar High School is considered to be the major social event of the year in Lourenço Marques. Apart from the teachers, students and their families, only the highest members of colonial society are admitted to the hall, to be honoured with the presence of the very Governor General. Despite all this, Dona Violante thinks, she, her husband and her daughter – simple mulattos – will be there thanks to Celina having reached the seventh year of secondary school.

As if echoing her thoughts, Dona Celeste comments: 'Oh, what a thing education is. How could Violante ever have dreamt of one day going to the banquet at Salazar High School! But how your daughter has succeeded ...'

'Are you also going?' interrupts Leonor, eyes shining with excitement. 'Show us the dress you're going to wear, come on, let's see!'

Dona Violante goes to the room to fetch the dress of black crepe, very sober, its only touch of colour being a long lilac shawl which goes with it.

'You won't be behind those whites,' says Leonor, looking at it approvingly.

'All that sacrifice was worthwhile,' agrees Dona Celeste eagerly.

And, in agreeing, she includes the exhausting work, nights without sleep and all the hardships her friend had put herself through for Celina to be able to study.

'The sacrifices have not ended yet,' replies Dona Violante with pride. 'If Celina passes, she's going to continue her studies. Now that she's come this far...'

'How will she continue her studies if Mozambique doesn't have a university?' asks Dona Celeste.

'She'll go to Portugal. Now that she's come this far, she'll go the whole way,' concludes Dona Violante, turning to take the dress back to the room.

The other two women cannot find the words to express their admiration for such a spirit of sacrifice.

'Is it true that the Governor also goes to the banquet?' asks Leonor a little later, returning to the topic of the banquet, having an infinite interest in it.

'He goes every year,' says Dona Violante, with all the assurance of a mother of a matriculant.

At that point the three begin commenting on the personal life of the Governor General: a lazy and poisonous man, distinguished only by his unrestrained passion for horses and beautiful mulatto women. He even sends for lovers in his official car and then, obviously, lets them come in at the back entrance of Ponta Vermelha Mansion.

'I pity his wife,' says Dona Violante, pursing her lips. 'He could at least deceive her with other white women. But with women of an inferior race, that takes the cake.'

Dona Celeste and Leonor obviously agree, as they are also convinced of the inferiority of their own kind, even if as in Leonor's case this is only a pretence as she has seduced the husbands of many a white woman. And their commentary only ends when, already close to lunch-time, both of them leave, wishing Dona Violante the greatest success at the banquet.

'Like Celina you ought to be happy,' says Leonor on her way out.

Meanwhile Celina is busy in the majestic hall of the high school and is not as happy as all that. She is now a good-looking young woman with all the vigour of her twenty years. She commands unusual charm and the features so marked in mulatto women. Yet she is not beautiful, due to a strange expression in her eyes, simultaneously distrustful, hard and passive. Eyes which reflect uneasiness of spirit and, because of this, are unpleasant to look at.

While the shouts and bursts of laughter of the final year students fill the large space where the banquet will take place, Celina tries to get involved in the lively atmosphere felt on the eve of the great event. Nevertheless, as always when she is among her fellow students, she feels tormented and has the acute sensation of her outward appearance being false and too happy, leaving a bitter taste deep inside her. She concentrates on her job of arranging flowers to decorate the hall. Aware of the absolutely farcical role she plays in this situation, with great astonishment she hears her name in a loud bellow: 'Student Celina de Sousa and Student Jorge Vieira are called to the headmaster's office!' shouts one of the teachers who has just entered the hall.

A sudden silence follows the words of the teacher who, irritated that nobody is responding, repeats himself in a very serious and offended tone. Only then does Celina put down the flowers she is arranging and, trembling inside, go to the teacher. Now the fright has given way to panic, because the headmaster sees fit to call up students only in very serious cases. And the fact that Jorge Vieira, the only student of colour besides herself, is also summonsed, does not bode well. Scared to death and a little embarrassed, both of them follow the teacher, leaving behind them a murmur of curiosity.

'The students you wanted to see are here, sir!' announces the teacher respectfully, ushering them into the headmaster's office.

The headmaster is seated at his desk and responds with a curt nod of his head. He is a dry and thin man, with the air of someone who is always bored with the things and people around him. He seems so distant and so absorbed in what he is writing that, for a moment, Celina doubts that he has really called for them.

'We need to talk,' says the headmaster at last, putting his pen on the blotting pad.

Celina and her fellow student stand in front of his desk, not daring to look at one another.

'I want to tell you that you cannot go to the matric banquet,' continues the headmaster calmly, resting his short-sighted vision on the students.

Celina cannot believe what she is hearing. Her temples throb and an uncontrollable nausea numbs her feelings. She remains standing with difficulty, hearing the voice of the headmaster which sounds so gentle, so distant . . .

'Undoubtedly you understand,' he continues. 'There are certain unpleasant things I need to do from time to time. The Governor General
himself is coming, as are people who are not used to socializing with
people of colour. And you will also not have wanted to sit and chat in
their midst! To avoid irritation on all sides, we thought it better if you did
not come to the banquet. It would be very annoying if...'

Celina and her fellow do not dare answer back, crushed by that calm
voice, distant, full of authority. They both wish the headmaster would
finish his monologue and let them leave.

'You may go,' he orders finally, returning immediately to his writing.

At the same time, in Celina's house, Dona Violante and her husband
are having lunch, talking nervously about the banquet the next day, to
which they are looking forward with a mixture of pride and apprehension.
The absence of their daughter doesn't bother them. She told them she
would probably arrive much later because of preparations for the banquet.
Anyway, it would take a great deal for them to imagine that, while they
are having lunch, the girl is wandering the streets, trying to gather the
courage to face them and repeat what the headmaster has said to her.
Besides, since that declaration, in a soft and distant voice, that she could
not go to the matric banquet, Celina has been wandering in a semi-
conscious nightmare. After leaving the headmaster's office she did not
return to the majestic hall. She left the high school quickly and walked
aimlessly down the streets. And when, tired and lightly feverish, she
finally returns home, her father has already left for work and her mother
is resting in her bedroom.

When, much later, Dona Violante goes again to work in the sewing
room, it takes a while before she notices that Celina's gown, which she
had left hanging up, is gone. Smiling to herself, she goes to the little room
where her daughter sleeps, as she thinks Celina has taken the gown,
perhaps to admire it better.

But what she sees on opening the door leaves her dumb with fright
and indignation. Sitting on her bed with a pair of scissors, Celina is cutting
up her beautiful white gown.

'Are you mad?!' shouts her mother, recovering from the first moments
of shock.

Celina doesn't answer, doesn't even raise her eyes. Calmly, determined,
she continues to slice the dress into little pieces which are strewn on the
floor like fragile and vaporous clouds, scattered by the breeze.

Mia Couto

The Russian Princess

Translated from the Portuguese by Luís Rafael

Mia Couto was born in 1955 in the northern port-city of Beira, Mozambique,
but lives as a journalist in Maputo. He has been a director of the Mozambique
Information Agency and is noted for his regular 'cronicando' newspaper
columns in *Notícias*, which use literary forms to comment on current affairs.
The first of his several collections of stories was first published in Mozambique
in 1986 and is now available in English as *Voices Made Night* in a translation
by David Brookshaw. Other items in English have appeared in *Critical Quarterly, Third World Quarterly* (1990) and *New Era* (1991). 'The Russian Princess'
first appeared in an English version by Luís Rafael in *Staffrider,* Johannesburg,
in 1993, was collected by Bartlett in *Short Stories from Mozambique,* and has
since been considerably revised for inclusion here. It is also in Brookshaw's
second collection of Couto stories, *Every Man is a Race* (1994), also available
in the Heinemann African Writers Series. The original story opens with an
epigraph from a Portuguese government report of 1946 on the Manica gold-
fields to the effect that, thanks to wild rumours of a strike, all attempts were
being made by entrepreneurs not so much to extract the gold, but to exploit
those who came in search of it.

Luís Rafael is a Mozambican-born South African, currently living in Lisbon,
who has contributed translations of several Portuguese-language authors from
Africa to journals, including an early version of Couto's 'Caramel Rose' to *Soho
Square* (1992).

I'M SO SORRY, FATHER, I'm not kneeling properly. You know, Father, it's
my leg: it doesn't really go with the rest of my body, this very thin leg
that I use on my left.

I've come to confess sins from long ago. My soul's like blood trampled
upon. I'm even scared to remember them. Please, Father, listen to me at a

slow speed. Be patient. It's a long story. Like I always say: the path the ant makes never ends close by.

Maybe you don't know it, Father, but at one time this town had another life altogether. There was a time when many people from faraway places arrived here. The world's full of places, most of them foreign ones. There're so many of them. The whole of Heaven's filled with their flags. I can't imagine how the angels get around without knocking into all those flags. What d'you say? I must walk inside the story? Yes, I'll walk in. But don't forget: I did ask for a lot of your time, a small lot of your time. You see, Father, life takes a long time.

I must continue, then. At that time a Russian lady also arrived in the town of Manica. Her name was Nadia. They said she was princess in the land where she came from. She came with her husband Yuri, who was also Russian. The two of them came for the gold, like all the other foreigners who came to dig out the riches from under our soil. But like our elders always say: don't run after the chicken with salt in your hand. You see, Father, those mines were the size of a speck of dust. You blew once and there was nothing.

But those Russians did bring with them the bits and pieces of their previous way of life – the luxuries of old times. You should have seen their house, Father. It was full of things. And houseboys? There were more than many. I was already 'assimilated' and I became the head of the houseboys. D'you know what they called me? General Foreman. That was my rank; I was a somebody. I didn't work: I made others work. I was the only one who attended to the Master and Milady. They spoke to me in a good way, always with respect. Whenever they requested something from me I shouted at the houseboys and ordered them to do it. Yes, I shouted. That was the only way they obeyed. No one started getting that tired feeling just because they felt like it. Or don't you think that when God threw Adam out of Paradise he didn't give him a few kicks?

Those houseboys hated me, Father. I could feel their anger when I took their holidays away from them. I didn't mind. In a way I even liked not being liked. Their anger made me feel fat inside. I felt almost – almost like the boss. I was told that it's a sin to enjoy bossing people around. But I think it's this leg that gives me wicked advice. I've got two legs: one belongs to a saint, the other to the devil. How can I walk in one direction?

Sometimes I overheard the houseboys talking in the back rooms. They were angry about lots of things. They spoke through clenched teeth. As soon as I walked in they'd shut up. They didn't trust me. But I was flattered with the way they distrusted me: I was the master of that fear which made me feel so small. They took revenge. They made fun of me. They were always copying my limp-limp. The bastards laughed. I'm sorry I used a swearword in this place where you're supposed to show respect. But I feel this old anger like it's still happening. I was born with this defect. It was a punishment God had in store for me even before I was made into a person. I know God's all-powerful. But still, Father, d'you think he was fair to me? Am I offending the Holiest One? Well, I am confessing my sins. If I cause too much offence now then Father can add more on the forgiveness side later on.

All right, I'll continue. The days never changed in that house. Sad and quiet. The Master left early for the gold mine – the gold plot, we called it. He only came back at night. The nightest of the night. The Russians never had visitors. The others, the English, the Portuguese, those never stopped by. The princess lived inside her own sadness. She dressed up for visitors even when she was alone at home. I think she visited herself. She always spoke in whispers. If you wanted to hear what she was saying you had to put your ear really close. I would move closer to her, her thin body – I've never seen skin as white as hers. That whiteness took to frequenting my dreams. Even today, the fragrance of that colour makes me shudder.

She had this habit of lingering behind in the small hall and staring at the clock. She would listen to the dials and the time going drip-drip-drip. It was a clock she'd got from her family. I was the only one allowed to clean it. If that clock were to break, Fortin, it would be as if my whole life had broken. That's what she was always saying to me. I was advised to be careful.

On one of those nights I was lighting the coals in my room at the back. That's when I saw a shadow behind me and got a fright. I looked again and saw that it was Milady. She'd brought a candle with her and she walked very slowly towards me. She looked at my room while the light was dancing on all four corners. I didn't know what to do. I was even embarrassed. She'd always seen me in the white uniform that I used for work. And here I was in shorts. With no shirt on, with no respect at all. The princess walked around and then, much to my surprise, sat on my mat. Have you ever? A Russian princess sitting on a mat? She stayed there for a long time, just sitting, and continuing to sit. Then she asked me a question in her funny way of speaking Portuguese: '*So you leeve ghere ah-fter all?*'

I had no answer for her. I even thought she was sick. Her head was getting places all mixed up.

'Milady, it's better for you to go back to the house. This room's not so good for Milady.'

She didn't respond to that. She asked another question: *'Is it goot enough for you?'*

'It's enough for me. All we need is a roof to protect us from the sky.'

She undermined everything I was so sure of. She said only animals hid themselves in holes. Each person is its own place – the place from we start sowing our lives. I asked if there were blacks in her country and she laughed and laughed. Oh, Fortin, you ask such odd questions! I was surprised: if there were no blacks then who did all the heavy work? Whites, she said. Whites? She was lying, I thought. After all, how many laws are there in the universe? Could it be that misfortune wasn't distributed according to race? No, I'm not asking you, Father. I'm thinking aloud.

That's how we spoke that night. When she was by the door she asked me if I would show her the hostels where the others lived. At first I said I wouldn't. But deep down I wanted her to go there. So she'd see something more wretched than my own life. And so I obliged. We set out in the dark towards the place reserved only for domestic servants. Princess Nadia was filled with sadness when she saw how they lived. She was so shaken that she began to swop languages. She went skipping from Portuguese back to Russian. Now she understood why the Master wouldn't let her go out. Why he'd never given her permission. It's only so I wouldn't see this misery, she said. I noticed that she was crying. Poor lady. I felt sorry for her. A white woman, so far away from her own people, there in the middle of the bushveld. Yes, for the princess it must've been bush, all of it. The surroundings of the bush. Even the big house always tidied according to her own customs, even her house was a bush-house.

When we returned I pricked myself on one of the micaia thorns. The thorn got deep into my foot. The princess tried to help me but I didn't want her to: 'You can't touch this leg of mine, Milady . . .'

She understood. She tried to console me; said it wasn't a defect at all. I shouldn't be ashamed of my body. At first I didn't like it. I thought she felt pity for me. Compassion. Nothing more. But after a while I was so lost in her sweetness that I forget the pain on my foot. It seemed like that leg that moved all over the place wasn't mine any more.

It was from that night onwards the princess started to go out. She started to visit the areas around. She took advantage of the Master's absence and she asked me to show her all the footpaths. One day, Fortin, we'll leave early and go to the mine. Her wishes frightened me. I knew Master's orders. The lady wasn't allowed out.

Until one day the whole thing exploded: 'The other servants have told me that you have been taking walks with the Madam.'

Bastards. They'd complained about me. So I'd know that I was no different from them: I was reduced to size by the same voice. Jealousy is the worst type of snake: it bites with the victim's own teeth.

And so, at that moment, I took a step back: 'It's not because I want to, Master. It's Milady that tells me to.'

See what I did, Father? All it took was a second and there I was accusing Milady, betraying her confidence.

'It's the last time it happens. Do you hear that, Fortin?'

We never took to the roads again. The princess asked me, she insisted with me. Only for a short distance, Fortin. But the spirit had left me. And she went back to being a prisoner in the house. She looked like a statue. Even when the Master came home at night she continued to look at the clock in silence. She seemed to see a time that only those who were absent could see. The Master didn't even bother with her: he'd walk straight to the table and ask for a drink. He drank, he ate, he drank, he ate. He didn't notice Milady. It was like she was *sub-existing*. He didn't hit her. Beating up the wife wasn't a thing a prince did. They'd never hit or kill someone, they'd give orders for somebody else to do it. It's we who are destined to work for others that are the hands of their dirty wishes. I always beat up people when I was told to do so. I was a whirlwind of beatings up. I only hit people of my race. Now I look around me and there's no one I can call brother. Not one person. Those blacks don't forget. They're full of grudges, this race of mine. You're also black, Father. You know what I mean. If God's black, Father, then I'll sizzle: I'll never be forgiven. Never ever. What d'you say? Mustn't I talk about God? Why's that, Father? D'you think he can hear me here, so far away from Heaven, and me so small? Can he hear? Wait, Father, I must just straighten the way I'm sitting. Blasted leg. It never wants to obey me.

All right, I'm ready to confess more things. It was like I said. Or more correctly: like I was saying. The house of the Russians was storyless. Nothing happened. Only Milady's silence and her whispers. And the clock, which was like a drum sound in the hollow.

Until one day the Master shouted at me about something urgent: 'Call the servants, Fortin. Quick. I want them all outside.'

I got them all together, the houseboys and the kitchen totos and even the fat cook, Nelson Machine.

'We're going to the mine. Quick. Get on the wagon.'

We got to the mine, were given spades and began to dig. Once more the roof of the mine had collapsed. There were men under the ground we were walking on. Some of them were dead already, others were saying goodbye to dear life. The spades went up and down. Nervous spades. We began to see arms coming from the inside of the sand – they looked like roots made of flesh. There were shouts, there was a whole mix up of different commands and there was dust. The fat cook next to me was pulling an arm, trying to get all the strength to tug out the entire body. But I tell you what: it was a loose arm, it had already been torn away from its body. The cook fell. He was still holding that chunk of arm in his hands. Sitting just like that he burst out laughing. He looked at me and his laughter was filled with tears. Fatty looked just like a lost child sobbing away.

I couldn't cope, Father. I unabled myself to cope. I know I sinned: I turned my back on all that misfortune. There was too much suffering. One of the houseboys tried to hold me. He insulted me. I turned my face. I didn't want him to see that I was crying.

That year the mine fell a second time. Again, this second time, I walked away from the job of saving lives. I'm no good, Father, I know it. But you've never seen a Hell like that one. We pray to God to save us from Hell when we die. But what difference does it make? We already live in Hell, we walk on its flames and our souls have got all its scars. That's what it was like over there. It was like a farm of blood and sand. We were scared even to walk. Because death was burying itself inside our own eyes. And she was pulling our soul down with her many arms. Why is it my fault? Be honest with me, why is it my fault that I was incapable of shaking little bits of people in a sieve?

I'm not a rescue man. Things happen to me, I don't make things happen. I was thinking about these things on my way home. My eyes didn't even look to the front. It as though I was walking inside my own tears. Then, all of a sudden, I remembered the princess. I seemed to hear her voice asking for help. It was as if she was there, beside each tree, begging on her knees – like I'm doing now. But once again I wouldn't let myself help anyone. Goodness wasn't for me and I walked away.

Back in my room I found it difficult to listen to the world all around me – so full of the beautiful sounds of nightfall. I hid myself in my own arms. My thoughts were locked in a dark room. That's when her hands came. Slowly they unloosened the obstinate snakes that my arms had become. She spoke to me as if I were a child, the child she'd never had: '*Zhere was êksident in mine, yes?*'

I answered with my head. She pronounced terrible curses in her own language and then left. I went with her. I knew that she suffered more than I did. The princess sat in the lounge and waited for her husband to return. She sat in silence. When her master returned she got up slowly. She was holding the glass clock in her hands. The one she had entrusted me to take special care with. She lifted the clock well above her head and with all her strength threw it on the ground. Pieces of glass were scattered everywhere – the floor was covered with glittering grains. She then moved on to break the chinaware. She did this slowly and without shouting. But I knew those bits of glass were cutting her soul open. The Master, yes, he shouted. First in Portuguese. He commanded her to stop. He shouted in their own language. She didn't even hear. And d'you know what she did? No, Father, you can't imagine it. It's even difficult for me to have to tell it. The princess took her shoes off, she stared at her husband and began to dance on top of the broken pieces of glass. She danced, danced, danced. The amount of blood she left behind, Father! I know about it, I was the one who cleaned it up. I took a cloth and cleaned the floor like I was caressing Milady's own body, like I was consoling all her many sorrows. The Master told me to get out and to leave everything as it was. But I refused to. I've got to clean up this blood, Master, I said. I was speaking back to him in a voice which didn't even seem to be mine. Was I showing disobedience? Where did I get that strength that held me close to the ground and made me a prisoner of my own will?

And that's what happened, even though it doesn't sound like the truth. Then all of a sudden a lot of time went by. I don't know if it was because of the glass, but on the next day the lady got sick. She was laid to bed in a separate room. She slept alone. She rested on the sofa while I made the bed. We spoke. The topic was always the same: she remembered things from her country – the lull-lullabies of when she was child.

'This sickness, Milady, I'm sure it's from missing something too much.'

'*My life is zhere. Man I love ghe is in Russia, Fortin.*'

My mind danced way – I was pretending. I didn't want to understand.

'*Ghis name is Anton. Sat is only mwaster of my gheart.*'

I'm imitating the way she spoke. It's not that I want to make fun of her. But that's how I keep her confession, the one about that man she loved. Other secrets came along – she was always offering me the memories of that love she kept so hidden. I was scared in case anyone overheard our conversations. I got the job done quickly so I could get out of that room. But one day she gave me a sealed envelope. It was something I had to be very secret about. No one was allowed to suspect. Ever. She told me to post the letter at the post office in town.

From that day onwards she started giving me letters. One followed the other, and the other, and another. She wrote while she was lying down. The writing on the envelope was shaky because of her high temperature.

But Father: d'you want to know the truth? I never posted those letters. None at all. Not even one. I have sinned and I suffer for it. It was fear that stopped me from obeying like I should have – fear of being caught red-handed with that burning evidence.

The poor lady treated me with all the goodness in her. She believed I was making a sacrifice for her. She'd give me the letters and I'd begin to shake: it was like my fingers were holding the fire. Yes, what I said was correct: the fire. Because that's where all those letters ended. I threw them all in the kitchen coal-stove. All Milady's secrets were burnt over there. I'd hear the fire and it sounded like her own sighs. Bloody hell, Father, I'm getting a cold sweat just from talking about these things that make me feel so ashamed of myself.

And that's how life went on. The lady had less and less strength. I'd walk in the room and she'd look at me. It was as if those blue eyes pierced through me. She never asked if a reply had come. Nothing. Only those eyes questioned me in silent despair, those eyes that had been snatched away from the sky.

The doctor was coming every day. He'd leave the room and shake his eyes. He didn't think there was any hope. The whole house was dark. The curtains were always closed. There were only shadows and silence. One day I noticed that the door was open by a half slit. It was Milady peering to see. She waved at me; and I went in. I asked her if she was getting better. She didn't reply. She sat in front of the mirror and put scented rice powder on her deathly face – she was cheating death of its colour. She painted her lips, but she took a long time to get the paint on the respective lips. Her hands were shaking so much that she made a red scratch on her nose and on all around the chin. If I'd been a woman I would have helped but I was a man. I just looked. And kept to myself.

'Is Milady going out?'

'*Vee go to si-tation. You end me.*'

'To the station?'

'*Yes. Anton comes on ttrain.*'

She opened her bag and showed me a letter. She told me it was his reply. It had taken long but eventually she'd received it. She was shaking the envelope, like children do when they're scared their fantasies will be taken away. She said something in Russian. Then she spoke in Portuguese: Anton was coming on the Beira train. He was going to take her away from there to a very far place.

The lady was raving, I'm sure. It was all make-believe. How could she have got a reply? Wasn't I the one who used to collect the post? And hadn't the lady not left the house for much more than many days? And what's more: weren't the letters addressed to the fire?

We went out to the street, she holding on to me. I was her walking-stick until we got close to the station. It was here, Father, that I committed my worst sin. I'm very hard on myself. I don't give myself a chance. Yes, I'll defend myself against anything except myself. That's why this confession is stealing some of the burden away. I can already count on God being my side. Don't you think I'm right, Father? Then, listen.

The princess's skin was tight against my own body – I was sweating her own sweat. The lady was on my lap, the whole of her – her whole abandoned self. Who was that Anton if not I? Yes, I was the one who made himself into the writer of that letter. Was I deceitful? At the time I was in favour of it. After all, there wasn't much left of Milady's life. What did it matter if I helped her fantasies a little? Maybe – who knows – that bit of madness would help to heal the wound that was stealing her body away from her. But, Father, have you considered what I was really trying to be? Was I, Duarte Fortin, general foreman of the houseboys, running away with a white woman, and a princess at that? As if she would have wanted to go with me, a man with my colour and with unequal sized legs. There's no doubt about it. I have the soul of an earthworm. I'm really going to crawl in the other world. My sins ask for more than many prayers. Pray for me, Father, don't stop praying for me! Because I haven't told the worst.

I was carrying the princess through an out of the way path. She didn't notice that we'd made a detour. I took the lady to the river-bank. I laid her on the soft grass. I went to get some water from the river. I wet her face and her neck. She replied with a shiver – that mask of rice powder was beginning to crack. The princess breathed with difficulty. She looked around and asked: '*It is si-tation?*'

I decided to lie. I told her it was right there, on the side. We were by the shade only to hide from the other people who were waiting on the station platform.

'They mustn't see us. It's better to wait for the train from this hiding-place.'

The poor woman, she thanked me for all my concern. She said she'd never known a man with such goodness in him. She asked me to wake her up when it was time; she was very tired, she needed to rest. I continued to look at her and to feel the nearness of her presence. I saw the buttons of her dress. I could imagine what sort of fire lay beneath them. My blood was running fast. At the same time I was tormented by fear. What if the Master caught me in the middle of the grass with his lady? There was only one thing: he'd aim the black muzzle of his gun and shoot. It was the fear of being gunned down that put a stop to me. I took too long. I was just looking at the woman on my lap. That was when the dream began to run away from me once again. D'you know what I felt, Father? It felt as if she didn't have her own body: she was using mine. D'you understand, Father? That white skin of hers was mine, that mouth was mine, both those blue eyes were mine. It was like we were one soul distributed between two opposite bodies: male and female; one black, one white. You're not convinced? But you should know this, Father: it's opposites that are always the most similar to each other. You don't believe me. Look: isn't fire that's most similar to ice? They both burn and it is only through death that man can walk inside the fire and the ice.

But if I was her, then my second body was dying. That's why I felt so weak. I had given up. I fell down on her side. Neither of us moved. She had her eyes closed. I was trying to avoid falling asleep. I knew that if I closed my eyes I would never wake up again. I was much too much inside this; I couldn't afford to go further down. There are times when we become very similar to the dead and that's what gives the dead their strength. That's what they don't forgive in us: it's that we, the living ones, are so similar to them.

And d'you know how I saved myself, Father? I put my hands in the hot ground, like those dying miners had. My roots connected me again with life. That's what saved me. I got up. I was sweating. I had a temperature. I decided to get out of there at once. The princess was still alive and she motioned me to stop. I didn't pay attention. I went back home with the same tightness in my heart that I'd had when I abandoned the survivors on the mine.

When I got there I told the Master that I'd found Milady dead by a tree near the station. I went with him so he'd see I was telling the truth. The princess in the shade could still breathe. When the Master leaned down she held his arms and said: 'Anton!'

The Master heard that name which wasn't his. Even so, he kissed her on the forehead – in a way which showed he cared. I went to fetch the wagon and when we lifted her up she was already dead – as cold as all non-living things. A letter fell from her dress. I tried to catch it but the Master was quicker. He looked at the envelope with surprise and then peered into my face. I had my chin down. I was worried in case he asked. But the Master crumpled up the envelope and put it in his pocket. We returned home in silence.

I ran away to Gondola the next day. I've been there ever since – working for the railways. Now and then I come to Manica and stop by at the old cemetery. I kneel in front of Milady's grave and I tell her I'm sorry, what for I don't know. No, actually I do know. I ask her to forgive me for not being the man she was waiting for. But that's all pretending. Father, you know how my kneeling here is all a lie. Because, you see, when I'm standing in front of her grave I can only remember the taste of her body. That's why I'm confessing to this bitterness that has taken away my love for life. There's not much time to go before I have to leave this world. I've already asked God for permission to die. But it looks like God doesn't pay much attention to those kinds of requests. What d'you say, Father? I shouldn't talk like this. Like I'd given up all hope. That's how I remember myself, a widower of a woman whom I never had.

I feel so insignificant now. D'you know what's the only thing that brings joy to my heart? It's when I leave the cemetery and go walking in the dust and the ashes of that mine of those Russians. The mine's closed. It closed down when Milady died. I walk there all alone.

Then I sit on an old trunk and look at the back of me so I can see the tracks I've left behind. And d'you know what I see? I see two kinds of tracks, but both of them made by my own body. Some are of a big foot, a masculine foot. The others are footprints from a small foot, a lady's. They're the footsteps of the princess, the one that walks by my side. They're her footsteps, Father. That's the one thing I'm dead certain of. Not even God can change this certainty I have. Maybe God won't forgive any of my sins and maybe I'll be in for hell-fire. But I don't care. I'll see her footsteps there, in the ashes of Hell. They'll be walking on my left side.

José Eduardo Agualusa
The Day They Arrested Father Christmas

Translated from the Portuguese by Luís Rafael

José Eduardo Agualusa was born of Portuguese parents in Huambo, Angola, in 1960, and has studied agronomy in Lisbon, where he has produced several novels dealing with his African life. In 1990 he published a first collection of short stories, which won several literary awards. His 'The Fall of Santa-Maria' has appeared in an English translation in *The Kalahari Review* (April 1994); 'The Day They Arrested Father Christmas' first appeared in *Pública* in Lisbon in 1999. His translator here, Luís Rafael, has the following explanatory note to the story: 'The allusion at the end is to Saint Elizabeth of Aragon (1271–1336), wife of King Denis of Portugal, who much against her husband's wishes used to feed the poor. The legend goes that, caught by the king who challenged her to reveal what she had in her bag, the bread had indeed been transformed into roses.'

OLD PASCOAL had a long beard, white, very white, and it fell unevenly over his chest. It wasn't the fashion; it was just that he didn't care; it was a sign of his own wretchedness. But it was thanks to that beard that he got a job. Because of that and because he was born an albino – with his gecko-skin and the blink of his tiny pink eyes which were always hidden behind a pair of dark sunglasses.

At the time he'd really given up all hope of getting a job. He was sure he would die soon in some street in the city, more out of sadness than of hunger itself, because the soup the General gave him every night fed him, as did the bread-crusts that he found now and then in the rubbish bins. At night he slept in the beer hall, right under the billiard table, all huddled inside a blanket, another favour from the General. He dreamt of the swimming-pool.

He had worked at the swimming-pool for forty years, ever since the day he started off as a janitor. He knew how to read, he could count and he remembered all the prayers he had learnt at the Mission, not to speak of honesty, hygiene and a love for work. The whites liked him. It was always Pascoal come here, Pascoal go there. They gave him the little children for him to look after, some even invited him to play soccer (he was a good goalie), others told him secrets; they also asked to use his room when they were courting each other.

Pascoal's room was next to the men's changing rooms. That was his house. The whites slapped him on the back: 'Pascoal, the only black man in Angola with a swimming-pool in his house.' They would laugh: 'The whitest black man in Africa.' They told him jokes about the albinos: 'D'you know that chief who was asked to give a speech at the Day of the Nation? Yeah, the guy got on to the platform, cleared his voice and said: "Here in Angola we're all Portuguese – whites, blacks, mulattos and albinos. We're all Portuguese."'

The blacks, on the other hand, did not like Pascoal. The women cursed him, they spat on the floor when he walked past or, worse still, they pretended not to see him at all. The kids used to climb over the wall before dawn and jump into the pool. He had to get out of bed, still wearing his underpants, so he could get them out of there. One day he bought a shotgun, a second-hand vacuum pump. He began to shoot at them from behind the acacia trees.

When the Portuguese left, Pascoal knew that his happy days were over. He witnessed with sadness the arrival of the guerillas, the shots in the sky, the ransacking of the houses. What hurt him the most was having to see them take over the swimming-pool. Comrade here, Comrade there, as if no one had a name. The children, the same children that Pascoal had got rid of with the shots from his vacuum pump, pissed in the pool from the diving board. Until one afternoon when there was no water. It didn't come the next day, or the one after, or ever again. The swimming-pool wilted. It turned yellow, a dull yellow, it turned green; and suddenly it was filled with frogs. At first Pascoal tried to combat the invasion of frogs by using his shotgun. It didn't work. The more frogs he killed, the more frogs there were, huge-sized happy frogs that sang until dawn on those nights when the moon was out, drowning the echo of gunshots in the distance and the barking of dogs.

Some kind of sleeping sickness fell on the houses and the city began to die. Africa – let's call it that – once again took over what had been hers. Wells were dug out in the backyards. Fires were lit up in the gardens. The grass burst through the tar, it invaded the sidewalks, the walls, the courtyards. Women pounded wheat in the halls. Fridges were used as shoe-racks. Pianos made excellent rabbit warrens. Generations of goats grew up eating libraries, very erudite goats they were, especially when it came to French literature, although others were more specialized in finance and architecture.

Pascoal emptied out the water in the swimming-pool and cleaned it. He put all his money together and bought chickens. He apologized to the swimming-pool. 'My friend,' he said, 'it's only for a few months. I'm going to sell the eggs and the chicks and then I'll buy good water and I'll buy chlorine. You'll see. You'll be as beautiful as you used to be.'

The time that was to come was worse still. One afternoon soldiers came and took away the chickens. Pascoal didn't say anything. He should have said something perhaps. 'This albino's acting all smart,' said one very irritated soldier. 'He must think he's white. He's an imitation white.' They hit him. They left him for dead in the swimming-pool. Months later more soldiers came. They had been told that an albino who raised chickens lived there and, as they found no chickens, they beat him up as well.

The war had returned in all its fury. Planes bombarded the city, or what was left of it, for fifty-five days. On the thirty-sixth a bomb destroyed the swimming-pool. For weeks Pascoal drifted in and out of the rubble. One day three men appeared in a Land-Rover – a white man, a mulatto, a black man – all of them wearing a suit and tie. 'It was urbicide,' said the mulatto, making a big sign with his hand. Pascoal didn't know what the word meant but he liked it. 'It was urbicide,' he repeated, and even today, when he remembers the swimming-pool, he mulls over that word for hours. 'It was urbicide.'

An army made of very foreign-looking white men all wearing blue helmets took him to Luanda one morning as dawn was breaking and the rain was falling. He was in hospital for two days. Here they tended to his wounds and gave him food. Then they told him to go. The old man began to live in the street. One day, it was in December, the Indian from the supermarket in Mutamba came to speak to him. 'We need a Father Christmas,' he said. 'With you we'd save on the beard. What's more, you're the Nordic type. It would look like the genuine thing. We're giving three million a day. Is that good enough for you?'

His job was to stand in front of the supermarket dressed up in a type of red pyjamas and with a hood on his head. As he was very thin, they had to tie two pillows around his belly. Pascoal suffered with the heat; he sweated the whole day under the sun, but for the first time in many years he felt happy. Dressed like that, with a bag in his hand, he gave presents to small children (presents which a Swedish NGO had given to the

Ministry of Health) and invited the parents to go inside the store. 'I'm a Cambulador Father Christmas,' he explained to the General. The job of cambulador was a real one and existed in Angola into the second half of the century: a cambulador was someone hired to stand outside the door of commercial establishments and entice clients to walk in.

Every day Pascoal got to like his job more and more. The children ran to him with open arms. The women laughed; they winked at him as though they were sharing a joke (they never smiled though). Men greeted him with respect: 'Good afternoon, Father Christmas! How is the situation with the presents this year?' The old man enjoyed it, especially the signs of surprise on the faces of the young children. They made a circle around him. They asked for permission to touch the bag. 'Father Christmassy,' asked a very weak-looking small child, 'pleeeze give me a balloon.' Pascoal had strict instructions to give condoms only to children accompanied by adults, and even then a lot depended on what sort of aspect the adults had. The contract made it quite clear: he had to get rid of the street kids.

At the end of the second week, after the shop had closed for the day, Pascoal decided not to take off his disguise and, dressed in that scandalous attire, went to the beer hall. The General saw him but said nothing. He served him his soup in silence.

'There's too much misery in this country,' said the old man. 'Crime pays.'

That night he didn't dream of the swimming-pool. He saw a very pretty lady who had come down from heaven and was standing next to the billiard table. The lady wore a long dress with small shiny gems and she had a golden crown on her head. The light reflected off her skin, like a lamp.

'You are Father Christmas,' said the lady. 'I have sent you here to help the homeless children. Go to the store, hide the toys in your bag and distribute them among the children.'

The old man woke up startled. All around the billiard table and in the thickness of night there was a cloud of bright dust. He covered himself with the blanket again, but he couldn't get back to sleep. He got up, put on his Father Christmas suit and went out into the street. He was in Mutamba in no time. The square was deserted and the store shone as brightly as a UFO. There were Barbies in the main window display; each had their own dress but they all had the same annoying smile. Another display had the mechanical monsters, the toy guns, the electric cars. Pascoal knew that if he broke the glass of the window display he would be able to get his hand to the door. He took a stone and broke the glass.

He was about to come out, his bag already full, when a policeman arrived. At that instant he noticed that behind the policeman, on the street corner, an acacia tree was filled with light. Pascoal saw the lady smiling at him; she was floating above the flames of flowers. The policeman didn't seem to notice anything. 'You shameless old man,' he shouted. 'You're going to tell what you've got in that bag.'

Pascoal felt his mouth opening against his will; he heard himself saying, 'They're roses, sir.'

The policeman looked at him, confused: 'Roses? This old man's lost it . . .' He gave him a slap on the back.

Then he took out a pistol from the holster, pointed it in his face and shouted: 'So they're roses! Show me these roses.'

The old man hesitated for a second. He turned to look at the acacia tree in full bloom and he saw the lady again and she was smiling at him; she was a most beautiful woman, she was like a whole festival of light unto herself. He took the bag and emptied it out at the feet of the policeman.

They really were roses – plastic ones. But roses all the same.

Yvonne Vera

Independence Day

Yvonne Vera was born in Bulawayo, Zimbabwe, and during the liberation struggle until 1980, and after it, spent several years in exile as a doctoral student at York University, Toronto, where she wrote many of the early short stories included in her first collection, *Why Don't You Carve Other Animals* (Baobab, 1992). Her terse, unsparing 'Independence Day' is taken from there. She has since published several novels, including *Under the Tongue* (1996), which was the winner for the Africa region of the Commonwealth Writers Prize the following year. Her latest novel is *Butterfly Burning* (1998). She is at present the director of the National Gallery in her home town.

'MOVE BACK! MOVE BACK!' the policemen shouted.

Today they were lining the main street in the city to see the Prince who had come from England to give their country back to them. At midnight.

The woman took shelter in the green space in her head, and waited. The children, released early from school, were standing along a stretch of empty road, books held above their heads casting inky shadows on their faces. The sun shone brightly on the tarred road. A policeman stood on the broad yellow centre line, his starched cap exploring the distance. Policemen in heavy brown boots and khaki uniforms, holding guns and batons, told the children to move back. The Prince from England would not like to be crowded upon.

On the other side of the road women were dancing and singing traditional songs, under the towering gum-tree. Sweat poured down their faces as they welcomed the future. The policemen with guns and batons told them to move to the back of the crowd or line up with the rest of the people. One gave them tiny flags to wave, a new flag for a new nation. While waiting for the Prince, sent by his mother the Queen, the woman held a branch from a jacaranda bush over her tired face, and stayed shielded in the green space in her head.

A limousine came down the street that was lined with exploding

purple jacarandas. Children broke into screams, thinking it was the very
important person who had come all the way from England to give them
back their country. The woman watched the car drive up, and then heard
the excitement die down. This was not the moment. It was just another
car.

'We shall not know which car the Prince is in when he finally drives
by,' a man said. 'For security reasons. But we have to wave at all the cars
as they drive by. One of them has the Prince.'

'You mean we shall not see the Prince?' the woman asked, perplexed.
She had woken up very early, to see the man who had the power to give
them back their country. She heard the sound of sirens, and saw policemen rush by on motorbikes, followed by several cars moving slowly
behind.

'Stay back! Stay back!' the policemen shouted to the excited students
who extended their arms and waved their tiny flags in front of the stream
of passing vehicles.

'Which car has the Prince?' asked the woman.

'Certainly not the first or the second one, for security reasons,' the man
answered. 'And certainly not the last, it's too obvious.'

It must be the third then. The woman looked hard through the heavily
tinted windows, but saw nothing. Still, everyone waved and shouted.
They saw only their own excited faces, intercepted among reflections of
purple jacaranda blooms. Along that very road the Prince surely had
passed. If they had not seen him, maybe he had seen them. 'Did you see
the Prince?' they asked each other on the way home. Later, some of them
would see him at the stadium, at midnight. The woman would not go.

*

The man kept one arm around the woman, while with the other he held
a bottle of cold beer. He had the television on, and insisted that he would
watch the Independence celebrations first. He had already given her the
money, and she kept it knotted in a yellow handkerchief which she had
tied on the strap of her bra. The stadium, usually reserved for soccer
matches, was filled to capacity. First there was traditional dancing in
the middle of the stadium. The woman withdrew into the safe space
in her mind, and watched the pictures go by on the screen.

The new Prime Minister gave a long speech, and people clapped and
shouted. They raised their fists in jubilation. The new Prime Minister
spoke into a microphone. The women continued dancing while the Prime
Minister was speaking. The people waved their flags when they were told

everything would be changing soon. Jobs and more money. Land and education. Wealth and food. The woman saw the Prince sitting quietly, dressed in spotless white clothing. They said his mother could not come. But in these matters he was as important as his mother. The new Prime Minister said something about the Prince, and everyone cheered.

The man watching the screen went to the kitchen for another beer. He was going to celebrate Independence properly: with cold beer and a woman. Now it was ten minutes to midnight. She must take her clothes off. The screen flashed the ticking minutes. The Prince and the new Prime Minister walked to the large flagpole in the middle of the stadium. The old flag was flapping in the air, the new one was hanging below. The man pushed the woman on to the floor. He was going into the new era in style and triumph. She opened her legs. It was midnight, and the new flag went up. The magic time of change. Green, yellow, white. Food, wealth, reconciliation.

When he was through he sent her home. When he awoke he preferred the whole house to himself. They had met under the jacarandas, waiting for the English Prince.

In the morning she saw miniature flags caught along the hedge: the old flag and the new.

Musaemura Zimunya

A Pineapple Incident

Musaemura Bonas Zimunya was born in 1949 in Mutare; in 1975 he moved to England to continue his education at the University of Kent at Canterbury. Currently he lectures in English at the University of Zimbabwe, Harare. Well known as a poet and cultural commentator, in 1993 he put out with Longman Zimbabwe his first collection of over a dozen varied pieces, *Nightshift and Other Stories*, in the Zimbabwe Writers series. 'A Pineapple Incident' is from there.

HARARE HAS BOASTED one precarious claim above all the other cities of Africa and, indeed, the whole world, which the city fathers have vigorously promoted ever since the heyday of settler rule when it used to be called Salisbury. This is the claim of being 'The Sunshine City'. And now, as in those dark days when it was christened by colonists, the idea is to lure moneyed tourists from cold and depressing climes of Europe and America. Of course, it is a precarious claim because there are more than a dozen other cities in Southern Africa alone which passionately claim that their sunshine is the best on the forex market.

Because this claim is boosted by corresponding campaigns in the media, journals, magazines, on T-shirts and billboards, its spirit permeates the character of the men and women, boys and girls of this city. The idea that Harare's sunshine is the best transforms into the claim that its citizens are the best. So you will see it in the politicians, policemen, civil servants, workers, thieves, thugs and of course even prostitutes. They, like Phaeton, begin to believe they are children of the sun-god, divine heirs of the light of life. Which makes them cocky, arrogant, boisterous, chest-beating; in short, thoroughly presumptuous and know-all.

Should you decide to attend a political rally, you will be severely assaulted by the rhetoric of a bigoted and vainglorious politician on issues he least understands. Should you challenge a policeman, he will throw you into a filth-ridden cell and, being drink-besotted, he will forget all about you when he wakes up in the morning. And, should you be so unlucky as to need a birth certificate or a passport, you will have to hurdle over a mile-long queue and then settle with a bribe-eyed civil servant.

And as for the thugs, thieves and prostitutes, they are so proud of their professions that they have formed their own unions whose acronyms make such ridicule of our sanctified revolutionary parties.

All this in the Sunshine City.

Nevertheless, while Harare's citizens may be truly intoxicated with their false heritage, there is, however, a fruit which, were they true artists and children of the sun, they would worship because it has drunk of the sun and is, therefore, a divine symbol of sunshine. This fruit is none other than the pineapple, born of the *ananas*, which makes the theme of this little story.

It happened at a disused parking lot, now overgrown since the beginning of the summer rains, just outside a suburban shopping centre in the month of December in 1989, a few days before Christmas. You may well have heard that December is pineapple time in Harare, being right in the heart of the sunshine months. On roadsides, in vegetable stalls and at the big Mbare Msika, you will see these huge orange-ripe grenade-shaped fruits that only explode juice and sweetness with each crunch, leaving an even sweeter aroma in your hands.

And so, you may now visualize in this disused park a young pineapple seller wearing a pair of khaki shorts and a shirt all red with earth including his hands and legs, feet buried deep in the pineapple load in the trailer of a green seven-ton lorry. The boy, who must be barely twelve – I guess the size of David when he met Goliath – looks young and simple, though his hands and legs are taut with strength from regular and heavy work.

He and the lorry driver, servants of a hard taskmaster, have come all the way from Chirinda, near Chipinge, a tiring distance of some nearly five hundred kilometres away on a rickety old Albion truck. At first, there are very few customers, two or three feet below him, raising their hands to him as though they were praying, their fingers clutching their money. They hand him variously a blue two-dollar note, a red ten-dollar note and, in some inconsiderate cases as the crowd grows larger, a twenty-dollar bill. This, for a green and half-ripe or yellow or hard or soft pineapple, depending on size and quantity. As his customers swell in numbers, something of a frenzy seems to catch them.

Calmly the young pineapple boy obliges and sometimes looks slow and overwhelmed by the hands of these worshippers of pineapple below him. He is not trained in the crude bustle and tumble of the Sunshine

City. But in his humble, rustic way he offers his pineapples to all, great and small, knowing that a sweet fruit such as the *anana* sells itself without the vulgarity of street vendors. In any case, he is also careful not to make enemies of the citizens of Harare as, according to the City Fathers, selling pineapples from the roadside is a grave criminal act for which the whole lorry-load could be confiscated.

Indeed, in 1989, the forces of law and order would descend heavily on any vendors – as they were derogatorily termed – who sold anything from pavements and roadsides. Thus in Harare the pineapple is as good as exotic. For Harare may boast of its sunshine, but that sunshine has not the sap of sweet pineapple in it. The small town of Chipinge and the little village of Chirinda on the south-east border with Mozambique, somewhere in the Eastern Highlands have, however, come to terms with the fruit of the sun. Harare is only fair streets, rising blocks, a lot of alleyway garbage, crowded bus stops and even more crowded job centres, national registration offices, you name it. And while Chipinge may be small, rustic, backward and unheard of, it, however, is the land of the pineapple and tea.

Out of the black, muddy and red soil comes the pineapple. Where there is more than just attractive weather. There is rich sun and warm rain which go to making the pineapple flourish and bear the fruit whose sweetness lures Hararians to suburban roadsides. On the rugged hills and muddy red soils people have learnt to grow the sweetest fruit in the land. The farmer has learnt the patience of the gods. For he knows that he is not master of the seasons, though he has conquered many an adverse drought over the years. His hands may be rugged and callous but his heart is human, while Harare's children are soft of hand and hard of heart. And so it was with the pineapple incident.

At first the pineapple boy was a stranger in Harare where he was always on the look-out for the forces of Law; those violent men wielding vicious batons and handcuffs. If they missed you with one thing, they got you with the other. He and the driver would, therefore, never park their seven-ton lorry in the heart of Harare. There they were sure to be arrested and all their *ananas* would be 'dumped', which was a euphemism for wanton sharing of confiscated goods among the lucky relatives and friends of the forces of law from Bikita. And besides, their master would 'shoot' them if that ever happened.

Anyway, the pineapple boy knew the value of his fruit among the people of Harare, whatever their crudity and roughness. And so, as business became more brisk with more than ten customers lining up before the trailer at any moment, he also felt lighter, as though he had spring in his hands and legs. Money was coming like leaves.

All seemed to be going well until a short man with a stubbly moustache and a bold and shiny pate came along and started asking some awkward questions. The pineapple boy had received a twenty-dollar bill and was looking all over his pockets for change, with little progress. Nervously his hands moved from one shirt pocket to another, then to his trouser pockets, right and left, back and front and then all over again in great confusion. All this was made worse by the fact that from the top of the lorry he was also keeping a wary eye on the men of law and order. It wouldn't do to be arrested now, just as he had sold so many pineapples. They would take his money as well.

Just at the time when he seemed to have only managed to pull out many notes and was holding them in both hands, with another stuck between his lips, this newly arrived customer yelled at him angrily, 'I said how much are they, or don't you know?'

Of all human beings, this was one kind the pineapple boy had always hoped and prayed to avoid, particularly at a time when he felt great distress that things had gone out of hand. He gave the citizen a simple pleading look which meant, 'Take it easy man, can't you see I can't open my mouth? Besides I am serving another customer.'

'Damn these rustics. Mfana, can't you just tell me the price of these rotten apples of yours? I can't wait here for ever, you know? And if you don't know how to run a business in Harare, go back to Mozambique!' He was pacing about, very agitated.

At last the pineapple boy managed to remove the bill from his lips, then appeared to have recovered from his great confusion and began counting the change. As he did so, he was dropping it into the hands of a white woman below who seemed anxious to depart from such a 'rude' crowd.

'O my God!' exclaimed the bald-headed citizen, feigning yawning. 'You shouldn't be selling your rotten pines or apples in this city anyway, do you hear? All I am asking is how much you're earning from selling those rotten things and you start a monkey dance with dollar bills, eh?'

The young scavenger went down on his knees, counted four pineapples, and gave them to the white woman who promptly disappeared from the scene, cluck-clucking. At the same time, the stubbly moustached citizen seemed determined to get something from the boy.

'Boy, who do you take me for, village headman or jungle idiot? I can have you arrested, right now. You will die in jail, little boy, selling pineapples without a licence.'

'Eighty cents for the big ones and sixty cents for the smaller ones,' he finally managed to say, though no one seemed to hear him.

Unfortunately, by that time the irate citizen had already made up his mind to sort the boy out. He pulled a two-way radio out of the inner pocket of his jacket and started talking to his colleague, who was invisible, with great force and agitation. In no time a cream Peugeot 504 with unmistakable number plates pulled up and out emerged men who looked well-spruced up with jackets and ties. Each one was wielding a walkie-talkie and speaking into it. They had arrived at the scene of the crime and had caught the criminals red-handed. The culprit boy couldn't believe his eyes when one of these men went over to the driver, told him he was under arrest and ordered him to follow him to the police station with his pineapples. And, not to be outdone, the bald-headed man jumped up on the back of the truck and, after jostling the pineapple boy, he handcuffed his hands behind his back.

Then, in a gesture that many will not find it easy to forget, he split a pineapple with the force of his bare hands, forcing a shower of juice on to his jacket, tie and face and, with both his lower and upper lips drawn to his gums, he sank his rusted dentures into the juicy fruit.

Paul Tiyambe Zeleza

Blood Feuds

Paul Tiyambe Zeleza was born in 1955 in the old Salisbury, Rhodesia (now Harare, Zimbabwe), of Malawian parents. He graduated from the University of Malawi's Chancellor College in 1976, pursued his career at London University and Dalhousie and taught at Trent University, Ontario. His memorable first collection of youthful stories (*Night of Darkness*) appeared in the Malawian Writers Series in 1976. He has since published a novel and a further collection, *The Joys of Exile* (1994), with House of Anansi in Concord, Ontario, in the same year in which he won the Noma Award for Publishing in Africa for a work on African economic history. He has contributed to *Women's Studies Quarterly* and he is the director of the Centre for African Studies of the University of Illinois at Urbana-Champaign.

FOR SURE they had their squabbles. But they were the usual squabbles among friends. They went through all those moments of loneliness and sometimes utter despair that everyone in exile goes through. But they always pulled through, sustained by their longing for home. They never doubted they would return one day.

That was all my father and Uncle Phala dreamed about: the return to their native land. They talked about home all the time. How they grew up. The games they used to play. The schools they went to. The struggles they waged for freedom.

'You kids have no idea what we went through to get rid of the British,' Uncle Phala used to tell us at the slightest opportunity. He proudly wore his limp, which he said he got from an injury he suffered during an anti-government riot in the turbulent fifties. Not to be outdone, my father was obliged to show us a scar on his back, which he got from beatings in jail.

'I was in jail for a week,' he would say proudly, 'not like others who only got injured in a riot.' My father would pull his face at Uncle Phala. Over the years his jail term lengthened into a month, six months, then a year.

'Don't listen to him,' Uncle Phala would interrupt spiritedly. 'He fell from a tree. That's how he got that scar!' And he would break into his infectious belly laugh.

'Don't mind him. He got his injury while chasing goats!' my father would retort, also laughing. And they would go on like this.

To say that my father and Uncle Phala liked each other would be an understatement. They behaved like inseparable twins. They called each other brother. It was only when I was a teenager that I learned that Uncle Phala was, in fact, not my real uncle. He and my father had met in the mining compound where I was born and grew up.

We shared a flat the size of a matchbox. My brothers and sisters and I grew up and went to school with Uncle Phala's children. We were like one big extended family. When we finished school, most of my brothers and I became miners and lived in the mining compound.

My father and Uncle Phala took an active part in the mining compound's Home Burial Society. This was a welfare association that helped workers from home in times of crisis, especially funerals. That is how they started getting involved in exile politics. Many years later they joined the National Redemption Movement, an organization formed by exiles opposed to the government back home. My father and Uncle Phala never regarded themselves as exiles. That term was reserved for the educated elite. Nor did they regard themselves as refugees. Refugees were destitute people, mostly women and children, fleeing war and famine. They thought of themselves as ordinary migrant workers.

But ordinary they were not. At least not in the eyes of their colleagues. They were both good organizers and eloquent speakers. When I was a young boy I sometimes used to accompany them to the beer hall where they held their meetings. Whenever my father or Uncle Phala rose to speak, the hall fell silent and everyone listened to them as keenly as we listened to the headmaster during school assembly. They had a way with words and proverbs. After they finished speaking, everybody would clap and sometimes stand up and cheer. I felt so proud of them. When they retired as miners at the age of fifty, as required by the company, they began working full-time for the movement, which grew rapidly, thanks to a large exile community.

Over the years the news from home became more depressing. We heard of widespread arrests, repression and corruption. It was not the government that my father and Uncle Phala had fought for.

'When they first came to power,' my father remembered, 'we loved them. We loved the government. We thought it was ours.'

I recall Uncle Phala telling us when we were small about the day of independence.

'Everything seemed so beautiful that day. The sunshine felt a little gentler, the skies were bluer, the vegetation greener and the air smelled fresher. The moonlight even appeared brighter. Our flags fluttered from street lamps and the colonial towers and buildings. Just before midnight the Union Jack was hauled down and our flag was hoisted to deafening applause from the crammed stadium. We cheered and savoured every word our leader spoke. He roared like a lion. We called him 'the saviour'.

Like so many people from all over the country, my father and Uncle Phala scraped together every penny to go and attend the independence celebrations in the capital, to witness history in the making. But they left the country a couple of years later, as so many others had done before them, to look for jobs in the mines of Zimbabwe.

Before leaving for the mines my father worked on a tobacco plantation. He lost his job when the owner of the plantation left for Europe and sold it to one of the new ministers who preferred to employ workers from his region. Uncle Phala lost his job because he was a union organizer at his factory. The new government banned trade unions, saying there were no more enemies for them to fight now that independence had been won.

The exiles learned to live with the bad news that came from home. They would discuss it, amplify it and pass it on. But it remained distant, something they did not actually experience. Exile removed the sting of immediacy. Thus exile, with all its pain, was also a shield. It was a mask behind which they could dream and hide from themselves and avoid taking complete charge of their lives.

I did not think of myself as one of them. Of course, I regarded where my parents came from as my country of origin, although I had never been there. But I also felt strongly attached to Zimbabwe, the place of my birth. At home we spoke my parents' language; elsewhere we used one of the local languages.

I never really had to think much about my *real home* until I was a grown-up. It had never really mattered when I was a child. Sure, the other kids would sometimes call us by whatever abusive term was currently fashionable against 'foreigners'. But it never stuck. Not so in later years. It was partly age, I suppose. As one grows older things tend to stick a little more, to hurt a little deeper.

The situation in Zimbabwe was also changing. People were becoming more nationalistic, less inclined to think of themselves as *Africans* and more as *Zimbabweans*. I guess all that singing of the national anthem, watching national parades and celebrating national days were having the desired effect. We became 'foreigners', even those of us who were born in Zimbabwe, when it came to dispensing jobs and the other privileges of uhuru, and to finding scapegoats for the mounting economic and social problems.

That is when I became more involved in the National Redemption Movement. Our community gradually turned inward, became more self-contained. As far as possible, we kept together, supported one another and married among ourselves.

I married Uncle Phala's eldest daughter, Mwali, to the great satisfaction of both our parents. 'We are now real brothers!' the two men announced happily at the wedding reception.

I began to miss my native land as much as my father and Uncle Phala. I wanted to know more about it. So I asked questions and devoured any information I could get from books, newspapers and magazines. I dreamed of the shimmering lake with its golden sand beaches, the cascading rivers, the rolling hills and mountains, and the cool green highlands. A land, as my father and Uncle Phala remembered it, of neat villages, handsome cities, safe streets and smiling faces. Not this semi-arid wasteland only fit for exile.

We hoped and dreamed. In the meantime I grew older. I had three children. My father and Uncle Phala began to look like the grandfathers they were. They continued to play an active role in the movement, but the situation seemed as intractable as ever. None of us thought it would change soon, although we did not doubt that change would eventually come. But nobody could have foreseen the suddenness with which the thirty-year-old regime began tottering a few years later.

Discontent had, of course, been simmering for years. It was the church leaders who brought it into the open. One Easter Sunday priests read a pastoral letter in churches throughout the country. The letter did not make outlandish demands. It called for simple things like social justice, the rule of law and respect for human rights. But the letter hit the nation like a volcano. No one within the country had ever publicly made these demands before. The letter was confiscated. Distributing it became an act of subversion. Some church leaders were arrested and threatened with dire consequences.

But it was too late. The die had been cast. Students took over from where the priests had left off and added their youthful vigour and impatience. They demonstrated, rioted and demanded free and fair elections and the release of all political prisoners. The universities and colleges were closed and the students were sent home. That only served to spread the discontent, for the students carried the message back to their home regions.

Then the workers joined the fray. They went on strike, asking for a living wage. The security forces tried to break one strike gathering, but they only succeeded in shooting scores of workers and setting the whole country on fire. Even foreign governments and lending institutions that had long supported the regime began to see the writing on the wall and threatened to cut off aid.

I had never seen my father and Uncle Phala so excited. They became glued to the radio and television. For some reason I was not as excited as I thought I would be. I had become so used to hoping and dreaming about the seemingly impossible that the impending reality of return frightened me. Exile had always been my life. It was all I knew.

There were several developments that reinforced my unease. The community began to fracture between those who wanted to return and those who were not so keen. These conflicts were also played out in families. Before long they spilled into the movement itself. That year's general assembly was rent by strife over whether or not to turn the movement into a political party, the ideological orientation of the party and the distribution of leadership positions to satisfy the various constituencies of age, gender and ethnicity. By the end of the meeting the movement had split into three factions. It was sad to watch.

But this did not prepare me for what awaited us in our beloved native land. The country was physically beautiful all right, but that was about it. We first went to my father's village. I was disappointed. It was a run-down collection of mud dwellings. I met some of my uncles and aunts for the first time. They all looked much older than my father, although they were younger than he was. They were nice and friendly, but that is as far as they could take their hospitality. It was the same at my mother's village, which was located a few miles away.

I felt like a stranger. They called us machona, meaning the long lost people. As machona, we were expected to shower them with gifts, far more than the migrant labourers who returned every two years or so carrying huge suitcases filled with second-hand clothes inside and blankets strapped outside. Not to mention radios, watches, sunglasses and other fanciful trinkets that they distributed to eager relatives. For a couple of months they would live like chiefs. Then their money ran out and they would embark on another trek to Zimbabwe. We disappointed them.

I had a suspicion that this may have been one of the reasons why my father had not returned for so long.

I also began to understand that we were no different from the people of Zimbabwe. In our community we used to poke fun at what we thought were their petty ethnic prejudices and squabbles. We prided ourselves in being above that, for our community contained people who came from different regions and ethnic groups back home. My father and Uncle Phala were a good example. My father was from the south and Uncle Phala from the north. But this is not what I found. I heard the same petty prejudices and squabbles.

In fact, it was more serious than that. Both the discredited regime and the opposition parties seemed bent on stoking the fires of ethnic antagonism, perhaps because neither had a real agenda for change apart from advancing the personal ambitions of their respective leaders. Anybody who could convince his wife, children, clan and drinking mates seemed to think they could form a party.

As active as my father was, he soon got involved in politics. At first he concentrated his energies on establishing a business. He had come back with all his savings, which he used to set up a grain mill and a grocery store. He was approached to join one of the parties in the region and take up a leadership position. He resisted for a while, only because, I suspect, he did not want to appear too eager.

'Well, I can't let these people down,' he said, finally relenting. 'They need a man of my experience for leadership.' It proved good for his business. Many of the local businesses were owned by northerners. Resentment against them was strong and growing.

A few weeks later I went with my family to visit Uncle Phala. We were well received. Uncle Phala proudly introduced me to his relatives. I liked his village better. It was not as dilapidated and the people did not look as miserable. We decided to settle there and start a business. I bought two trucks to transport fish between the lake and the capital. It turned out to be a lucrative business.

My father was not pleased with the decision when I returned for a brief visit. He said I was betraying my people.

'But, Father,' I protested, 'we're living with Uncle Phala. He's your "brother", remember?'

'Uncle Phala is all right. It's his people who aren't. I don't trust them.'

'I can't believe you, of all people, saying that.'

I did not tell Uncle Phala about my father's objections. He was pleased with our decision.

'You're my favourite son. You've been good to my daughter.' Uncle Phala did not have a son. All of his eight children were girls.

Like my father, he had also started a business, which was doing quite well. Before long he, too, was approached by the region's leading party to join. And like his 'brother', he played coy for a while.

So it was that the two most important men in my life became entangled in the new politics. The parties tried to outdo each other in seeing which one could organize the biggest demonstrations and rallies, not which one had the best programme for transforming the country. The political prisoners still languishing in jail were almost forgotten, except by their relatives, especially their mothers, who organized a daily vigil outside the high court. It was later violently broken up by the police. And none of the opposition parties pressed for a national conference to hammer out a new constitution and the terms of the transition from a dictatorship to a democracy.

It was difficult not to get caught up in the frenzy, but I tried not to. I missed the disengaged politics of exile. In this politics there was no hoping, no dreaming, just scheming and plotting. It was raw and real. Too raw, as it turned out.

A couple of months before the elections were held to elect a new government, violence erupted. It was not clear who started it. In the months that followed, people from the north and south traded accusations. Each community started chasing the 'foreigners' in their midst. Church leaders and other neutral observers blamed the government for fomenting the troubles. The government, of course, denied any responsibility. The 'saviour', now a doddering old man who could hardly walk and sneeze at the same time, said the violence vindicated him. It showed that multi-party politics were as foreign to the country as winter.

One morning we were woken up by a loud explosion. I looked out of the window. My trucks had been set ablaze. We all knew why, but we conveniently blamed it on thieves. It was less painful that way. We should have seen it coming, but we clung to the hopes and dreams of exile. Reality had now caught up with us. That evening Uncle Phala spoke what was on our minds.

'You're not safe here. Maybe you should go home.'

'I thought I was home,' I sighed, more in sadness than anger.

'So did I. This isn't the country your father and I left thirty years ago. They've created a monster. It will devour us if we don't watch it, even after they're gone.' For the first time he looked very old.

'We'll be out of here as soon as we can.'

He shook his head. 'You'll go alone. Mwali and the children will be as unsafe in your home as you are here.'

'But I can't leave my family behind.'

'It's for their own good, and for your own good, too,' he said sadly. 'Believe me.'

'It's not right,' I murmured. 'It's just not right.'

He nodded, but did not look at Mwali or me.

Mwali and I spent a sleepless night discussing the matter. We decided that we would either stay together or leave together. Nothing would separate us.

But we did not have time to communicate our decision to Uncle Phala, for early the next morning we heard noises from a large crowd that was chanting with great excitement.

'We want the southerner!' they screamed. 'We want the southerner! Give us the southerner!'

'Hide under the bed quick,' Mwali whispered.

The chanting came closer. Some people started banging on the door. Then the chants and banging stopped. We heard Uncle Phala's voice. 'He sneaked away last night!'

'No!' the crowd yelled with disappointment. 'We want the southerner!'

'You know how these southerners are!' Uncle Phala bellowed. 'They're spineless cowards. They may be good with books and monopolize the teaching and clerical jobs in this country, but that's all they can do. They can't fight. That boy may have balls, but he has the guts of a woman.'

The crowd laughed.

'Leave the house alone.' Suddenly he called out Mwali's name. 'Come and tell these brave sons of the north where your spineless husband is.'

I could not believe what he was saying. Had he gone crazy?

'What should I do?' she begged me.

'I don't know. What's wrong with your father? I thought he loved me. He told me so himself.'

'Mwali! Please come out and tell these men where your good-for-nothing husband went.'

I lost my temper. 'Go. He's your father.' I pushed her and she started crying. 'Go, I said!'

'Don't scream. They'll hear you.' She tried to collect herself. 'Please stay where you are. Don't move,' she said as she reluctantly made for the door.

'See, she's crying,' Uncle Phala said when she came out. 'I told her not to marry a southerner!' The crowd began to disperse, cursing southerners. Moments later Mwali returned, looking both shaken and relieved.

I stayed indoors the whole day. Later Uncle Phala came to me. His face was visibly distressed. 'I'm sorry I had to say all those things.'

'So you didn't mean it,' I said curtly.

'Of course not.' He was holding back tears. 'That was the only way I could save you, by talking their kind of language. You'll always be my favourite son, no matter what.'

I do not know how long we sat there, staring listlessly at the walls. We all yearned for the bad old days of exile.

I escaped that night, and my people were relieved to see me.

'I always told you that northerners are cruel savages,' my father reprimanded me. I could not remember him ever saying that. But I was in no mood to argue with him. I just wanted to sleep and dream of the simpler days of exile.

The elections were held on schedule. The old governing party just barely managed to scrape through, thanks to the splintered opposition. The opposition parties contested the results and refused to recognize the government. As the politicians squabbled, the army moved into the vacuum and terrorized the country into an uneasy calm.

It seemed secure enough for me to ask Mwali and the children to come. They were accompanied by Uncle Phala.

When the two old men met, they shook hands and hugged heartily. For a while it all seemed like the old days, except that they both looked so much older now. They had lost a lot of weight. Uncle Phala's limp seemed to have gotten worse. My father complained of poor hearing and failing eyesight.

But it was not the old days. They had little to talk about. It was painful to watch. There was none of that old intimacy, and the banter was gone. The days of exile now seemed so remote and unreal. And yet we had been back for about a year.

Uncle Phala only stayed a couple of days. He left early in the morning. We all accompanied him to the bus station, except for my mother who was not feeling well. My father and Uncle Phala hugged in silence for what seemed like a long time. From the steps of the bus Uncle Phala waved to us with his cane. We waved in return. Then he staggered into the bus and never looked back.

Peter Clarke

The Changing of the Season

Peter Clarke was born in Simon's Town near Cape Town, South Africa, in 1929. Largely self-taught, as a graphic artist and book illustrator he has held several one-man exhibitions of his work since 1957; as a poet he has been widely published in reviews. Under the pen-name of 'Peter Kumalo' in the 1950s he twice won awards in the *Drum* short story contest, and his sketch, 'Death in the Sun', was taken from there by Langston Hughes for inclusion in his *An African Treasury* (1960); another sketch was included in Richard Rive's *Modern African Prose* (1964). *Plain Furniture* – a selection of his prints, poems and prose pieces – appeared in 1991 (from Snailpress). 'The Changing of the Season' gave its title to a collection of prize-winning stories published by COSAW in Johannesburg in 1995.

WE OPENED OUR BOOKS, looked at words and sentences and became involved in the process of learning while our teacher stood by the blackboard explaining things.

At the time it did not occur to us that a great deal of what we were forced to learn in school would eventually become more or less meaningless in our daily lives. Many of the facts that we memorized were not worth remembering. It had nothing to do with us. For instance, one looked at the atlas and certain names stood out. On the map of Africa one noticed Suez, the Straits of Gibraltar, Dakar, Gulf of Guinea, Congo River, Benguela, the Cape of Good Hope which was within travelling distance – even by donkey cart if one had the patience and the time – Mozambique, Dar es Salaam, Zanzibar, the Horn of Africa. Apart from the Cape of Good Hope, which is situated in this country in which we live, nothing was real. Nothing existed. We would never travel there from this poor little rural village somewhere in South Africa that the world did not know of and never would know existed. All those places on the map could be places imagined, places that were real only in the geography of the mind. For instance, the Horn of Africa was only a term that suggested something else to us country children. Cattle. A bull's horn. 'Horing' –

Penis Erection – a masculine organ of stiffened flesh and hot pumping blood.

Sitting in the school benches we thought about the Horn of Africa, suggestive as it was of something else. We looked at each other, lowered our heads and sniggered silently so Meneer wouldn't notice.

At certain times of the year we had to write tests. There were those individuals who came first and those who followed. There was even the person who, naturally, came last. It was important to pass examinations. Still it wasn't a matter of life and death. But it was agonizing.

It became a kind of ritual having to recite the times table: two twos are four, three twos are six and so on – then being called on to say recitations and to be the first to expose your knowledge, or lack of it at the time, because yours was the surname beginning with A, Abrahamse, Adams, Adonis, Appollis. It was inconvenient but it wasn't the end of the world. If your surname began with A and you were stupid you were the first to hold out your hand to get caned. You suffered the indignity, but you got it over and done with.

If your name began with a letter far down in the alphabet – like Z for Zondi – you were the last to be called to show you were as bright as everyone else or as stupid or worse. There was nobody after Zondi. He was always the last person to be called. Being last has its disadvantages, too. Zondi was usually so tense at that stage that he couldn't help farting. He couldn't very well ask to leave the room even if he genuinely needed to get to the lavatory. He wasn't always believed. Nobody takes jesters seriously. Jesters aren't supposed to reveal their true feelings, otherwise who would we laugh at?

As we grew older it seemed as if Zondi was meant to be last. I used to wonder about that piece in the Bible where it says those that are last shall be first and those who are first shall be last. Did it mean things always worked out just that way it is stated there? Does it mean really that? And Zondi? Where did he fit into the scheme of things? Zondi would joke about it. One thing about him, he was stupid in school, but he had a sense of humour. He could laugh at himself. He had a way of saying things.

'It gives me breathing space if I'm last,' he would say.

But for what? I would wonder. For what?

During our early school years, when we pupils had running races he would not be first even though he was bigger than most of us. He was so clumsy, when we were involved in football on the school's playground he'd miss the ball and, kicking gravel, would cut his big toe early in the game. When we sang hymns or school songs he'd be the one who'd finish last, singing a little off-key as well, so his voice was always being noticed. It was that kind of voice, deep, from all the smoking, they said. He was the only one who was left-handed in the class and the teacher struggled to get him to write with his right hand. Trying to get him to do it that way was a waste of time. Poor Zondi. He certainly wasn't clever. But the thing is he also had a way of complicating things at times by just being himself.

As the years went by I wondered if he sometimes wondered why things weren't always right for him and if he ever thought about being first for a change, instead of always last.

It was Andries Hendriks who said, 'Sometimes things are meant to be that way and you can't change it. No one can change it.'

'You mean,' I asked, 'this being the way he was?'

'Ja,' said Andries. 'Certain things are set out that way.'

'Ach, man, I wonder. Maybe if he gave himself a chance he'd have seen he wasn't all that stupid as he thought he was. This thing about always having to be last can be a lot of nonsense. Surely a person can also be first for a change? Sometimes?'

'I don't know. Maybe.'

'But the Bible does say so, and if the Bible says so it must be so.'

We thought about that for a while because whenever the Bible is mentioned people tend to think more seriously, whether they're clever or not.

Dolphie Arendse looked at us. 'Perhaps,' he suggested, 'it would have been different if he believed that everything didn't have to be the way it was.'

'Yes,' said Lukas Francke, 'maybe that was it. He had to think differently.'

We sat there reminiscing on the river bank, Andries, Dolphie Arendse, Lukas Francke and I. The water flowed by as it had four to five years ago when we were innocent youngsters and Zondi was still living here and a part of our daily lives. Now we were young men with muscles where there had been nothing before and moustaches starting to grow. Wild oats were being secretly sown, with nothing being said about it, even to friends. Things had changed from the days when, as they say, we were still children with milk behind the ears. That was the time when the grown-ups would say to us, 'muisdrolle uit die peper' (little mice-droppings). We had grown up, become older and had had and were having certain experiences. So even though we were the same people, we weren't the same innocent children of a few years ago. Things had changed. I sighed.

'Remember when we were still really youngsters,' I said, 'the way we used to come to the river and have good times here?'

'Yes, we had a lot of fun.'

'Even though we sometimes didn't get a chance to come to the river because we had to stay out of school to go and work on the Boere's farms to pick apples and mielies or help during the harvest with the onions in order to earn extra pennies for the family. I won't ever forget that.'

'Me neither. All that going to work on the different farms. Extra pennies. But there was also time when we had fun.'

'Yes. Yes. Sometimes getting up to all kinds of mischief. The good things, the not so good things, the funny things.'

We laughed, remembering the past, even the silliness that went into discovering what life was all about and who we were.

'Yes ... and Zondi was part of it too, hey?'

'Uh. Neither will I forget how annoyed Meneer used to get when he had a school that was half empty. "Learning is so important," he used to say.'

'Ja. I remember him saying that more than once, wanting to drum it into our young minds. Meneer knew that the Boere knew it too. But there was absolutely nothing he could do to prevent his schoolchildren going by the lorryload to work on their farms.'

'It's so sad. Not that being book-educated was going to get us plaas-japies anywhere.'

'But all Meester just wanted was for us to learn and not be altogether stupid.'

'That's the honest truth. Remember how he used to say learning is far more than just being able to sign your name? I used to feel sorry because Meester really cared about us.'

'True, yes. He really cared. He didn't want us to grow up and still be stupid. That's why he used to say it's not a crime to be a farm worker, but it is a crime to ignore books. That is why he used to cane us like that when we didn't learn what we were supposed to learn. Perhaps that's the reason too why he started to drink like that, worrying about the future of the children he taught.'

'Ach, shame. And the school not full every day too during the picking season.'

'Yes. We worked even though we schoolkids were supposed to be attending classes. But at least we got time to play also. Sometimes.'

'Sometimes, yes.'

'Playing games. Making tiny oxen and ox-wagons out of clay, and toy cars and lorries from scrapwire. Wrestling and learning to swim naked in the river . . . and seeing who had the biggest cock among us.'

We laughed, thinking about the things young boys get up to.

'Remember that time when Gielie told us how he'd heard his father and his mother's brother, his Uncle Stoffel, and their men-friends talking one night when they were having a braaivleis. Everything was going jolly and the dop had trekked – you know how the Boere like to get together and braai meat and drink beer and wine and get gesuip otherwise their braaivleises aren't braaivleises. That's the time they forget themselves and their tongues get loose and you hear all kinds of things coming out. Gielie said Oubaas Coen and Gielie's Oom Stoffel and the others were talking from below the waistline and out of the trousers and he heard his Oom Stoffel boast that he, Oom Stoffel, was proud of the fact that he had a big horing, bigger than anybody else's there that night. Gielie said his father laughed and then told his Oom Stoffel, "O Here, Stoffel. If you've got such a big horn, it means only one thing. There's Kaffir blood in you some-where," and he laughed his head off. Gielie's Oom Stoffel was drunk and he got so angry that the other ouens had to come in between, all because of what was said.'

'Instead of him just being proud to have a big cock, Kaffir blood or no Kaffir blood.'

'Yes. That's the way they are. I remember Gielie telling us that story about his Oom Stoffel and what Oubaas Coen had said about people with Kaffir blood.'

'Stupid, hey?'

'Damn stupid. Sies!'

'Hm. White people!'

'Yes, I remember that day. I remember how Gielie looked at Zondi, standing here naked on the river bank after we'd been swimming, and Zondi saying, ever so unexpectedly, "Maar jy moet my pa sinne sien. [But you should see *my* father's.] There's something for you. His is bigger than anybody else's. There's the real Horn of Africa."'

There was an explosion of laughter at what Zondi said, thinking of the Horn of Africa in our school atlas and what it always implied to us. We had burst out laughing because it was funny Zondi suddenly saying what he said. It wasn't quite the kind of thing you said about your father . . . although, of course, it would be wonderful had it been true. Then he could really be proud of his father, the biggest in the whole of Africa. Truly, a big black horn of Africa. We laughed. In our child-minds each of us wondered if this was true, each of us thinking it might well be so. The thought of it was spicy and the conversation with Gielie's Oom Stoffel and Oubaas Coen and Zondi's Pa thrown in was so ridiculous we couldn't help laughing. We sat there on the river bank in the heat, a group of naked boys amused at what had been said, all of us laughing, finding it funny . . . except Gielie. He wasn't laughing.

Unexpectedly our humour had separated us from Gielie. We had been together. We had taken it for granted that he would go on being a part of all of us just as we had always been, a close-close group, Andries, Lukas, Dolphie, Zondi, Gielie and I. But just then Gielie was quiet; with us, yet not part of us. He was alone. A barrier suddenly existed between him and us, a barrier created by what had been said and by our humour and the sound of our laughing voices. Gielie looked hurt and it was strange to us because we had expected him to laugh also, not to sit there looking the way he did. This was so strange to us. The truth was we didn't realize he would feel insulted at the thought of having Kaffir blood in him. We had forgotten he was White. And then this business too of Zondi saying what he did about his father.

Gielie had sat there quietly, perhaps not knowing what to say. Then he said, lamely, 'Ja. But your father's only a Kaffir and my father's a White man.'

'Yes . . . then Zondi said, "Au! Yes! But my father is big and when I'm grown up, this," playing with his cock in the palm of his hand, "this is going to be even bigger than it is now."' He laughed, loudly, brazenly, his teeth white in contrast with the darkness of his skin. We had laughed with him because it was all so funny, this talk about that part of the human body that was never exposed to the world when one was grown up because it was so private. Everyone laughed . . . except Gielie. In the midst of us, he had turned into an outsider.

We didn't have to make peace between the two, the White boy who was going to grow up and be baas one day and the taller Black boy who was just going to grow big and be a labourer for the rest of his life. But we knew things weren't going to be the same after this incident. A seed had been planted from which terrible snagging thorns would grow between us, tearing at friendships, eventually choking to death what had been beautiful.

'Things started changing afterwards, didn't they?' Lukas said. 'What with Gielie going to the High School for the Whites in town and him coming home only at weekends. Remember how moody he'd be, sometimes okay with us, sometimes otherwise?'

'Yes,' I replied. 'Sometimes just all that sitting around the place with those lekker story books in which there were pictures of White men and women half naked falling in love with each other, or the men moering each other up over women that one or the other got in the end.'

'Ach, those picture love-story books are a lot of nonsense.'

'Ja,' Andries recalled, 'but after looking at those books, Gielie would sit about with his hands in his pockets.'

'He and his pimples ... and his hands in his pockets,' I commented.

We, who had already had certain experiences, laughed. Then we were serious.

'Yes, it wasn't quite the same any more. Things were changing. He was getting other ideas.'

'But in between we still had good times, hey? We and Zondi and Gielie, swimming in the river at weekends.'

'We still swimming kaalgat, but he wearing swimming trunks ... as if he wanted to hide something from us. What I don't know.'

'Poor fellow.'

'We and Zondi still sometimes went on hiking trips to the mountain with him.'

'Not we with him. Him with us,' Lukas said quickly. 'Gielie would go with us. But it wasn't quite the same. Something was lost that none of us could ever replace.'

'It definitely wasn't the same from that time when Oubaas Coen told us to start calling Gielie Baas Gielie, was it?'

'No. It definitely wasn't the same. That day Oubaas Coen was so angry that the spit was flying when he said, "Hoor'ie, hoor'ie ... from today there's no more Gielie. You Hotnots ... and you, Kaffir," he said, giving Zondi a look that I've never seen him give anybody before, "you all call Gielie Baas Gielie, understand?"'

'Yes, and we could only mutter, "Ja, Oubaas." We couldn't say anything else.'

'We understood because I think we all told ourselves, "Yes. From today on Gielie is a White man."'

We understood Oubaas Coen to say Gielie and we were different, while at the same time he had attempted to really plant the idea into our heads, to bury it there, that we and Zondi weren't the same either. Zondi was different. There was a difference of blood. Oubaas Coen had called him 'Kaffir', telling us all what he really thought of him.

Life suddenly became then like the remembrance of green fields where now there were rank-smelling weeds and thorn-bushes growing uncontrollably. A shadow had moved over the day. From then we were to see less and less of Gielie. He wasn't a part of our lives any more. He had become White.

What had happened with Gielie was bad, so we didn't expect anything worse to happen. When it did, it was terribly unexpected.

There was the time when the Government started to come and check up on people living in farm villages. This had to do with races that different people belonged to ... as if that had been important before. I'm sure nobody's pure. All of us in this country have got all kinds of blood in us. Instead of worrying who's got what kind of blood in them we should just get on with living our lives and doing what we've got to do. That's all. But along come these bastards with their notebooks and forms and things, asking all kinds of questions, wanting to know where people were born and when, wanting to know about papers and passes and things. Zondi's father was told he was Xhosa and as this was a Coloured work area – my God, at the time we didn't know there was something like that! – they belonged in a Bantustan.

'I remember,' Dolphie mused, 'how Zondi told us that they were told they had to go and live in a Xhosa homeland, just like that. He looked like someone who had stepped into shit and couldn't get it off his shoes.'

'Can you imagine? What kind of stupid thing was this? Go and live in a homeland!'

'It isn't Christian coming from White people. Breaking up a family, any family, is evil.'

'I say it's the work of the devil, whether he's White or not. That's what it is.'

'They had always lived here and been part of us,' Dolphie said. 'Couldn't someone do something about it?'

'We couldn't do anything, could we? And Oubaas Coen told everyone even he couldn't do a thing. He said he couldn't very well go against the Government and what the Government said. "The law's the law," he said. Those were his very words.'

'Almost like Pontius Pilate. Washing his hands. None of his business.'

'Huh. If you ask me, he didn't care,' Lukas suggested.

'Perhaps not,' I said. 'Maybe he reckoned there were enough of the

Hotnots around here to do the dirty work. But if more were needed there were those still sitting on the school-benches that could be kept out of school when there were onions or potatoes to be harvested and apples, peaches and pears to be picked. Extra pennies, you know. Poor people always needed money to keep going.'

'We must really stop screwing and having so many babies. We're always going to know hardship.'

'Yes, problems. Cheap labour,' Lukas said. 'Hell.'

'Oubaas Coen votes for the Government,' I said. 'We don't. We don't even have a vote. Not even our fathers who are old enough to vote. Shit!' For a moment I sat there thinking how mysteriously God works His wonders. A person is so often puzzled by the strangeness of being alive.

'Shame. Sometimes I think about old Zondi and his Pa and Ma and his sisters and I wonder what happened to them? They were so much a part of us that there was actually a pain in my heart when they were forced to go away from here.'

'That's how I felt too,' said Andries. 'All of us.'

'Yes,' we said.

'Strange how their house collapsed shortly after they left, hey?'

'Yes, during the first rain ... damn strange ... almost as if it had given up the ghost because the people who had lived there weren't living there any more.'

'My folks said it was the first and only house Zondi's father and mother had lived in ever since they were married,' I told everyone.

'The first and the last,' Dolphie said. 'The first and the last.'

'Yes,' Lukas said. 'It's damn sad what they've done to us people, not only here but all over the country.' He sighed.

'Yes. It is damn sad,' Dolphie said. 'But one shouldn't give up hope. Things don't always stay the same. Look,' he said, 'even at the change of seasons. Everything. Everything changes when it has to, even though certain things take much longer than others. If it has to change, it has to change ... and if it has to, it will.'

Relaxing on the bank we looked at the river flowing and thought about Dolphie's words and what he'd said. Things change when they have to, everything, as if according to an unwritten law.

Sheila Roberts

Sweetness

Sheila Roberts was born in Johannesburg, South Africa, in 1937, and undertook her further studies at UNISA in Pretoria. She has published several novels and her collections of short stories date from *Outside Life's Feast* (1975) to *Coming In and Other Stories* (Justified, 1993), from which 'Sweetness' is taken. 'Sweetness' had first appeared in the long-lived South African review *Contrast* (number 59 in July 1985) and won her the Thomas Pringle Award for Fiction in that year; later it was included in *Triquarterly*, number 69 (Spring–Summer 1987), the issue devoted to New Writing from South Africa. She emigrated to the United States in 1977 and is a professor of creative writing at the University of Wisconsin, Milwaukee.

AFTER KEEPING HER MOTHER four days in capricious labour, Clare chose to be born on 29 January 1914, the very day that Gandhi chose to leave South Africa for India, never to return. So on the night of 29 January, Clare's mother, a sturdy eighteen-year-old, slept the sleep of exhaustion and disillusion, and General Smuts, rid of a troublesome mystic, slept the sleep of relief.

Clare's mother was Dutch, *her* mother, she always boasted, having twice met and talked with Queen Juliana of the Netherlands. The grand-mother, the acquaintance of a queen, could substantiate her grandeur by showing her possessions: some fine old pieces of jewellery and crystal and a set of beautiful Dutch stamps, all of which, she said, she was saving for Clare. To Clare's unremitting disappointment and to her young mother's secret satisfaction, a loitering miner out on strike stole the valuables from the grandmother's bedroom on the night of 15 March 1922, having first tied up the grandmother with her own Lyle Thread stockings. At eight years Clare received her first intimation that her childlike conviction of a foreordained distinction awaiting her might be misconceived.

Clare's father was a skinny Englishman with tired-lidded eyes and a cleft chin, a kind of watered-down working-class Douglas Fairbanks. He had come to Johannesburg to find a job on the mines, had married the stalwart Dutch girl several years his junior and had proceeded to give her a baby every two years for the next twenty years, starting with Clare who had not wanted to be born. In return for these unwelcome favours, the Dutch girl perpetually fulminated and stormed at him, beat Clare cruelly with a rawhide whip kept hanging behind the kitchen door for that purpose, threw cups and saucers at the walls, and on occasion was known to dump her husband's warm plate of dinner in his lap. When the tenth child was five, he died, emaciated and disoriented, having been slowly strangled by the black lung contracted underground. Clare had loved her father. He never beat her unless her mother forced him to. She remembered once that he had spilled some sugar he was putting into his tea and how, under her mother's raucous impatience, he had winked at Clare and whispered, 'It's good sometimes to spill a little sweetness.'

Clare remembered that miners' strike of 1922, when her inheritance was stolen. When in 1984 the SABC ran a docudrama about it, Clare, now shrunken and ill, had felt herself to be more than usually tremulous. She suspected that the SABC was showing the movie for *her* specifically – that a public acknowledgement of her experiences might be the long awaited distinction. She attended very closely to the TV images, would not allow her husband to talk during the show, and waited for the telephone to ring so that someone could question her on the veracity of something. Of course the phone did not ring, and of course Clare had known and knew very little about that huge disturbance. All she did recall was wandering out in the street when she heard shots in the distance and banging and shouting a few doors down. She saw Mr Koekemoer and Mr Luyt throw old furniture and woodslats into the street and thought they were angry. But when she saw Barnie Koekemoer and Boetie Luyt come out to help their dads, she was able to distinguish between violent ill-temper and urgent strategy. She went to help. Later, her mother, furious because Clare had 'interfered' with the neighbours, tied her right leg to the kitchen table with a length of rope and kept her there for two days, declaring that *that* would teach her to wander. For two days Clare had to crouch under the table at mealtimes and eat her food from a plate on the floor like a dog, keeping her eyes watchfully on the many legs surrounding her like jail bars in case someone inadvertently or on purpose kicked her.

As things turned out, there was no fighting on their street, but an unexploded bomb was dropped into their back garden, smashing several ripe pumpkins into a vast pink sticky pitted obscenity.

At seventy, trembling, Clare watched the SABC's show but would not admit to herself that the colours and significance of history had evaded her.

By the time she reached adulthood, Clare knew that the distinction she believed life would bestow on her would not come in the form of a grandmotherly gift, nor in the form of expansive motherly love, nor from her own energetic action, for her flesh and bones had been infused with a timidity akin to embalming fluid. Or rather, having lived for twenty-four years in the path of her mother's siroccos, her possible leaves and branches of enterprise had become sclerotic.

In 1938, hearing on the wireless names like Rhineland, Sudetenland, Czechoslovakia and an infinite repetition of the opinions of Germany, Britain, France and Russia, she grew to suspect that her distinction might come through travel, though each time she stared at a tiny hazy newsprint map she would feel the sensation of a rope tied round her right ankle. But she fantasized that someday someone would put a boat ticket into her hand, help her on board and send her off somewhere.

That geographically expansive year of 1938 she met a daring blond young goldminer, the owner of a monstrous Harley Davidson, part animal part machine. Every Saturday Wally the miner took her on the back of his bike to the bioscope and bought her a bag of chocolate creams. She would eat them all, not saving any for her grey-haired but still raving mother and her noisy siblings. And as the last one melted between tongue and soft palate, she would think, *Sweetness, Sweetness.* In 1939 Wally and Clare married and Clare felt (only momentarily, but not for the last time) that her bond with Wally might be her distinction. When Wally joined the army in 1942 to be part of the South African contingent of 'Tobruk Avengers', Clare realized enviously that she was still waiting for her own miraculous chance to travel – imaginary rope or no imaginary rope.

Wally returned from North Africa and Italy in 1945 an enthusiastic and unashamed drunkard. Brandy, sugar and water was his staple, the bread-and-butter of his imbibing, but he constantly experimented with other liquors and liqueurs, particularly on weekends. At one time it was eggnog and kirsch that he mixed while extolling their strengthening properties, another it was vodka laced with kümmel, and for several months he went for 'kleiner-kleiners', which are a shot of brandy swallowed fast followed by a more leisurely pint of beer. When he was trying out unusual mixtures or when he took to wine for a time, he would insist that Clare taste the drink to learn appreciation, and later offered the glass to the children, three little girls born in 1939, 1942 and 1946. In Italy, he maintained, the children drank wine and it was good for them. When the Nats got in in 1948 he made them all drink Van der Hum in celebration, even the two-year-old who then amused them all by dancing giddily.

The extended families on both sides deplored Wally's drunkenness openly. They all took turns to nag, coax, cajole and threaten, and tried to shore up the sagging boughs of Clare's passivity so that she would stand against Wally's addiction. But she merely listened to their indignation, nodding and murmuring, but could not oblige them. What she did, however, was turn to the little girls. At bedtime she would tell them stories of her childhood and youth, of how her mother had mistreated her, and how neither happiness nor anything of distinction had ever come her way. She spoke slowly and softly. Hardly understanding her, the girls were nevertheless moved to a deep childish pity, and as the years went by they took more and more of the household tasks off her hands. And more and more Clare discovered she had headaches, wonderful dank headaches that sent her to lie on a bed that metamorphosed into a darkened cave smelling of vinegar.

Her one consolation during those years of Wally's rowdiness and the wasting of his wages on drink was the vaguely bitter distinction she achieved by being the wife of a man of lost potential. Wally's family started the story that grew into an indestructible legend: that Wally had been a clever lad, and a bright young man, one who had been going to make a success of something some day, but that he would never do it now because of the drink. *Wally could have been a fine man and a good provider*, they would say to Clare, whereupon she would feel a mantle of dignity settle on her shoulders. Again she would nod and murmur, as if she had known all along of the potential, as if she had chosen her husband with acute discrimination.

As soon as they were old enough to get jobs, the three girls (variously glutted from having had to serve as parents to their parents) each left home in turn. Out in the world they hoped to rid themselves of a confused inner weightiness and to grow young, light and easy. Eventually the eldest left for England and the two younger ones for Australia.

When the last girl left Wally gave up drinking, not out of grief over losing his children but because he had been shocked sober by Prime Minister Verwoerd's assassination. He felt that the country now needed his full attention. He started learning Afrikaans – belatedly and badly. Clare, now fifty-two, found an uninebriate, politically muddled but verbose Wally very tedious. She hated to have the editorials from *Die Volksblad* read out to her in a halting Afrikaans which she did not understand even when it was unhalting.

She retreated more frequently into subterranean headaches. She also began answering more diligently the letters from her daughters. She suggested with increasing directness that she should visit them in turn, but either they did not comment on her suggestion or they kept pointing out that they had no place for a guest in their one-room apartments. Noleen, the eldest, salved her conscience each time she did not take up her mother's self-invitation by sending home parcels of good English chocolates. The word *sweetness* still came to Clare as she ate them all – alone and methodically – but not as mellifluously as before. When her insistence that mothers and daughters should not be separated for too long became strident – she even underlined the words on the page – she merely succeeded in delaying her daughters' replies. Every day she visualized herself in a neat beige suit, carrying a fine leather overnight bag, boarding a large plane for London or Sydney. She saw herself as distinguished, even beautiful, as she crossed the expanse of an air terminal.

Over the years Clare grew smaller and more simian, though she was unaware of this. Whenever Wally took photos of her to send to her daughters, she would write behind them: *Supposed to be me! Supposed to be me!* Several times she argued that Kodak had sent back the wrong photos. During those years she once again enjoyed a dubious distinction, that of being married to the fittest old man in the neighbourhood. Wally had diverted all the enthusiasm he had felt for alcohol into personal fitness programmes. He had trimmed down, firmed up and put on a healthy glow to his relatively unlined face. His once blond hair had turned a brilliant admirable silver, and his long brisk walks around the neighbourhood earned him many acquaintances. Even the dogs seemed to like him. People she had never met stopped Clare at the shops, saying *Your husband is wonderful!* The family all said behind their hands, *Hasn't Clare aged?*

By 1976 when the Soweto riots broke out, the two daughters in Sydney had given Clare seven grandchildren between them, children she had only seen in bad reciprocal photographs, the sun in their eyes, all frowning, all blonde, all looking alike. Noleen in London had remained single, having had her fill of what Americans call nurturing (a word absurdly suggesting that human beings are as pleasant as gardens). Clare grew obsessed with the idea of visiting Noleen. As time passed, Noleen's spinsterhood made her age unnaturally in Clare's mind's eye until Noleen seemed her contemporary. She visualized them as two lone elegant women together in London. In the shops. In the parks.

In 1976 Wally gave up fitness for target practice. He also bought a thoroughbred Alsatian which he named Lucia after a woman he had known in Italy. He had her spayed when she was still pre-oestrous to make her wild, and took her to killer-training school. Clare hated Lucia.

One day in 1979 Clare tripped over a rucked mat and fell, startling Lucia, who promptly bit Clare several times in the head. The doctor who was called in to stitch the wounds was so appalled by the length and depth of the gashes that he notified the police. A magistrate ordered Wally to have Lucia destroyed, but Wally's lawyer managed to get the sentence commuted to defanging. With a defanged Lucia back in the house even before Clare's bites were healed, she felt the first stirrings of an indignation rendered quiescent almost sixty years previously by her mother's rawhide whip. This little sprout of indignation pushed her to pack a suitcase and keep it in readiness under her bed.

By 1984 when the SABC broadcast its programme on the 1922 miners' strike, Lucia had been run over and Wally had had to have his bottom lip removed because of cancerous growths. He looked a little doglike himself without the lip but was still spry and shock-haired. He nattered all day in Afrikaans about two things only: the Great Depression and how he had retained his job, and his experiences in Cairo and Rome during the war. Clare never listened. But the two daughters from Sydney did visit that year, frightening Clare. They had both grown into stocky loudmouthed women, both uncannily like Clare's own mother. She would become dumb and wide-eyed in their presence. But her indignation was growing.

One spring morning, still in 1984, Clare went into town by bus. She withdrew a large sum of money from the savings account. Then she went by taxi to the South African Airways office and bought a return ticket for London. She had no intention of returning, but not wanting to get into a debate over legitimacy and sponsorship, she paid the fare. Using the same waiting taxi, she returned to Eloff Street where she bought an expensive beige suit from an exclusive boutique. Two weeks later she left the house silently at dawn while Wally was still asleep in his bed and walked to the corner phonebooth. There she phoned another taxi. As she was about to climb into the vehicle, she fell. She seemed to lie hazily on the sidewalk for a long time, but then with a lightened sensation and the awareness of bright sunshine, she was lifted up and driven away. She enjoyed gliding over the smooth tiles of the airport and with quiet excitement boarded the aircraft. There was a momentous roaring as it taxied down the runway. She was a little startled, however, when the stewardess who had been offering her candy to chew for take-off changed her uniform for a white coat and drew a syringe out of the air. Clare fell asleep with the strong sensation that there were ropes tying both her feet. When she woke much later and was introduced to a sweet-faced middle-aged woman named Noleen, she was convinced she had arrived.

Hennie Aucamp

Poor Old Joe

Translated from the Afrikaans by Johann Rossouw

Hennie Aucamp was born in the Eastern Cape, South Africa, in 1934, and has recently retired from lecturing in education at the University of Stellenbosch; the prolific and consummate short story writer of the Afrikaans language, he has published over a dozen collections, as well as cabaret scripts and textbooks on writing short stories. In 1983 Tafelberg issued a selection from these in English translation as *House Visits*. 'Poor Old Joe' (the title relies on a reference to the Stephen Foster song) first appeared as one of a pair in the Cape Town journal, *New Contrast* (in June 1993), and is a typical example of his use of the short short form.

Johann Rossouw trained as a philosopher at the University of Pretoria and UNISA, and works as a librarian at the French Institute of South Africa in Johannesburg. Usually he translates French texts into Afrikaans, but here has ventured into rendering Afrikaans into English.

> I'm coming, I'm coming,
> For my head is bending low,
> I hear their gentle voices calling,
> 'Poor Old Joe' . . .

POOR OLD JOE made his appearance in our town on a Sunday evening. It was a clever marketing ploy by the laundry in the main street, since many students have to walk past it on their way to church, and back again from the church to the café where coffee is always to be had after the service.

The lit display window of the laundry already drew attention as all other lights there are normally off on a Sunday evening. What made groups of people and individuals come to a perplexed standstill, noses against the glass, was the man-sized figure which stood half-bent over a washing tub, scrubbing washing with slow, mechanical movements on a washboard. The tub, which stood on a table, was brimming with suds and every now and then a soap bubble would drift away and disappear into nothing. There was also a packet of washing powder on the table proclaiming this legend: *Our washing is whiter than snow.*

The man-puppet was a black man who looked exactly like nineteenth-century American caricatures of Negroes. Somebody baptized him Poor Old Joe there and then, and this name was accepted by the whole community as fitting and correct.

There was something chillingly real about Joe. The mechanics which controlled his arm movements were also connected to his jaw muscles. Each time that he straightened up, his thick lips pulled open and a groan escaped from his throat.

Joe was a festive attraction until the burglaries started. A wave of burglaries in the well-heeled part of town: perfectly executed, as if planned by a professional criminal. And then the rape which nearly became a murder. Old Missus Neethling was found smeared with blood in her back garden, half covered under dry plane-tree leaves. But whether or not she was in her right mind is another matter. She insisted that none other than Poor Old Joe had assaulted her, still with his overalls and chequered cowboy shirt on and his arms covered up to the elbows with soapsuds.

It was clear that Poor Old Joe had to be eliminated. Old Missus Neethling's story was of course pure nonsense, but what the psychologists and the sociologists of the university realized was that there might well have been a link between Poor Old Joe and all the burglaries. Joe had come to activate something among the underprivileged – call it a group recollection of a slave past, or rebelliousness against a political dispensation, or just a low self-image. Somebody even started a thesis on the Joe case, but never completed it; and Poor Old Joe, imported from New Orleans, became forgotten in Mr Silverberg's attic.

Until the 1976 uprisings, that is.

Those of the Far Right among the students had, who knows how, found out about Old Joe, went to dig him up from under dust and cobwebs and carried him carefully, like mature wine, down the brickwork staircase.

But first there was a march by extreme Left students, with some brown and black activists among them. These individuals were summarily removed by the police because they apparently weren't bona fide students.

And then the Far Right-wingers started with a counter demonstration.

They marched silently through the streets, those at the front with a platform or stretcher lifted above their heads, three bearers on each side of this pallet. On top of the pallet, probably tied down lightly, stood Poor Old Joe painted enamel-black for the occasion, the lips scarlet, the teeth whiter than soap powder. Those who had experienced Semana Santa in Spain say it looked like a holy procession, just a pity that there weren't any candles.

Next to the main street the crowds packed on the pavements; there were even spectators in the windows and on balconies. From one of the windows 'Vrysta-a-at!' was shouted, and then Joe was shot at.

He jerked, staggered and fell.

Feet kept on milling around him, until someone shouted, 'Ugh, look at that blood!'

A Catholic miracle?

One doesn't exactly want to make oneself guilty of sacrilege, but the truth remains: Poor Old Joe lay dead still in a puddle of blood, be it human blood or ox-blood.

Ivan Vladislavić

The WHITES ONLY Bench

Ivan Vladislavić was born in Pretoria, South Africa, in 1957. After studying at the University of the Witwatersrand in Johannesburg he became an editor at Ravan Press. His first collection of short stories was *Missing Persons* (David Philip, 1989). His 'The WHITES ONLY Bench' won him the Thomas Pringle Award in 1994 and is included in his collection of 1996, *Propaganda by Monuments*. He lives in Johannesburg as a freelance editor. Recently he has contributed stories to the anthologies *Obsession* and *Sex, Drugs, Rock 'n' Roll*.

YESTERDAY OUR VISITORS' BOOK, which Portia has covered in zebra-skin wrapping-paper and shiny plastic, recorded the name of another important person: Coretta King. When Mrs King had finished her tour, with Strickland herself playing the guide, she was treated to tea and cakes in the cafeteria. The photographers, who had been trailing around after her trying to sniff out interesting angles and ironic juxtapositions against the exhibits, tucked in as well, I'm told, and made pigs of themselves.

After the snacks Mrs King popped into the gift shop for a few memen-toes, and bought generously – soapstone hippopotami with sly expressions, coffee-table catalogues, little wire bicycles and riot-control vehicles, garish place-mats and beaded fly-whisks, among other things. Her aide had to chip in to make up the cost of a set of mugs in the popular 'Leaders Past and Present' range.

The honoured guests were making their way back to the bus when Mrs King spotted the bench in the courtyard and suggested that she pose there for a few shots. I happened to be watching from the work-shop window, and I had a feeling the photographs would be exceptional. A spring shower had just fallen, out of the blue, and the courtyard was a well of clear light. Tendrils of fragrant steam coiled up evocatively from a windfall of blossoms on the flagstones. The scene had been set by chance. Perhaps the photographers had something to prove, too, having failed to notice a photo opportunity so steeped in ironic significance.

The Star carried one of the pictures on its front page this morning. Charmaine picked up a copy on her way to work and she couldn't wait to show it to me.

The interest of the composition derives – if I may make the obvious analysis – from a lively dispute of horizontals and verticals. The bench is a syllogism of horizontal lines, flatly contradicted by the vertical bars of the legs at either end (these legs are shaped like h's, actually, but from the front they look like l's). Three other verticals assert their position: on the left – our left, that is – the concrete stalk of the Black Sash drinking fountain; in the middle, thrusting up behind the bench, the trunk of the controversial Kaffirboom; and on the right, perched on the very end of her seat, our subject: Mrs King.

Mrs King has her left thigh crossed over her right, her left foot crooked around her right ankle, her left arm coiled to clutch one of our glossy brochures to her breast. The wooden slats are slickly varnished with sunlight, and she sits upon them gingerly, as if the last coat's not quite dry. Yet her right arm reposes along the backrest with the careless grace of a stem. There's an odd ambiguity in her body, and it's reflected in her face too, in an expression which superimposes the past upon the present: she looks both timorous and audacious. The WHITES ONLY sign under her dangling thumb in the very middle of the picture might be taken up the wrong way as an irreverent reference to her eyes, which she opens wide in an expression of mock alarm – or is it outrage? The rest of her features are more prudently composed, the lips quilted with bitterness, but tucked in mockingly at one corner.

The photographer was wise to choose black and white. These stark contrasts, coupled with Mrs King's old-fashioned suit and hairdo, confound the period entirely. The photograph might have been taken thirty years ago, or yesterday.

Charmaine was tickled pink. She says her bench is finally avenged for being upstaged by that impostor from the Municipal Bus Drivers' Association. I doubt that Strickland has even noticed.

There seems to be a tacit agreement around here that *Mrs* King is an acceptable form, although it won't do for anyone else. When I pointed this out, Charmaine said it's a special case because Mr King, rest his soul, is no more. I fail to see what difference that makes, and I said so. Then Reddy, whose ears were flapping, said that 'Mrs King' is tolerated precisely because it preserves the memory of the absent Mr King, like it or not. He said it's like a dead metaphor.

I can't make up my mind. Aren't we reading too much into it?

*

Charmaine has sliced the photograph out of the unread newspaper with a Stanley knife and pinned the cutting up on the noticeboard in Reception. She says her bench has been immortalized. 'Immortality' is easy to bandy about, but for a while it was touch and go whether Charmaine's bench would make it to the end of the week.

We were working late one evening, as usual, when the little drama began. The Museum was due to open in six weeks' time but the whole place was still upside down. It wasn't clear yet who was in charge, if anyone, and we were all in a state.

Charmaine was putting the finishing touches to her bench, I was knocking together a couple of rostra for the Congress of the People, when Strickland came in. She had been with us for less than a week and it was the first time she had set foot in the workshop. We weren't sure at all then what to make of our new Director, and so we both greeted her politely and went on with our work.

She waved a right hand as limp as a kid glove to show that we shouldn't mind her, and then clasped it behind her back. She began to wander around on tiptoe, even though I was hammering in nails, swivelling her head from side to side, peering into boxes, scanning the photographs and diagrams pinned to chipboard display stands, taking stock of the contents of tables and desks. She never touched a thing, but there was something grossly intrusive about the inspection. Strickland wears large, rimless spectacles, double glazed and tinted pink, and they sometimes make her look like a pair of television monitors.

After a soundless, interrogative circuit of the room she stopped behind Charmaine and looked over her shoulder. Charmaine had just finished the 'I', and now she laid her brush across the top of the paint tin, peeled off the stencil and flourished it in the air to dry the excess paint.

I put down my hammer – the racket had become unbearable – and took up some sandpaper instead. The people here will tell you that I don't miss a thing.

Strickland looked at the half-formed word. Then she unclasped her hands and slid them smoothly into the pockets of her linen suit. The cloth was fresh cream with a dab of butter in it, richly textured, the pockets cool as arum lilies.

'What are you doing?' Strickland asked, in a tone that bristled like a new broom.

Charmaine stood back with the stencil in her hand and Strickland had to step hastily aside to preserve a decent distance between her suit and the grubby overall. Unnoticed by anyone but myself, a drop of white paint fell from the end of the brush resting across the tin on to the shapely beige toe of Strickland's shoe.

The answer to Strickland's question was so plain to see that it hardly needed voicing, but she blinked her enlarged eyes expectantly, and so Charmaine said, 'It's the WHITES ONLY bench.' When Strickland showed no sign of recognition, Charmaine added, 'You remember the benches. For whites only?'

Silence. What on earth did she want? My sandpaper was doing nothing to smooth the ragged edges of our nerves, and so I put it down. We all looked at the bench.

It was a beautiful bench – as a useful object, I mean, rather than a symbol of injustice. The wooden slats were tomato-sauce red. The arms and legs were made of iron, but cleverly moulded to resemble branches and painted brown to enhance a rustic illusion. The bench looked well used, which is often a sign that a thing has been loved. But when you looked closer, as Strickland was doing now, you saw that all these signs of wear and tear were no more than skin-deep. Charmaine had applied all of them in the workshop. The bruised hollows on the seat, where the surface had been abraded by decades of white thighs and buttocks, were really patches of brown and purple paint. The flashes of raw metal on the armrests, where the paint had been worn away by countless white palms and elbows, turned out to be mere discs of silver paint themselves. Charmaine had even smeared the city's grimy shadows into the grain.

Strickland pored over these special effects with an expression of amazed distaste, and then stared for a minute on end at the letters WHI on the uppermost slat of the backrest. The silence congealed around us, slowing us down, making us slur our movements, until the absence of sound was as tangible as a crinkly skin on the surface of the air. 'Forgive me,' she said at last, with an awakening toss of her head. 'You're manufacturing a WHITES ONLY bench?'

'Ja. For Room 27.'

Strickland went to the floor plan taped to one of the walls and looked for Room 27: Petty Apartheid. Then she gazed at the calendar next to the plan, but whether she was mulling over the dates, or studying the photograph – children with stones in their hands, riot policemen with rifles, between the lines a misplaced reporter with a camera – or simply lost in thought, I couldn't tell. Did she realize that the calendar was ten years old?

Charmaine and I exchanged glances behind her back.

'Surely we should have the real thing,' Strickland said, turning.

'Of course – if only we could find it.'

'You can't find a genuine WHITES ONLY bench?'

'No.'

'That's very hard to believe.'

'We've looked everywhere. It's not as easy as you'd think. This kind of thing was frowned upon, you know, in the end. Discrimination I mean. The municipalities were given instructions to paint them over. There wasn't much point in hunting for something that doesn't exist, so we decided at our last meeting – this was before your time, I'm afraid – that it would be better if I recreated one.'

'Recreated one,' Strickland echoed.

'Faithfully. I researched it and everything. I've got the sources here somewhere.' Charmaine scratched together some photocopies splattered with paint and dusted with fingerprints and tread-marks from her running-shoes. 'The bench itself is a genuine 1960s one, I'm glad to say, from the darkest decade of repression. Donated by Reddy's father-in-law, who stole it from a bus stop for use in the garden. It was a long time ago, mind you, the family is very respectable. From a black bus stop – for Indians. Interestingly, the Indian benches didn't have INDIANS ONLY on them – not in Natal anyway, according to Mr Mookadam. Or even ASIATICS. Not that it matters.'

'It matters to me,' Strickland said curtly – Charmaine does go on sometimes – and pushed her glasses up on her nose so that her eyes were doubly magnified. 'This is a museum, not some high school operetta. It is our historical duty to be authentic.'

I must say that made me feel bad, when I thought about all the effort Charmaine and I had put into everything from the Sharpeville Massacre to the Soweto Uprising, trying to get the details right, every abandoned shoe, every spent cartridge, every bloodied stitch of clothing, only to have this Jenny-come-lately (as Charmaine puts it) give us a lecture about authenticity. What about our professional duty (Charmaine again)?

'Have we advertised?' Strickland asked, and I could tell by her voice that she meant to argue the issue out. But at that moment she glanced down and saw the blob of paint on the toe of her shoe.

I had the fantastic notion to venture an excuse on Charmaine's behalf: to tell Strickland that she had dripped ice-cream on her shoe. Vanilla ice-cream! I actually saw her hand grasping the cone, her sharp tongue curling around the white cupola, the droplet plummeting. Fortunately I came to my senses before I opened my big mouth.

*

It was the first proper meeting of the Steering Committee with the new Director. We hadn't had a meeting for a month. When Charlie Sibeko left in a huff after the fiasco with the wooden AK47s, we all heaved a sigh of relief. We were sick to death of meetings: the man's appetite for circular discussion was insatiable.

Strickland sat down at the head of the table, and having captured that coveted chair laid claim to another by declaring the meeting open. She seemed to assume that this was her prerogative as Director, and no one had the nerve to challenge her.

The reportbacks were straightforward: we were all behind schedule and over budget. I might add that we were almost past caring. It seemed impossible that we'd be finished in time for the official opening. The builders were still knocking down walls left, right and centre, and establishing piles of rubble in every room. Pincus joked that the only exhibit sure to be ready on time was the row of concrete bunks – they were part of the original compound in which the Museum is housed and we had decided to leave them exactly as we found them. He suggested that we think seriously about delaying the opening, which was Portia's cue to produce the invitations, just back from the printers. Everyone groaned (excluding Strickland and me) and breathed in the chastening scent of fresh ink.

'As far as we're concerned, this date is written in stone,' Strickland said, snapping one of the copperplate cards shut. 'We will be ready on time. People will have to learn to take their deadlines seriously.' At that point Charmaine began to doodle on her agenda – a hand with a stiff index finger, emerging from a lacy cuff, pointing at Item 4: Bench.

Item 2: Posters, which followed the reports, was an interesting one. Pincus had had a letter from a man in Bethlehem, a former town clerk and electoral officer, who had collected copies of every election poster displayed in the town since it was founded. He was prepared to entrust the collection to us if it was kept intact. Barbara said she could probably use a couple in the Birth of Apartheid exhibit. We agreed that Pincus would write to the donor, care of the Bethlehem Old Age Home, offering to house the entire collection and display selected items on a rotating basis.

Item 3: Poetry, was Portia's. Ernest Dladla, she informed us, had declined our invitation to read a poem at the opening ceremony, on the perfectly reasonable grounds that he was not a poet. 'I have poetic impulses,' he said in his charming note, 'but I do not act upon them.' Should she go ahead, Portia wanted to know, and approach Alfred Qabula instead, as Ernie suggested?

Then Strickland asked in an acerbic tone whether an issue this trivial needed to be tabled at an important meeting. But Portia responded magnificently, pointing out that she knew nothing about poetry, not having had the benefit of a decent education, had embarrassed herself once in the performance of her duties and did not wish to do so again. All she wanted was an answer to a simple question: Is Alfred Qabula a poet? Yes or no?

No sooner was that settled than Strickland announced Item 4: Bench, and stood up. Perhaps this was a technique she had read about in the business pages somewhere, calculated to intimidate the opposition. 'It has come to my attention,' she said, 'that our workshop personnel are busily recreating beautiful replicas of apartheid memorabilia, when the ugly originals could be ours for the asking. I do not know what Mr Sibeko's policy on this question was, although the saga of the wooden AK47s is full of suggestion, but as far as I'm concerned it's an appalling waste of time and money. It's also dishonest. This is a museum, not an amusement arcade.

'My immediate concern is the WHITES ONLY bench, which is taking up so much of Charmaine's time and talent. I find it hard to believe that there is not a genuine example of a bench of this nature somewhere in the country.'

'Petty apartheid went out ages ago,' said Charmaine, 'even in the Free State.'

'The first Indian townships in the Orange Free State were established way back in October 1986,' said Reddy, who had been unusually quiet so far, 'in Harrismith, Virginia and Odendaalsrus. Not many people know that. I remember hearing the glad tidings from my father-in-law, Mr Mookadam, who confessed that ever since he was a boy it had been a dream of his to visit that forbidden province.'

'I'll wager that there are at least a dozen real WHITES ONLY benches in this city alone, in private collections,' Strickland insisted, erasing Reddy's tangent with the back of her hand. 'People are fascinated by the bizarre.'

'We asked everyone we know,' said Charmaine. 'And we asked them to ask everyone they know, and so on. Like a chain-letter – except that we didn't say they would have a terrible accident if they broke the chain. And we couldn't find a single bench. Not one.'

'Have we advertised?'

'No commercials,' said Reddy, and there was a murmur of assenting voices.

'Why ever not?'

'It just causes more headache.'

'Oh, nonsense!'

Reddy held up his right hand, with the palm out, and batted the air with it, as if he was bouncing a ball off Strickland's forehead. This gesture had a peculiarly mollifying effect on her, and she put her hand over her eyes and sat down. Reddy stood up in his ponderous way and padded out of the room.

Pincus, who has a very low tolerance for silence, said, 'Wouldn't it be funny if Charmaine's bench turned out to be the whites' only bench?'

No one laughed, so he said 'whites' only' again, and drew the apostrophe in the air with his forefinger.

Reddy came back, carrying a photograph, a Tupperware lunch-box and a paper-knife. He put the photograph in the middle of the table, facing Strickland. She had to lean forward in her chair to see what it was. I wondered whether she fully appreciated the havoc her outsize spectacles wreaked on her face, how they disjointed her features. She looked like a composite portrait in a magazine competition, in which some cartoon character's eyes had been mismatched with the jaw of a real-life heroine.

Everyone at the table, with the exception of our Director, had seen this routine before. Some of us had sat through it half a dozen times, with a range of donors, do-gooders, interest groups. For some reason, it never failed to involve me. I also leant forward to view the eight by ten. No one else moved.

I looked first at the pinprick stigmata in the four corners.

Then I looked, as I always did, at the girl's outflung hand. Her hand is a jagged speech-bubble filled with disbelief. It casts a shadow shaped like a howling mouth on her body, and that mouth takes up the cry of outrage. The palm Reddy had waved in Strickland's face was a much more distant echo.

I looked next at the right hand of the boy who is carrying Hector Peterson. His fingers press into the flesh of a thigh that is still warm, willing it to live, prompting the muscle, animating it. Hector Peterson's right hand, by contrast, lolling numbly on his belly, knows that it is dead, and it expresses that certainty in dark tones of shadow and blood.

These hands are still moving, they still speak to me.

Reddy jabbed the photograph with the point of his paper-knife. 'This is a photograph of Hector Peterson, in the hour of his death,' he said. Strickland nodded her head impatiently. 'The day was 16 June 1976.' She nodded again, urging him to skip the common knowledge and come to the point. 'A Wednesday. As it happened, it was fine and mild. The sun rose that morning at six fifty-three and set that evening at five twenty-five. The shot was taken at ten fifteen on the dot. It was the third in a series of six. Hector Peterson was the first fatality of what we would come to call the Soweto Riots – the first in a series of seven hundred odd. The photographer was Sam Nzima, then in the employ of the *World*. The subject, according to the tombstone that now marks his grave, was Zolile Hector Pietersen, P-I-E-T-E-R-S-E-N, but the newspapers called him Hector Peterson and it stuck. We struck out the 'I', we put it to rout in the alphabet of the oppressor. We bore the hero's body from the uneven field of battle and anointed it with English. According to the tombstone he was thirteen years old, but as you can see he looked no more than half that age ... Or is it just the angle? If only we had some other pictures of the subject to compare this one with, we might feel able to speak with more authority.'

This welter of detail, and the offhand tone of the delivery, produced in Strickland the usual baffled silence.

'Not many people know these things.' Reddy slid the point of the knife on to the girl. 'This is Hector's sister Margot, aka Tiny, now living in Soweto.' The knife slid again. 'And this is Mbuyisa Makhubu, whereabouts your guess is as good as mine. Not many people know them either. We have come to the conclusion, here at the Museum, that the living are seldom as famous as the dead.'

The knife moved again. It creased Mbuyisa Makhubu's lips, which are bent into a bow of pain, like the grimace of a tragic mask, it rasped the brick wall of the matchbox house which we see over his shoulder, skipped along the top of a wire gate, and came to rest on the small figure of a woman in the background. 'And who on earth do you suppose this is?'

Strickland gazed at the little figure as if it was someone famous she should be able to recognize in an instant, some household name. In fact, the features of this woman – she is wearing a skirt and doek – are no more than a grey smudge, continuous with the shadowed wall behind her.

I looked at Hector Peterson's left arm, floating on air, and the shadow of his hand on Mbuyisa Makhubu's knee, a shadow so hard-edged and muscular it could trip the bearer up.

The child is dead. With his rumpled sock around his ankle, his grazed knee, his jersey stuck with dry grass, you would think he had taken a tumble in the playground, if it were not for the gout of blood from his mouth. The jersey is a bit too big for him: it was meant to last another year at least. Or is it just that he was small for his age? Or is it the angle? In his hair is a stalk of grass shaped like a praying mantis.

'Nobody knows.'

Strickland sat back with a sigh, but Reddy went on relentlessly.

'Nevertheless, theories were advanced: some people said that this woman, this apparent bystander, was holding Hector Peterson in her arms when he died. She was a mother herself. She cradled him in her lap – you can see the bloodstains here – and when Makhubu took the body from her and carried it away, she found a bullet caught in the folds of her skirt. She is holding that fatal bullet in her right hand, here.

'Other people said that it didn't happen like that at all. Lies and fantasies. When Nzima took this photograph Hector Peterson was still alive! What you see here, according to one reliable caption, is a critically wounded youth. The police open fire, Hector falls at Mbuyisa's feet. The boy picks him up and runs towards the nearest car, which happens to belong to Sam Nzima and Sophie Tema, a journalist on the *World*, Nzima's partner that day. Sam takes his photographs. Then Mbuyisa and Tiny pile into the back of the Volkswagen – did I mention that it was a Volkswagen? – they pile into the back with Hector; Sam and Sophie pile into the front with their driver, Thomas Khoza. They rush to the Orlando Clinic, but Hector Peterson is certified dead on arrival. And that's the real story. You can look it up for yourself.

'But the theories persisted. So we thought we would try to lay the ghost – we have a duty after all to tell the truth. This is a museum, not a paperback novel. We advertised. We called on this woman to come forward and tell her story. We said it would be nice – although it wasn't essential – if she brought the bullet with her.'

'Anyone respond?'

'I'll say.'

Reddy opened his lunch-box and pushed it over to Strickland with the edge of his palm, like a croupier. She looked at the contents: there were

.38 Magnum slugs, 9 mm and AK cartridges, shiny .22 bullets, a .357 hollow-point that had blossomed on impact into a perfect corolla. There were even a couple of doppies and a misshapen ball from an old voor-laaier. Strickland zoomed in for a close-up. She still didn't get it.

'If you'll allow me a poetic licence,' Reddy said, as if poetic licence was a certificate you could stick on a page in your Book of Life, 'this is the bullet that killed Hector Peterson.'

*

So we didn't advertise. But Strickland stuck to her guns about the WHITES ONLY bench: we would have the real thing or nothing at all. She made a few enquiries of her own, and wouldn't you know it, before the week was out, she turned up the genuine article.

The chosen bench belonged to the Municipal Bus Drivers' Association, and in exchange for a small contribution to their coffers – the replacement costs plus ten per cent – they were happy to part with it. The honour of fetching the trophy from their clubhouse in Marshall Street fell to Pincus. Unbeknown to us, the Treasurer of the MBDA had decided that there was a bit of publicity to be gained from his Association's public-spirited gesture, and when our representative arrived he found a photographer ready to record the event for posterity. Pincus was never the most politic member of our Committee. With his enthusiastic cooperation the pho-tographer was able to produce an entire essay, which subsequently appeared, without a by-line, in the *Saturday Star*. It showed the bench in its original quarters (weighted down by a squad of bus drivers of all races, pin-up girls – whites only – looking over the drivers' shoulders, all of them, whether flesh and blood or paper, saying cheese); the bench on its way out of the door (Pincus steering, the Treasurer pushing); being loaded on to the back of our bakkie (Pincus and the Treasurer shaking hands and stretching the cheque between them like a Christmas cracker); and finally driven away (Pincus hanging out of the window to give us a thumbs-up, the Treasurer waving goodbye, the Treasurer waving back at himself from the rearview mirror). These pictures caused exactly the kind of headache Reddy had tried so hard to avoid. Offers of benches poured in from far and wide. Pincus was made to write the polite letters of thanks but no thanks. For our purposes, one bench is quite enough, thank you.

You can see the WHITES ONLY bench now, if you like, in Room 27. Just follow the arrows. I may as well warn you that it says EUROPEANS ONLY, to be precise. There's a second prohibition too, an entirely non-racial one, strung on a chain between the armrests: PLEASE DO NOT SIT ON THIS BENCH. That little sign is Charmaine's work, and making her paint it was Strickland's way of rubbing turpentine in her wounds.

When the genuine bench came to light, Charmaine received instructions to get rid of 'the fake'. But she refused to part with it. I was persuaded to help her carry it into the storeroom, where it remained for a month or so. As the deadline for the opening neared, Charmaine would take refuge in there from time to time, whenever things got too much for her, and put the finishing touches to her creation. At first, she was furious about all the publicity given to the impostor. But once the offers began to roll in, and it became apparent that WHITES ONLY benches were not nearly as scarce as we'd thought, she saw an opportunity to bring her own bench out of the closet. The night before the grand opening, in the early hours, when the sky was already going grey behind the minedump on the far side of the parking lot, we carried her bench outside and put it in the arbour under the controversial Kaffirboom.

'When Strickland asks about it,' said Charmaine, 'you can tell her it was a foundling, left on our doorstep, and we just had to take it in.' Funny thing is, Strickland never made a peep.

*

I can see Charmaine's WHITES ONLY bench now, from my window. The Kaffirboom, relocated here fully grown from a Nelspruit nursery, has acclimatized wonderfully well. '*Erythrina caffra*, a sensible choice,' said Reddy, 'deciduous, patulous and umbrageous.' And he was quite right, it casts a welcome shade. Charmaine's faithful copy reclines in the dapple below, and its ability to attract and repel our visitors never ceases to impress me.

Take Mrs King. And talking about Mrs King, *Mr* King is a total misnomer, of course. I must point it out to Reddy. The Revd King, yes, and Dr King, yes, and possibly even the Revd Dr King. But Mr King? No ways.

It seems unfair, but Charmaine's bench has the edge on that old museum piece in Room 27. Occasionally I look up from my work-bench and see a white man sitting there, a history teacher say. While the schoolchildren he has brought here on an outing hunt in the grass for lucky beans, he sits down on our bench to rest his back. And after a while he pulls up his long socks, crosses one pink leg over the other, laces his fingers behind his head and closes his eyes.

Then again, I'll look up to see a black woman shuffling resolutely past, casting a resentful eye on the bench and muttering a protest under her breath, while the flame-red blossoms of the Kaffirboom detonate beneath her aching feet.

Chris van Wyk

Relatives

Chris van Wyk was born in 1957 in Soweto, and lives in Riverlea, Johannes-burg: through most of the 1980s he was editor of the creative journal *Staffrider*. He is a writer of children's books, and his first novel – *The Year of the Tapeworm* (1996) – was well received. His 'Relatives' was written for an anthology of stories for a new, post-apartheid South Africa (*Crossing Over*, 1995), and won him the SANLAM Award for Short Fiction of that year.

WHEN I WAS TWENTY-ONE I went down to the Cape to write a book. I had got it into my head that my first novel should be a family saga and that my own roots could be found in the arid dust of the Karoo, that famous semi-desert in the Cape, in a little dorp called Carnarvon.

I had first gone down to Cape Town for a week. How could one travel all the way to the Cape without a trip to the most beautiful city in the world, Table Mountain, the train ride from Simon's Town to the city meandering along the beach, the beautiful coloured girls with their lilting, singsong voices?

Then back to Hutchinson station in the heart of the Karoo to be picked up by my grandfather's younger brother, Henkie. A bigger version of my oupa, Uncle Henkie's other difference was that he had mischief in his eyes where my oupa had brooding shadows.

Then followed an hour's drive to Carnarvon by way of long, hot, dusty, pot-holed roads past waving, poor people on foot or pushing bicycles, and carrying bundles of wood or things wrapped in newspaper.

Carnarvon was a place in the middle of nowhere where nothing happened. Simple breakfasts, lunches and suppers were linked together by chains of cigarettes and conversations consisting of long, trailing life histories that made the old men in their elbow patches stammer and squint into the past from behind their thick spectacles, as they dredged up anecdotes from the dry riverbeds of history.

Oh, how wonderful it was listening to those minutely detailed sagas. But after two weeks I was bored out of my wits. The novel could wait,

I decided as I packed up and was driven back to Hutchinson station. The train from Cape Town – the very same one that had brought me there two weeks before – slid into the station. I bade Uncle Henkie goodbye with a promise that I would feature him prominently and truthfully in my novel.

When the train slithered out, I turned to the passengers in the compartment with whom I was going to spend the next sixteen hours or so on the way to Johannesburg.

There were three young men, two bearded, two chubby. (If you think I can't count, remember the riddle of the two fathers and two sons who each shot a duck. Only three ducks were shot. Why? Because one was a grandfather, the other a father and the last a son. The man in the middle was both a father and a son, got it?) All youthful and exuberant, they were drinking beer, straight from the can, and their conversation was full of the hammers and nails of their profession and punctuated with laughter and inane arguments. None of them swore and they all flashed smiles at me, accepting me into their midst with an easy friendliness.

'You been to Cape Town?' one of them enquired.

'Ja,' I said, shoving my bag into the space above the door among their own bags and stuff.

'Then you must've got your quota of ten girls,' he said with a wink.

Of course I knew exactly what he was talking about: in the Mother City there were at least ten girls to every boy. I gave them a supercilious nod, hoping to convey the impression that I had certainly got my fair share. The truth of it was very different. All I could truly claim was a brief encounter with Marina, a nurse from Tygerberg hospital. She had allowed me to kiss her in the back seat of her cousin's car, but my beer breath had proved too much for her and after administering a violet-flavoured Beechie, she bade me good night and told me to come and see her in the morning.

There were two other passengers in the compartment. They were not quite as friendly as the trio from the Cape. They sat huddled in a corner, muttering in undertones and casting sidelong glances down the green SAR leather seat at me and my new buddies. They were brothers. This was obvious from their identical features: sandy hair that had been cut so short that the hairs grew in sharp, italic spikes. They both had dark, brooding eyes and thick pouting lips. They wore khaki shirts and pants.

Try to describe people you meet on a bus or train it said in the writer's manual. I slipped a blank sheet into my mental typewriter and went to town:

They sit huddled in the corner of the compartment, bent so low in their conniving that they almost stick to the green SAR leather like two unsightly stains. They are identical but for the fact that there is a two or three year difference between them. Juveniles in khaki, they look like fugitives from a boy scout patrol, runaways not prepared to abide by the rules of the Lord Baden Powell. Stripped of their badges, their epaulettes, their scarves, banished to ride forever, second class on the Trans-Karoo.

As I've said, I was only twenty-one at the time.

I turned away from them and back to the three big men who were asking me questions as if I was an old buddy. I was surprised and pleased by this unexpected attention and friendliness. One of them glanced at his watch from time to time and stared out of the window at the scrub that made up the dry, lonely landscape of the Karoo. They asked me how my journey down to the Cape had been. They all seemed genuinely interested. One of them slid a can of beer across the little panelite table. They all sat forward to listen to what I had to say. I lit a cigarette, passing the pack around to my three friends. Then I began a story which I had already tested on my uncle in Carnarvon. There, among seasoned storytellers, it had passed my 'litmus' test – Listenable, Interesting, Telling, Meaningful, Unusual, Strange. I knew I had a winner:

*

On my way down from Johannesburg my travelling companion – no one else had been booked into our compartment – had been a Capetonian man. He travelled in a flamboyant striped yellow and white suit, every time he spoke he injected an air of drama into the compartment, and when he was quiet he seemed all the time to be sizing me up. I remember his name, Georgie Abrahams, from Elsies River.

As the train started its long journey out of Johannesburg station, Georgie began to tell me how he had once killed a man. Where? In a compartment exactly like the one he and I were sitting in, facing each other. Why? Because, Georgie was very eager to explain, this skelm tried to steal some of Georgie's possessions: food, money, an expensive watch? I can't remember what it was but Georgie caught him, beat him up, sliced him from his greasy fat neck down to his 'klein gatjie' – Georgie's words. He threw the remains of the dead man out of the window in the dead of night and wiped the blood carefully from the windowpane, the green leather seat, the floor. When the conductor questioned the whereabouts of the missing man, Georgie merely shrugged and uttered a melodious, 'How should I know? Nobody asked me to take care of him.'

But even as Georgie was relating this tale of theft and murder in all its horrific detail, I knew it was a lie, simply a more elaborate version of my mother's dire warnings to yours truly at seven, 'If you eat in bed you'll grow horns', or the more convincing, 'Go to bed with wet hair and you'll suffer from a smelly nose for the rest of your life.' Georgie was in fact warning me to stay clear of his luggage! And the story had quite an amusing ending. When we reached Cape Town station, a toothless woman in a lopsided jersey, stretched to twice its original size (which used to be XL) welcomed the murderer home with an unceremonious slap across his face, while I looked on together with a brood of his startled children who didn't know if they should laugh with delight at their Papa's homecoming or cry for the humiliating onslaught he was being subjected to.

'Ses maande en djy skryf niks, phone niks, not a blerry word van djou!' ('Six months and you don't write, don't phone, not a bloody word from you!')

*

My companions chuckled. They couldn't decide what was better, my story or my Cape accent.

I looked at the two sulking boys in the corner. They had followed the entire story, but they refused to laugh. So what! It hadn't been for their amusement anyway.

But then my journey took an unexpected turn. An hour or two from Hutchinson my three companions got up, stamped the pins and needles out of their feet, swept the crumbs from their pants and began to gather up their luggage. They shook my hand, slapped my back and said goodbye. And at the next station they were gone. It all happened so quickly that I was a little stunned. Now it was just me and the kids in khaki. And then a strange thing happened. I suddenly knew why they were dressed in khaki. In all probability they were from a Cape Town reformatory on their way home to Johannesburg! Why had I not realized this simple fact before? The answer was elementary. I had been far too preoccupied with my new friends to pay much attention to these two boys and there were no guardians in sight. But now that I was alone I focused my attention full square on these two, and in an instant I realized where they were from.

The two juvenile delinquents also seemed to undergo some transformation. They no longer muttered but spoke loudly, spicing their conversation with vulgarities. And, in an act of territorial imperative, they claimed more than their fair share of the confined space, stretching their stocky legs along the seats, putting their luggage everywhere, littering the floor with clothes and greasy food packets.

Then they began a conversation which froze my blood. Their brother, the leader of a gang, had been killed by a rival gang in a Johannesburg township called Coronationville. They had been given a weekend off to attend the funeral. They would bury their brother like the hero that he was, but they vowed to avenge his death before the soil on his grave hardened. They even had an argument about how this murder would be carried out, a slow cutting of the throat was the younger's plan. No, the elder brother disagreed, stab him about a hundred times, but from the ankles to the neck.

As these plans were being discussed they kept looking me straight in the eye as if challenging me to say anything in protest or disagreement. Each time I looked away, not daring to utter a word.

Meanwhile the train seemed to be riding into the sunset. A cool breeze replaced the warmth and the grim brothers felt the cold and pulled up the windows.

I began to worry. How could I spend an entire night in a pitch-black compartment with two juvenile delinquents! Maybe I could go out in search of the conductor and ask to be moved to another compartment. But if I did that my two little gangsters would know instinctively what I was up to. This also meant leaving my luggage unattended. As these thoughts went through my head, I looked down from the top bunk and saw the elder brother staring at me. He knows what I'm thinking, I thought.

Darkness came and we turned on the lights. A caterer opened our door and read out the menu for supper. The two boys ordered steak, buttered bread and potato salad. I had no appetite. The caterer left and I heard him whistling down the corridor and opening the compartment next door. My companions glared at me again. They seemed to know why I had not ordered a meal.

On my way down to the Cape, Georgie Abrahams had joked about committing murder. This time there was no such threat – towards me anyway. But for every dark kilometre to Joburg I felt that my home city was moving further and further away.

'You!' I looked down from the bunk. It was the elder brother who was demanding my attention.

'Ja,' I answered as casually as my voice would allow.

'Are you not Aunty Ria's child – grandchild?'

'Yes!' I could not believe my ears. Aunty Ria, as they called her, was indeed my grandmother and the mother of my own mother.

'I knew it was you when I saw you,' he said, not smiling but with some friendliness in his voice. His brother stared up at me with some interest.

'You're that clever boy who used to read books and write stuff, hey?'

'Yes, but who are you?'

'Me 'n him we Aunty Visa's grandchildren.'

Aunty Visa was my granny's sister.

'Then we're cousins!' I said. This wasn't quite true, but I was desperate to be as closely related to them as possible.

When their food arrived they insisted that I join them. And I did, for suddenly my appetite had returned.

*

I had forgotten all about my chance encounter with my two delinquent relatives until the other day, three years later.

I opened the newspaper and read a report about rampant gang crime in the streets of Western Township and adjacent Coronationville. The article spoke of streets running with the blood of gangsters, the death of innocents caught in the crossfire, the revenge killings, the tragic futility of it all. The writer paid particular attention to the two brothers who had been stabbed to death and who now lay dead in the same graveyard as their brother, killed three years before.

They had never reached twenty-one.

Acknowledgements

The publishers are grateful to the following copyright-holders for permission to reproduce their material:

for Naguib Mahfouz's 'Half a Day', translated by Denys Johnson-Davies, from *The Time and the Place and Other Stories*, copyright © 1991 by the American University in Cairo Press. Used by permission of Doubleday, a division of Random House, Inc.;

to Nawal El Saadawi for her 'The Veil' and to Shirley Eber for her translation;

to Granta and to Bloomsbury for Ahdaf Soueif's 'The Sandpiper', copyright © 1996 Ahdaf Soueif. By kind permission of Bloomsbury Publishers;

to Éditions Stock for the original of Rachid Mimouni's 'The Escapee' and to Quartet Books and Shirley Eber for her translation;

to Éditions du Sueil for Tahar Ben Jelloun's 'The Blue Viper', from *Le Premier Amour est Toujours le Dernier*, copyright © Éditions du Seuil, 1995, and to Anne Fuchs for her translation;

to *Jeune Afrique* for the original of Lotfi Akalay's 'Colour Blues' and to Pius Adesanmi for his translation;

to Don Burness for the original of Teixeira de Sousa's 'In the Court of King Dom Pedro' and for his translation;

to the Centre Togolais de Communication – Éditions Haho for Théo Ananissoh's 'Coming Home' and to Elsa Glenn for her translation;

to Éditions Sépia for Albert Taïeb's 'When a Dog is Worth Nine Children' from *Chroniques Abidjanes*, copyright © Éd. Sépia, 1995, and to Catherine Lauga du Plessis for her translation;

to Sylvie Kandé for her 'In this Goddamned Messed-up Land' and to Christopher Winks for his translation;

to Syl Cheney-Coker for his 'The Concert';

to Ama Ata Aidoo for her 'Lice';

to Tanure Ojaide for his 'God and His Medicine-men';

to Kanchana Ugbabe for her 'Exile';

to Guardian Newspapers Ltd. for Ben Okri's 'A Prayer from the Living', copyright © 1993 Ben Okri. All rights reserved. By kind permission of David Godwin Associates;

to Taban Lo Liyong for his 'The Big Swallow';

to Peter Nazareth for his 'Moneyman';

to Heinemann Educational Publishers, Oxford, for Ngugi wa Thiong'o's 'Minutes of Glory' and for M. G. Vassanji's 'Breaking Loose';

to SIDA, the Swedish International Development Authority, for Fatmata A. Conteth's 'Letter to my Sisters', from *Whispering Land: An Anthology of Stories by African Women* (Stockholm, 1985);

to Nuruddin Farah for his 'The Affair';

to Le Serpent à Plumes and to Abdourahman A. Waberi for his 'The Dasbiou Mystery' and to Anne Fuchs for her translation;

to L'Harmattan and to Idris Youssouf Elmi for his 'He Has Come Back' and to Chris Dunton for his translation;

to Groupe Hatier International for Francis Bebey's 'If Only the Gauls' from *La Lune dans un Seau Tout Rouge*, copyright © Hatier, 1980, and for E. B. Dongala's 'The Ceremony' from *Jazz et Vin de Palme*, copyright © Hatier, 1982, and to Norman Strike for his translation of both;

to Édouard J. Maunick for his 'Kala Who Dreams of Going to the Sea' and to Denise Godwin for her translation;

to *Revue Noire* for Michèle Rakotoson's 'Dolorosa' and for John Taylor's translation;

to Carole Beckett for Aboubacar Ben Saïd Salim's 'The Revolt of the Vowels' and for her translation;

to L. B. Honwana for his 'Rosita, until Death' and to Richard Bartlett for his translation of this and the following item;

to Lília Momplé for her 'Celina's Banquet';

to Mia Couto for his 'The Russian Princess' and to Luís Rafael for his translation of this and the following item;

to José Eduardo Agualusa for his 'The Day They Arrested Father Christmas';

to Yvonne Vera for her 'Independence Day';

to Longman Zimbabwe and to Musaemura Zimunya for his 'A Pineapple Incident';

to Stoddart Publishing, Toronot, for Paul Tiyambe Zeleza's 'Blood Feuds' from *The Joys of Exile* (Ananasi, 1994) and to the author;

to Peter Clarke for his 'The Changing of the Season';

to Sheila Roberts for her 'Sweetness';

to Hennie Aucamp for his 'Poor Old Joe' and to Johann Rossouw for his translation;

to David Philip, Publisher, for Ivan Vladislavić's 'The WHITES ONLY Bench' and to the author;

and to Chris van Wyk for his 'Relatives'.

Every effort has been made by the publishers to contact all copyright-holders; any inadvertent omissions are regretted and will be restituted at the earliest opportunity.

The publisher would also like to acknowledge the assistance of the French Institute of South Africa with regard to making the Francophone African writers in this anthology more readily available to English-language readers and to thank them for their generous support.